U.S. AIRCRAFT CARRIERS 1939-45

CASEMATE | ILLUSTRATED | SPECIAL

CASEMATE | ILLUSTRATED | SPECIAL

U.S. AIRCRAFT CARRIERS 1939–45

INGO BAUERNFEIND

Acknowledgements

Since writing a book is always a team effort, I would like to thank the following people and institutions for their support and advice during its completion: Russell Moore, Rolf Sabye and Chuck Myers at the U.S.S. *Hornet* Sea, Air and Space Museum; Daniel J. Lenihan (ret.) and Brett T. Seymour, National Park Service Submerged Resources Center; Pete Mesley, Technical Diving Instructor and Explorer; Dr. Art Trembanis, Coastal Sediments Hydrodynamics and Engineering Laboratory, University of Delaware; Ted Huetter, Museum of Flight, Seattle; Vincent Dhorne for creating aircraft profiles, and Ruth Sheppard, Isobel Fulton, and Todd Shugart and their colleagues at Casemate Publishers for making this book possible.

CISS0007

Published in the United States of America and Great Britain in 2021 by

CASEMATE PUBLISHERS

1950 Lawrence Road, Havertown, PA 19083, USA
and
The Old Music Hall, 106–108 Cowley Road, Oxford OX4 1JE, UK

Copyright © 2021 Ingo Bauernfeind

Hardback Edition: ISBN 978-1-61200-934-6
Digital Edition: ISBN 978-1-61200-935-3

A CIP record for this book is available from the British Library

Design by Battlefield Design
Color profiles by Vincent Dhorne

Printed and bound in Turkey by MegaPrint

For a complete list of Casemate titles, please contact:
CASEMATE PUBLISHERS (US)
Telephone (610) 853-9131
Fax (610) 853-9146
Email: casemate@casematepublishers.com
www.casematepublishers.com

CASEMATE PUBLISHERS (UK)
Telephone (01865) 241249
Email: casemate-uk@casematepublishers.co.uk
www.casematepublishers.co.uk

Facing Title Page: F4U Corsair fighters returning from a combat mission over North Korea circle the U.S.S. *Boxer* (CV-21) waiting to receive the permission to land. (U.S. National Archives)

Title Page: U.S.S. *Hancock* (CV-19) at a Pacific anchorage, 1944–45. (U.S. Navy)

Contents Page: A Grumman F8F Bearcat fighter in board U.S.S. *Valley Forge* (CV-45) in 1949. Despite its introduction into service in 1945, the Bearcat arrived too late to fight in World War II. (U.S. National Archives); Guadalcanal Invasion, August 1942: U.S. Navy ordnancemen of Scouting Squadron 6 (VS-6) load a 500-pound (227 kg) demolition bomb on a Douglas SBD-3 Dauntless fleet carrier U.S.S. *Enterprise* (CV-6), during the first day of strikes on Guadalcanal and Tulagi, August 7, 1942. Note the aircraft's landing gear and the bomb crutch, the bomb cart, and the hoist. (U.S. National Archives)

Contents

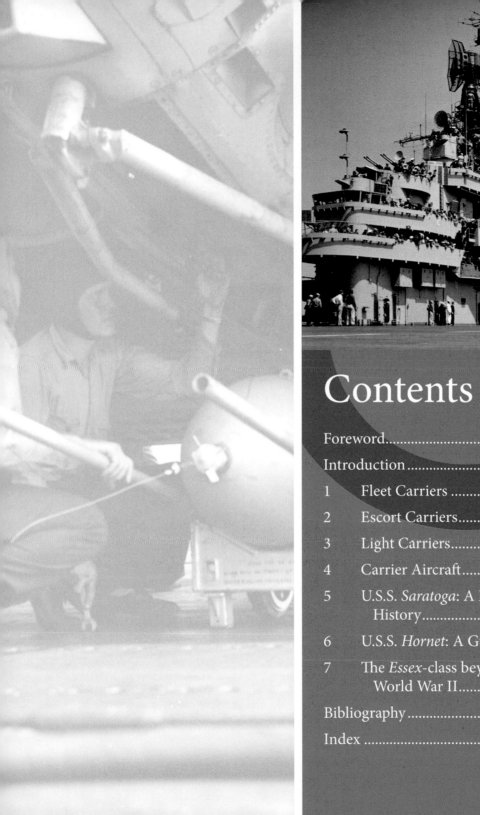

| Foreword

U.S.S. *Hornet* (CV-12) was the eighth and unfortunately the last of the American Navy ships proudly carrying the name *Hornet*. That she was to play a major role in my young life so many years after her heroics in World War II, was a destiny yet to be revealed. Her direct name predecessor, U.S.S. *Hornet* (CV-8) had participated in the famous Doolittle Raid and in the battle of Midway before she was sunk in the battle of the Santa Cruz Islands.

The new *Hornet* (CV-12) proved to be a worthy name successor, fighting in many of the major battles across the Pacific. But it was not only she and her sister ships of the *Essex*-class that made their important contribution to the Allied victory in World War II, but also the older fleet carriers as well as the smaller light carriers and escort carriers. From all their carrier decks, brave airmen took off to engage enemy aircraft, attack Japanese aircraft carriers and other warships, support amphibious landings, fight German U-boats and protect vital transatlantic convoys.

After World War II, most ships of the *Essex*-class, along with a few of the smaller carriers, now modernized or converted, served in the Korean and Vietnam Wars. By 1968, *Hornet*, after a few years in the reserve fleet, had been back in service for nearly 15 years. Her World War II sailors had long since returned to their homes and families. And yet, as a young sailor, I found it a humbling experience to walk down Pier 1 at the Long Beach Naval Shipyard, knowing her history, and that I was about to serve on board this ship for the next several years. And although the history was everywhere onboard, my encounters with World War II aircraft carrier veterans, including U.S.S. *Hornet* sailors, were still years away.

The experience of coming onboard that day in March 1968 was typical of any young sailor arriving at his first ship. I had completed the various schools and was a Quartermaster Seaman Striker. Once onboard and in my new division, it didn't take long to realize that of all the assignments onboard the ship, working up on the bridge was one of the most desirable jobs onboard. We of course reported to the Navigator, but also interacted with the various senior officers as well as our Captain when he was on the bridge.

Serving on a famous warship was a privilege and honor. *Hornet* was breathing history as she had an amazing World War II record, receiving nine battle stars and the Presidential Unit Citation, making her one of the most decorated carriers of the war. In her later years, she had a reputation as a well-run Navy ship. Clean, with a disciplined crew, and commanding officers who seemed to compliment *Hornet*'s honorable 195-year legacy (since the first *Hornet* of 1775.) I served under two such COs, Captain Stockton during the last Vietnam campaign, and Captain Seiberlich for the recovery of the command modules of the Apollo 11 and 12 moon landing missions, and the eventual decommissioning in June 1970.

After a stellar 27-year career, beginning in war, and ending in peace, on the morning of June 26, 1970, U.S.S. *Hornet* was ordered out of commission, and we became the last crew to serve on the last American Navy ship named *Hornet*.

In May 1995, *Hornet*, brought to Hunter's Point Shipyard south of San Francisco to begin her scrapping process, was towed to Alameda Naval Air Station's Pier 3 to be part of a historical display. Moored across the pier was the modern nuclear-powered aircraft carrier U.S.S. *Carl Vinson* (CVN-70). The old and the new. As it turned out, this gave the time and opportunity for a small group of enthusiasts to petition the Navy for transfer of *Hornet* to NAS Alameda for the purpose of becoming a maritime museum. I became aware of this, and after a meeting with the group, became part of the effort.

I was back on board my ship. This time instead of 2,500 young sailors, I met fellow Navy veterans, many of whom had served during World War II. Finally, I was able to walk the decks with sailors who could tell us what it was really like to serve on *Hornet* and other U.S. aircraft carriers during those dark days. We had first-hand accounts of their determination and challenges, the fear, and the sacrifices. Like us younger veterans, visitors were spellbound listening to their stories and asking for signatures on posters and photos posing with them. These sailors were once again being rewarded for their incredible service. Those men who had fought at Coral Sea, Midway, Iwo Jima or Leyte had passed the torch to new generations of aircraft carrier sailors and airmen who would fight in Korea or Vietnam.

More than 25 years have passed with hundreds of volunteers and a great staff having brought *Hornet* back to life as the U.S.S. *Hornet*, Sea, Air and Space Museum. Moreover, thanks to the efforts of numerous enthusiasts and organizations, three of her sister ships, U.S.S. *Yorktown* (CV-10), U.S.S. *Intrepid* (CV-11) and U.S.S. *Lexington* (CV-16), have also been preserved as floating museums. All these ships are memorials to all the men and their aircraft carriers who fought in World War II and subsequent conflicts. And although we have lost most of our World War II Navy Veterans, I will never forget their stories and their bravery which brought the world back from one of its darkest periods. My friend Earl Smith, who not only survived the attack on Pearl Harbor, but also the sinking of U.S.S. *Hornet* (CV-8), enjoyed his visits to the *Hornet* Museum even at his age of 92. He and so many others will always remain in my thoughts as Earl's and his shipmate's shared stories will help to keep their memory alive for generations to come.

Rolf Sabye

Former U.S.S. *Hornet* crew member (QM2 Navigation Division, March 1968–June 1970)

U.S.S. *Saratoga* (CV-3) under repair at Tongatabu, Tonga Islands, in September 1942, after being torpedoed by the Japanese submarine *I-26* on August 31. The torpedo struck her on the starboard side, just aft of the island, and flooded one fireroom, giving the ship a 4° list, but it caused multiple electrical short circuits. (U.S. National Archives)

| Introduction

"Where are the carriers?" or, "where is the next carrier?" These are the questions American presidents often ask when an international crisis or a new war is looming. An aircraft carrier is a very potent means of projecting power and one of the most powerful symbols of "gunboat policy." Often just the appearance of such a ship and its task group can cool down a situation before it escalates into a conflict as the combatants in a troubled region may realize that an aircraft carrier (armed with more than 80 aircraft) is a force that easily can overwhelm them. On the other hand, a carrier might heat up an already dicey situation, thus provoking the potential adversary to undertake unpredictable actions causing an unwanted and uncontrollable escalation. Therefore, the use of aircraft carriers has to be determined carefully by a president and his advisers. An aircraft carrier is basically a floating airport that can go virtually everywhere, launch its aircraft to destroy a variety of targets—warships, fortifications, production facilities or troops on land. Moreover, it can help to gain air superiority by hindering the enemy to launch his own aircraft or by destroying them in the air or on the ground.

These ships, often called super-carriers due to their size and striking capabilities, have their origin in World War II. During that epic conflict, two weapons systems proved their significant impact on the outcome of the war at sea. One was the submarine, which was able to cut the enemy's life lines, thus making it impossible for him to supply his army, navy and air force operations, feed his population and maintain his wartime production. Today, submarines, among them ballistic missile carrying variants, are among the most powerful and dangerous weapons in existence as they can fire a nuclear missile at the enemy while remaining hidden in the depths of the oceans.

The second weapon that proved its decisive potential during World War II was the aircraft carrier. It replaced the battleship as the surface warship of choice as it had a longer striking range than the battleship's artillery thanks to the range of its aircraft. During World War II, the air power provided by carriers was demonstrated by the British air raid on the Italian fleet in Taranto, the Japanese attack on Pearl Harbor, the battles of Coral Sea, Midway and Leyte, the U.S. invasion of numerous Japanese-held islands, as well as the bombardments of Japan. Even numerous powerful and well-protected battleships, among them the Japanese *Yamato* and *Musashi*, the largest ever built, fell victim to carrier-based aircraft.

When U.S. and Japanese carriers fought against each other during the battle of the Coral Sea in May of 1942, it was the first time that the ships of both fleets were not in sight with each other, as the range of their respective aircraft was significantly higher. During World War II, the aircraft carrier became the most powerful offensive weapon any navy could send into combat. After the attack on Pearl Harbor, U.S. aircraft carrier task forces made a vital contribution to defeating Japan's naval forces, island fortifications and even cities and production facilities on its homeland. Aircraft carriers also helped to defeat German U-boats in the Atlantic, thus enabling the Allies to send supplies to Great Britain and the Soviet Union, thereby laying the foundation for the 1944 invasion of Normandy and supporting the Russian advance towards Germany in 1945.

When the war ended, those battleships that had survived the conflict, were either scrapped or turned into museums, whereas the carrier, in particular the large fleet carrier, was further developed culminating in the present-day nuclear-powered 100,000-ton giants of the *Nimitz*- and *Gerald R. Ford*-classes. These modern ships and their crews are carrying on the tradition of the fighting World War II "flattops" and their brave sailors and airmen who endured and sacrificed so much to help make Allied victory possible.

One of the aircraft still aboard the wreck of U.S.S. *Saratoga* sunk at Bikini Atoll during the atomic tests of Operation *Crossroads*. (U.S. National Park Service, Submerged Resources Center)

Comparative Sizes of Carriers

Fleet Carriers:

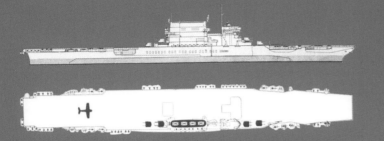

Lexington-class

Wasp

Ranger

Essex-class

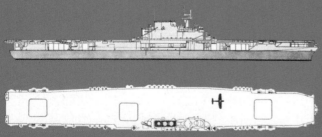

Yorktown-class

SCALE

| 0m | 50m | 100 m | 150m | 200m | 250m | 300m |

Escort Carriers:

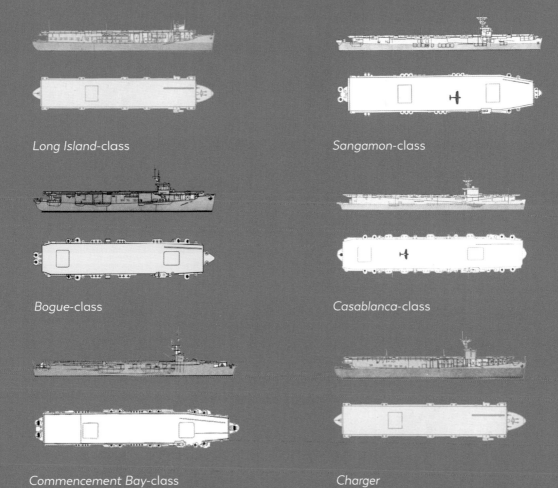

Long Island-class

Sangamon-class

Bogue-class

Casablanca-class

Commencement Bay-class

Charger

Light Carriers:

Independence-class

1
Fleet Carriers

Although the battleship had established itself as the most powerful warship in international fleets since the end of the 19th century, its age came to an end during World War II. A new type of ship, the aircraft carrier, of which the fleet carrier was the most powerful combatant, appeared on the stage of naval warfare, supplanting the time-honored battleship with its striking power. The first aircraft launch from a ship took place in the United States in 1910, when Eugene B. Ely took off in a biplane from a temporary ramp installed on the cruiser U.S.S. *Birmingham*. Since the ship did not have a landing platform or deck, the landing took place ashore. A short time later, however, Ely was able to land on the U.S.S. *Pennsylvania*, which was also equipped with a deck, thus proving that takeoffs and landings on ships were possible.

U.S.S. *Franklin* (CV-13) is floated out of her building dock immediately after christening, at the Newport News Shipbuilding and Drydock Company shipyard, Newport News, Virginia, on October 14, 1943. (U.S. National Archives)

The first aircraft takeoff from a ship took place on November 14, 1910. (U.S. Navy)

Ely's historic takeoff immortalized in a painting by John McCoy which is today part of the U.S. Air Force Art Collection. (U.S. Air Force Art Collection)

U.S.S. *Langley* shortly after her conversion to a carrier in 1924. (U.S. Navy)

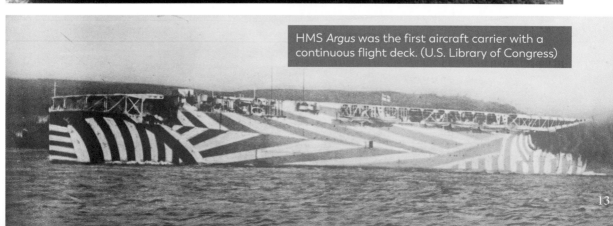

HMS *Argus* was the first aircraft carrier with a continuous flight deck. (U.S. Library of Congress)

The incomplete hull of U.S.S. *Saratoga* (CV-3) at the New York Shipbuilding Company shipyard, Camden, New Jersey, March 8, 1922. Construction had been suspended, pending her conversion to an aircraft carrier. Note barbette structures resting on blocks on her deck. (U.S. National Archives)

The precursors of later aircraft carriers were the so-called aircraft mother ships (seaplane carriers). They did not yet have a runway and could only get their planes into the air by catapult. After ditching, a crane took the aircraft back on board. During World War I, some of these ships saw combat action: the Japanese *Wakamiya* bombed German positions overseas at Tsingtau, China, in 1914, and the British HMS *Ark Royal* attacked Turkish fortifications at the Dardanelles the following year. In 1917, the Royal Navy installed a flight deck about 227 feet (69 meters) long on the cruiser HMS *Furious*. This deck already allowed takeoffs but did not provide landing facilities. The aircraft of *Furious* flew successful attacks against German zeppelin hangars in Tondern (Denmark). The first operational carrier to receive a full-length deck for takeoffs and landings was the Royal Navy's HMS *Argus*. However, the end of the war in November 1918 prevented its deployment. Germany's first aircraft carrier, a conversion based on the incomplete passenger ship *Ausonia*, was also not completed in time.

The U.S. Navy followed this development in the early 1920s by converting the coal freighter *Jupiter* into a carrier with a full-length deck and christening it the U.S.S. *Langley* (CV-1). The first carrier to be designed as such from the outset was the British HMS *Hermes*, but Japan was able to complete the *Hosho* more than a year earlier, in 1922, despite starting construction later.

After the experiences of World War I, which had been preceded by a massive maritime arms race, the leading naval powers of the time—the United States, Great Britain, Japan, France and Italy—adopted the Washington Naval Treaty in 1922. This agreement was intended to regulate the future size (35,000 tons), maximum armament (16-inch guns) and, above all, the number of battleships of all signatory nations in order to avoid a future naval arms race. It stipulated that the U.S. and Great

This photo illustrates the genesis of the *Lexington*-class aircraft carrier design. In the foreground is a model of the aircraft carrier design converted from the battle cruiser hull (background). (U.S. National Archives)

Britain should each have 525,000 tons, Japan 315,000 tons, and France and Italy 175,000 tons each for the total displacement of their battleship fleets.

In addition to a prescribed tonnage of battleships, the treaty also allowed each signatory nation to build aircraft carriers within a similarly fixed framework. Here, the U.S. and Great Britain were each granted 135,000 tons, Japan 81,000 tons, and France and Italy 60,000 tons each. Under the terms of the treaty, most fleets still had too many battleships and battle cruisers in 1922, some of which were still under construction. Although the treaty limited the maximum size per carrier to 27,000 tons, each signatory nation was allowed to have two carriers each with a displacement of up to 33,000 tons. This exception allowed the U.S. Navy and the Imperial Navy of Japan to complete some of their unfinished battle cruisers as aircraft carriers, although these ships exceeded the maximum displacement of 27,000 tons by more than 6,000 tons. On the American side, these were U.S.S. *Lexington* (CV-2) and U.S.S. *Saratoga* (CV-3). On the Japanese side, the battle cruiser *Akagi* and the battleship *Kaga* were selected. The Royal Navy decided to reconstruct the two "Great Light Cruisers" HMS *Courageous* and HMS *Glorious* and their already partially converted "half-sister" ship HMS *Furious* into full-fledged carriers. Their displacement of about 23,000 tons each was below the Washington Treaty's limit.

All of these first-generation fleet carriers completed during the 1920s served as active experimental platforms for developing launch and landing techniques and testing tactical mission profiles. Subsequent carrier designs benefited from the experience gained with these ships. In 1934, the United States also put into service its first carrier designed from the ground up, the U.S.S. *Ranger* (CV-4). Since the Washington Naval Treaty limited the size of international battleship fleets until the late 1930s, the construction and testing of new aircraft carriers took on increasing importance during this period. At the start of the Pacific War in December 1941, the U.S. Navy and the Japanese Navy each had seven fleet carriers, while the Royal Navy had eight:

Vought O2U-2 Corsair aircraft flying past U.S.S. *Saratoga* while preparing to land on board, circa 1930. Note the U.S. Marine Corps insignia painted under the rear cockpit. (U.S. Navy NH 94899)

United States		Japan		Great Britain	
Lexington-class	2 ships	*Akagi*	single ship	*Furious*	single ship
Ranger	single ship	*Kaga*	single ship	*Courageous*-class	2 ships
Yorktown-class	3 ships	*Ryūjō*	single ship	*Ark Royal*	single ship
Wasp	single ship	*Sōryū*	single ship	*Illustrious*-class	4 ships
		Hiryū	single ship		
		Shōkaku-class	2 ships		

During the Pacific War, the U.S. Navy was able to complete another seventeen operational fleet carriers (*Essex*-class), while Japan (*Junyo*-class, *Taihō*, *Unryū*-class and *Shinano*) and Great Britain (*Implacable*-class, *Colossus*-class and *Unicorn*) only seven each.

The U.S. Navy also laid down the three keels of the larger *Midway*-class during the war. However, these ships were not commissioned until after the end of the conflict (1945–1947). The Royal Navy also began construction of two more classes (*Audacious* and *Centaur*), but these, too, were not completed or ready for service until after the war. Japan was forced to stop building more carriers in the second half of the conflict due to shortages of materials and skilled labor but attempted to convert other types of ships into small and simplified carriers.

These naval powers built other small carrier classes in addition to fleet carriers and continued to use them during World War II. Germany, France, and Italy also began constructing carriers, but these ships did not participate in active warfare.

With some exceptions, fleet carriers had a standard displacement of about 20,000 to 40,000 tons, depending on the design, reached a top speed of over 30 knots, and could carry 50 or more aircraft. These values varied as some carriers were rebuilt several times during their active service to keep pace with advances in naval aviation. Lighter carriers such as the U.S. Navy's *Ranger* and *Wasp*, the Japanese *Ryujo*, and the British *Colossus* and *Unicorn* possessed the characteristics of fleet carriers (with limitations) despite their scaled-down designs. All three navies each protected their carriers with light side armor on the hull, antitorpedo bulges, and a lightly armored hangar deck. In addition, the ships all had strong to very strong air defenses to protect their vulnerable flight decks against enemy bombing. Armament often consisted of more than 100 gun barrels and included 20 mm and 40 mm antiaircraft guns, 5-inch (12.7 cm) general-purpose artillery, and in some cases large-caliber 8-inch (20.3 cm) guns for use against smaller ships (aboard *Lexington*-class).

The U.S. and Japanese carriers relied on as many aircraft as possible to mass strike power (*Essex*: 100; *Shōkaku*: 84). In order to be able to carry the aircraft's heavy weight, the designers of both navies dispensed with effective flight deck armor. The Royal Navy, on the other hand, placed great emphasis on protection and, starting with the *Illustrious*-class, used 2.5-inch (7.6 cm) armor to protect the flight deck. This reinforcement was to prove vital in the Pacific War in defending against kamikaze aircraft. However, due to weight, this additional protection limited the number of aircraft capacity. Designed to stow 48 aircraft in their hangars, the use of a permanent deck park allowed the succeeding *Implacable*-class to accommodate up to 81 aircraft, following the American practice.

Depending on the design of the individual carriers, their areas of operation and the aircraft available, the composition of the respective "air groups" (see Chapter 4) varied. During the course of the war, the number of fighter aircraft increased, especially on U.S. carriers, in order to be able to fend off the extremely dangerous Japanese kamikaze aircraft from 1944 onward before they could hit the carriers' flight decks.

Going into "Harm's Way"

The Japanese attack on Pearl Harbor on December 7, 1941, aimed to prevent the U.S. Pacific Fleet from interfering with Japan's imperialistic goal to occupy Southeast Asian territories (many of them under European rule) and control the region's natural resources vital to industrial and military production. In order to maintain unhindered access to this area, Japan established a protective island barrier, from the Kurile Islands (northeast from Japan) in the north through the Central Pacific, around the Dutch East Indies (present-day Indonesia) to the Burmese-Indian border. Besides neutralizing U.S. forces in Hawaii, the comprehensive plan also included the occupation of the islands of Wake, Guam, and strategic points in the Philippines (under U.S. control) and British Malaya (present-day Malaysia). Once this was accomplished, Japan expanded these holdings by invading Singapore and Hong Kong (British), the Dutch East Indies (present-day Indonesia) and other key islands.

On December 7, 1941, six Japanese aircraft carriers attacked the U.S. Pacific Fleet in Pearl Harbor. When a carrier-based aircraft dropped a 1,760 lb (800 kg) bomb on the battleship U.S.S. *Arizona* (BB-39), the forward magazines blew up, killing 1,177 crewmen. (U.S. Navy)

Map of the Pacific. (NASA)

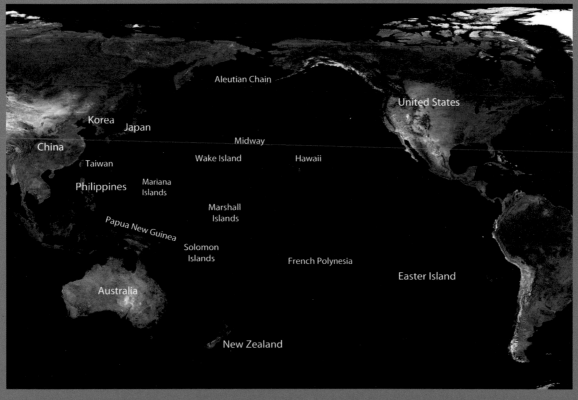

Although a number of battleships and other vessels were destroyed or damaged in Pearl Harbor, unharmed were the submarine base, the shipyard and fuel tanks as well as the carriers U.S.S. *Lexington* (CV-2) and *Enterprise* (CV-6) which were at sea during the assault. The seaplane tender (former carrier) U.S.S. *Langley* (CV-1) was in the Philippines, U.S.S. *Saratoga* (CV-3) in California, while U.S.S. *Ranger* (CV-4), U.S.S. *Yorktown* (CV-5), U.S.S. *Wasp* (CV-7) and U.S.S. *Hornet* (CV-8) were stationed on the U.S. East Coast. In May 1942, the Philippines finally capitulated. Thus, within the first five months of that, Japan's sphere of influence encompassed the Kuriles to the north, the Marianas, Marshalls, Gilberts, and Carolines in the Central Pacific, the Philippines, Indochina, Thailand, Burma, Malaysia, Borneo, the Dutch East Indies, and portions of China, New Guinea and the Bismarck Archipelago. During this period, the remaining American, British, Dutch, and Australian forces in the Pacific tried to consolidate their commands and coordinate the defense of their territories. Although unable to halt Japan's advances, several U.S. Navy carrier raids helped slow the process and also revealed weaknesses and strengths in the current methods for carrier operations. These missions were generally built around a task force consisting of one carrier plus escorts for protection. With Allied morale down, the U.S. Navy conceived a mission to raise their fighting spirit—a raid aimed against Japan itself.

"Doolittle Raid" (1942)

On April 18, 1942, Task Force (TF 16), built around U.S.S. *Enterprise* (CV-6) and U.S.S. *Hornet* (CV-8) carried out the "Doolittle Raid" attacking Tokyo and other targets in Japan. This joint Army-Navy effort was led by Army Air Force Lt. Col. James H. Doolittle and Vice Admiral William F. Halsey. Under this arrangement, 16 Army B-25 Mitchell medium bombers took off from *Hornet*'s deck, while her sister ship *Enterprise* provided defensive fighter coverage for *Hornet* as the task force had to venture far into enemy waters for the aircraft to be launched 600 nautical miles off the Japanese coast. The bombers, which could otherwise only take off from land, had sufficient range compared to carrier aircraft to reach and bomb various targets in Japan and then land in China. Landing again on U.S.S. *Hornet* was technically impossible; moreover, the valuable carriers could not stay too long in Japanese-controlled waters as

the Navy did not want to expose them to Japanese submarines. Immediately after the bombers had taken off, the carriers returned to Pearl Harbor. Although this mission did not cause any significant damage, it was considered a success as it boosted Allied morale and showed that the Japanese were not invulnerable. This was the first time that the Navy had utilized multiple carriers as part of a single task force.

Jimmy Doolittle (left) with his bomber crews shortly before the beginning of the "Doolittle Raid," the first U.S. attack on the Japanese homeland in World War II, aboard U.S.S. *Hornet*. Of the 80 men, 77 survived the mission. (U.S. Air Force)

Battle of the Coral Sea (1942)

In late April of 1942, the Japanese put together two invasion forces to land at Port Moresby (New Guinea) and on the island of Tulagi (Solomons) and a carrier force to prevent any interference from Allied naval forces. On May 7–8, 1942 after intercepting Japanese radio messages, the combined American-Australian Task Force (TF 17), commanded by Rear Admiral Frank J. Fletcher, including the carriers *Lexington* (CV-2) and U.S.S. *Yorktown* (CV-5), nine cruisers and 13 destroyers, engaged the Japanese carrier force in the Coral Sea, led by Vice Admiral Takeo Takagi, consisting of the fleet carriers *Shōkaku* and *Zuikaku*, the light carrier *Shōhō*, nine cruisers and 15 destroyers. For the first time, aircraft carriers played a decisive role in a naval battle: The two opposing fleets did not see each other as their aircraft were able to attack the enemy over long distances. Although *Lexington*, along with one destroyer and an oiler, was sunk and *Yorktown* heavily damaged, the Japanese Navy lost the light carrier *Shōhō* and one destroyer. With *Shōkaku* badly damaged and *Zuikaku*'s air group greatly reduced, both carriers would not be able to participate in the upcoming battle of Midway, whereas *Yorktown* was repaired. Moreover, the Japanese were denied access to strategically important New Guinea and thus an eventual hold on Australia.

During the battle of the Coral Sea, the Japanese aircraft carrier *Shōhō* being torpedoed by U.S. carrier aircraft in the late morning of May 7, 1942. (U.S. Navy)

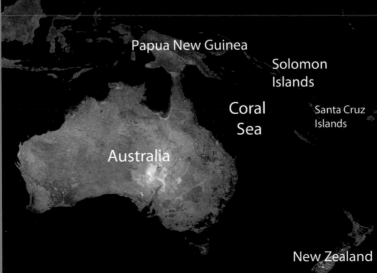

Map of the Coral Sea. (NASA)

Battle of Midway (1942)

From June 4 to 7, 1942, at the Midway Islands, the three U.S. fleet carriers, supported by bomber aircraft stationed on Midway, acting as the "fourth" American carrier, fought Japan's four fleet carriers to protect the archipelago from their access. During the course of the battle, U.S.S. *Yorktown* and one U.S. destroyer were sunk, but Japan lost all four carriers, one cruiser and a large number of experienced aircrews. Therefore, the intended invasion of Midway had to be abandoned. With such high losses in material and lives, Japan's margin of military superiority and their rapid advance through the Pacific were checked, thus marking the end of any real strategic offensive capability. During the subsequent war of attrition, Japan was not able to replace its losses, while the U.S. could through its superior industrial capacity.

The Japanese aircraft *Hiryū*, shortly before sinking during the battle of Midway. All in all, the Japanese Navy lost four of her fleet carriers (*Kaga*, *Akagi*, *Hiryū* and *Sōryū*) in this decisive engagement. (U.S. Navy)

Map of Midway. (NASA)

Following their rapid advance through the Pacific, the Japanese further secured their conquered territories and established additional controls around India, Australia and other Central Pacific islands. With Rabaul, New Britain and points along the northern shores of New Guinea (80 nm north-east from Australia) already occupied as a defensive perimeter, the Japanese aimed to further isolate Australia by disrupting British and American supply and communication lines in the South Pacific. This would entail securing access to Allied-held Port Moresby on New Guinea's southern coast and then advancing southeast into the Solomon Islands, New Hebrides, New Caledonia, Samoa and Fiji. Japan sought to remove the threat that U.S. carrier forces had posed to their recent Pacific conquests. Therefore, it was decided that after the New Guinea-Solomons campaign, future engagements against Midway (west of Hawaii) and the Aleutians (North Pacific) had to follow in order to lure U.S. carriers out into battle and to secure these areas as Japanese strongholds.

Carrier actions in the Doolittle Raid and the battle of the Coral Sea dominated the first months of the war, when U.S. Navy pilots flew relatively inferior aircraft including the Brewster F2A Buffalo and the Grumman F4F Wildcat fighter, the SBD Dauntless dive bomber, and TBD Devastator torpedo bomber. Most of these aircraft types would again play an important role in the upcoming battle at Midway.

Admiral Isoruku Yamamoto was the commander-in-chief of the Japanese Combined Fleet and therefore responsible for all naval operations in the Pacific. His American adversary was Admiral Chester W. Nimitz, commander-in-chief of the U.S. Pacific Fleet. Now, after Coral Sea, Yamamoto was even more determined to eliminate the threat of U.S. carriers by luring them into a battle at Midway. He was also aware that the U.S. had many more carriers under construction which eventually would shift the material superiority into America's favor. What he did not know was that U.S. intelligence had broken the Japanese naval code, thus knowing his plan to invade Midway (Central Pacific) and secure it as another stronghold (defensive perimeter) between Japan's offensive operations in the Southwestern Pacific and the U.S. Navy operating out of Pearl Harbor, Hawaii, in the East. Nimitz, knowing where the Japanese carriers would sail, dispatched Rear Admiral Raymond Spruance with the carriers *Enterprise* and *Hornet* to leave Hawaii and stop the Japanese fleet, which was commanded by Vice Admiral Chūichi Nagumo. His force included the four fleet carriers *Kaga*, *Akagi*, *Hiryū* and *Sōryū*, which had also previously participated in the attack on Pearl Harbor. Two days later, *Yorktown*, hastily repaired in just three days, followed with Rear Admiral Frank J. Fletcher on board.

After Midway, Japan was forced to cancel its plans to move beyond the Solomon Islands, and focused on strengthening its current holdings. This gave the Allies the opportunity to introduce some offensive measures into what had been a purely defensive strategy in their campaign to maintain some control in the Pacific. Therefore, Japan's major air base on Rabaul (New Britain, east of New Guinea) appeared to be a key launching point for any forthcoming advances as Allied control over this facility would ultimately open the way for a southern advance into the Japanese-held Philippines and subsequent assaults against Japan itself. As such, the Allies developed a strategy to establish airfields and advance bases throughout the Solomons, New Guinea, and the Bismarck Archipelago that could support a drive towards the capture of Rabaul. The first campaign phase focused on securing Guadalcanal, Tulagi, and Santa Cruz on the eastern end of the Solomons and Buna on the Papuan Peninsula in New Guinea. With operations being conducted out of Allied-held Port Moresby, the Papuan campaign would not require extensive additional naval support. However, taking Guadalcanal and the Eastern Solomons would first require amphibious landings supported by carriers and other warships.

Allied Counter-Offensive

The Allied counter-offensive in the South Pacific began in early August 1942 with Marine landings on Tulagi and Guadalcanal (Solomons), leading to stiff fighting for the latter island for six months until the Japanese withdrew north from the Papuan Peninsula in January 1943 and began evacuating Guadalcanal the following month. At the same time, their attempt to conquer New Guinea was effectively repelled, thus ending the immediate threat to Australia by depriving Japan of its air bases on the island's southern half.

In the six months that it took the U.S. and their allies to secure the waters around Guadalcanal and the Eastern Solomons, there were six major naval engagements including two aircraft carrier actions. On August 24–25, in the battle of the Eastern Solomons, the U.S. successfully repelled Yamamoto's plan to retake Guadalcanal when the fleet carriers U.S.S. *Enterprise* (CV-6) and U.S.S. *Saratoga* (CV-3), accompanied by a battleship, four cruisers and eleven destroyers engaged the Japanese landing force including the fleet carriers *Shōkaku* and *Zuikaku*, the light carrier *Ryūjō*, two battleships, 16 cruisers and 25 destroyers. During the fighting, the Japanese lost *Ryujo*, three other ships and a significant number of airmen, while the U.S. carrier *Enterprise* was heavily damaged, but still operational. On September 15, 1942, when the fleet carriers U.S.S. *Wasp* (CV-7) and U.S.S. *Hornet* (CV-8), along with the battleship U.S.S. *North Carolina* (BB-55) and 10 other warships, were escorting the transports carrying the 7th Marine Regiment to Guadalcanal as reinforcements, *Wasp* was torpedoed by the Japanese submarine *I-19*. When the fires on board got out of control, the ship was abandoned and scuttled by torpedoes from the destroyer U.S.S. *Lansdowne* (DD-486).

After landing troops on the island of Guadalcanal in preparation for a major offensive, Vice Admiral Nobutake Kondo's naval forces, including the fleet carriers *Shōkaku*, *Zuikaku* and *Jun'yō*, the light carrier *Zuihō*, four battleships, 10 cruisers and 22 destroyers, moved to the area to sink the remaining U.S. carriers (*Enterprise* and *Hornet*) there. While *Wasp* had been sunk a month earlier, *Saratoga* was temporarily inoperable after receiving a torpedo hit. On October 26, 1942, the Japanese engaged the U.S. naval forces commanded by Vice Admiral William "Bull" Halsey and Rear Admiral Thomas Kinkaid, of the carriers U.S.S. *Enterprise* (CV-6) and U.S.S. *Hornet* (CV-8), which were accompanied by one battleship, 10 cruisers and 22 destroyers. After an exchange of carrier air attacks, the U.S. vessels (including the damaged *Enterprise*) retreated after scuttling *Hornet*, which had sustained heavy bomb damage. The Japanese carrier forces also retired after suffering high aircraft and aircrew losses, and significant damage to the fleet carrier *Shōkaku* and the light carrier *Zuihō*. Although the U.S. Navy's losses were higher, it was able to replace these in the long run, while the Japanese could not. Deprived of many veteran pilots, Japanese carriers did not see any further action in the waters around Guadalcanal, thus finally giving the Allies the upper hand there. After fighting numerous battles at sea and on land over the course of 1943, which caused serious attrition to the Japanese, the U.S. Army and Navy brought the Solomons campaign to a successful completion and began driving the enemy out of New Guinea.

By mid-1943, the U.S. Navy's enormous construction program began to show its fruits as the new larger and faster fleet carriers of the *Essex*-class, the light carriers of the *Independence*-class (converted from cruiser hulls) and smaller escort carriers (converted from merchant ships) gradually were joining the fleet. Admiral Nimitz built various naval task forces around these new carriers, tailored in each case to the particular mission at hand. In the vast Central Pacific, these carrier task forces could provide both air and naval support for far longer leaps forward, while the entire Pacific fleet stood ready to confront the main Japanese fleet at any time.

Task Force

The Fast Carrier Task Force (TF 38 when assigned to the Third Fleet, TF 58 when assigned to the Fifth Fleet), was the U.S. Navy's main striking force in the Pacific from January 1944 through the war's end in August 1945. The task force was made up of several separate task groups, each typically built around three to four aircraft carriers and their supporting vessels which included cruisers, destroyers, submarines, minesweepers and the newly built fast battleships.

Air Group

Superior new aircraft that had been on the drawing boards in December 1941 were entering the U.S. Navy during 1943. The Carrier Air Group/Carrier Air Wing of an *Essex*-class aircraft carrier consisted of approximately 80 to 100 aircraft. Initially, the air wing consisted of Grumman F6F Hellcat and Chance Vought F4U Corsair fighters (from 1944) and Curtiss SB2C Helldiver dive bombers and Grumman TBF Avenger torpedo bombers. These aircraft proved to be superior to their Japanese counterparts.

The offensive in the Central Pacific began in November of 1943, following victories at Tarawa and Makin. During the invasion of the Gilbert Islands, the Navy relied on its growing fleet of aircraft carriers providing the air power necessary to seize air superiority from Japanese land-based aircraft and provide floating bases from which U.S. Marine Corps and Navy pilots could conduct devastating close air support missions on behalf of the assaulting ground forces.

With the successful invasion of the Marshall Islands in early 1944, the Central Pacific campaign proceeded apace including attacks on Truk, Guam, Saipan, and Tinian. South Pacific operations in New Guinea were completed in April 1944, when the Japanese troops there finally surrendered. U.S. naval forces then returned to the Central and Western Pacific focusing on the Marianas in June 1944. Located just 1,400 nautical miles southeast from Japan, these islands would serve as air bases for Army Boeing B-29 Superfortress bombers, enabling the U.S. to start a devastating bombing campaign against the Japanese home islands. The Japanese, who had been pushed farther and farther back in the months before, could not allow the enemy to launch air attacks against Japan from the Marianas. However, despite their losses in previous engagements, several new aircraft carriers and battleships, laid down in previous years, were now becoming operational. Therefore, Japanese naval leaders (Admiral Yamamoto had been killed when his aircraft was shot down in 1943) hoped to change the balance of power in favor of Japan in a decisive (and desperate) battle between the two navies in the Philippine Sea between the Marianas and the Philippines.

Battle of the Philippine Sea (1944)

On June 19–20, 1944, a superior U.S. naval force engaged a smaller Japanese fleet in the Marianas:

U.S. Navy	Japanese Navy
7 fleet carriers	5 fleet carriers
8 smaller carriers	4 smaller carriers
9 battleships	5 battleships
15 cruisers	13 cruisers
68 destroyers	31 destroyers
28 submarines	28 submarines
various support ships	various support ships

While the U.S. carriers could send some 900 aircraft into battle, the Japanese could operate about 450 carrier-based aircraft and an additional 300 aircraft based in the Marianas. The U.S. ships were commanded by Admiral Raymond Spruance and Vice Admiral Marc Mitscher, the Japanese fleet was led by Vice Admiral Jisaburō Ozawa and Vice Admiral Kakuji Kakuta. In this epic battle, the Japanese lost three carriers, numerous other ships, some 400 carrier-based aircraft and some 200 land-based aircraft. With the bulk of Japan's surface strength and naval air power destroyed, the fleet's remnants were forced to withdraw. The U.S., on the other hand, lost 123 aircraft but not a single ship and, through its numerical and technological superiority, was able to invade more Japanese-occupied Pacific territories, eventually leading to the recapture of the Philippines commencing at Leyte in October of 1944.

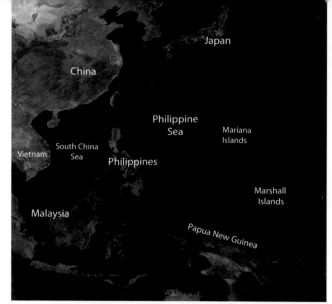

Map of the Philippine Sea. (NASA)

The Japanese aircraft carrier *Zuikaku* (center) and two destroyers under attack from U.S. carrier-based aircraft, during the late afternoon of June 20, 1944. *Zuikaku* was hit by several bombs during these attacks, but survived the battle of the Philippine Sea, June 1944. (U.S. Navy)

Sea and Air Battle of Leyte Gulf (1944)

The battle of Leyte Gulf, the largest naval engagement of World War II and one of the largest in world history, took place in the waters around the Philippines between October 23 and 26, 1944. This engagement was Japan's last attempt to halt the Allied advance in the Pacific and prevent Allied troops from landing in the Philippines. By that time, Japan had by far fewer aircraft carriers and battleships left than the U.S., underscoring the disparity in force strength at this point in the war. Regardless, Japan mobilized nearly all of its remaining major naval vessels in a desperate attempt to defeat the Allied invasion, but it was repulsed by the U.S. Navy's Third Fleet (Admiral William Halsey) and Seventh Fleet (Vice Admiral Thomas Kinkaid) including several Australian vessels.

"Great Marianas Turkey Shoot"

The aerial part of the battle of the Philippine Sea was nicknamed the "Great Marianas Turkey Shoot" by U.S. aviators for the severely disproportional loss ratio inflicted upon Japanese aircraft by U.S. pilots and antiaircraft gunners. The outcome is generally attributed to American improvements in training, tactics, technology, along with ship and aircraft design.

U.S. Navy (incl. Australian ships)	Japanese Navy
8 fleet carriers	1 fleet carrier
8 light carriers	3 light carriers
18 escort carriers	2 hybrid carriers/battleships
12 battleships	7 battleships
24 cruisers	20 cruisers
166 destroyers/destroyer escorts	35 destroyers
numerous submarines and support ships	various support ships
some 1,500 aircraft	some 300 aircraft

Map of Leyte Gulf. (NASA)

The battle included four main separate engagements: the battle of the Sibuyan Sea, the battle of Surigao Strait, the battle off Cape Engaño and the battle off Samar. It ended with an overwhelming victory for the quantitatively and qualitatively superior Allies, which lost the escort carrier U.S.S. *St. Lo* (CVE-63) after a kamikaze attack, the light carrier U.S.S. *Princeton* (CVL-23) and a few smaller ships. The Japanese lost four carriers, five battleships, numerous other ships as well as a large number of aircraft and aircrews. As a result of these losses, the Japanese Navy had effectively ceased to exist as a serious adversary and from then on was unable to exert any decisive influence on the further Allied advance against the Japanese home islands.

In January 1945, U.S. troops, supported by carrier-based aircraft and battleship gunfire, invaded Luzon in the Philippines, and fighting in the Southwest Pacific was largely over by February. Also in that month, the Marines seized Iwo Jima in order to secure the bomber routes to Japan, followed by the invasion of Okinawa in April and its final capture two months later, which eliminated the last impediment to an invasion of Japan itself. During these campaigns, Japanese "kamikaze" aircraft pilots sacrificed their lives by hitting American

The light carrier U.S.S. *Princeton* (CVL-23) afire during the battle of Leyte Gulf on October 24, 1944. The carrier (left) had been hit by a Japanese bomb, which caused fire and further explosions on board. It had to be scuttled as it could not be saved. Nevertheless, this engagement sealed the fate of the Japanese Navy as a fighting force. (U.S. Navy)

Defense against Aerial Attacks

By 1945, the U.S. Navy had developed a multilayer fleet antiair defense, integrating radar, fighter combat air patrols (CAP), and antiaircraft guns. Most combat ships possessed SK air search radar that could detect incoming aircraft, though not their altitude, to a range of 75–100 nautical miles. The use of destroyers along early warning picket lines extended this capability out to 150 miles. All carriers and many battleships, cruisers, and destroyers had shorter range SM or SP radar sets capable of identifying target direction and altitude, and fighter direction centers to vector CAP fighters to intercept. The fast carrier task forces maintained continuous CAP and all major landing operations enjoyed extended air coverage from escort carriers or land-based air units. Navy pilots averaged two years of training and 300 hours of flight time by mid-1944 before joining a carrier squadron, far exceeding the standards of their opponents.

The Navy had significantly improved the firepower and accuracy of its antiaircraft weaponry since the war began. On most warships, 5-inch/38 (12.7 cm) dual-purpose guns were used for long-range defense, while 40 mm and 20 mm automatic cannon batteries provided short-range coverage.

Radar and analog-computer-equipped dual-purpose fire directors were calculating range and bearing to automatically guide the 5-inch guns onto target. Manual and radar-guided antiaircraft gun directors were also added for the 40 mm batteries allowing them to be centrally controlled. 20 mm batteries received gyroscopically-stabilized gunsights computing elevation and traverse angles to lead incoming targets. By 1945, the number of antiaircraft guns per ship had increased drastically:

Fleet carriers	136 barrels	4 × 5-inch twins;
		4 × 5-inch/38 singles;
		17 × 40 mm quads;
		56 × 20 mm singles
Light carriers	42 barrels	2 × 40 mm quads;
		9 × 40 mm twins;
		8 × 20 mm twins
Escort carriers	37 barrels	1 × 5-inch single;
		8 × 40 mm twins;
		20 × 20 mm singles

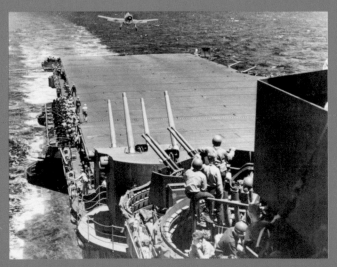

A view of the antiaircraft (AA) suite on the starboard side of the *Essex*-class aircraft carrier U.S.S. *Lexington* (CV-16). On the lower right is a Bofors 40 mm quadruple gun mount; in the center are a pair of turrets mounting dual 5-inch/38 dual (12.7 cm) purpose guns; and along the deck to the left is a gallery lined with Oerlikon 20 mm guns. In order to maximize the AA firepower, the Navy adopted circular task group antiaircraft dispositions with the highest value ships in the center and the screen and escorts deployed in concentric layers for an all-around defense in depth. The 5-inch batteries engaged attacking aircraft first at ranges of 12,000 yards or more due to their hitting power, special ammunition, and radar direction. The 40 mm and 20 mm guns provided close-in defense with massed automatic and aimed fire beginning at 3,000–3,500 yards. (U.S. Navy)

and Allied warships (primarily aircraft carriers) to stop or slow down the enemy's advance. U.S. carrier-based aircraft also succeeded sinking various Japanese battleships, including *Yamato* and *Musashi*, the largest of their type ever built. Next the Allies began preparations for a bloody invasion of Japan, which represented the largest amphibious operation ever conceived. However, due to the dropping of nuclear bombs on Hiroshima and Nagasaki in August 1945 and the subsequent Japanese surrender, this did not happen.

In December 1941, the U.S. Navy had entered the war with only eight aircraft carriers and some 5,000 aircraft. By mid-1943, at the start of the Central Pacific campaign, it operated 12 fleet aircraft carriers including the first *Essex*-class ships and 17 escort carriers, with 16 more ships completed and 16,000 aircraft operational by the end of the year. In 1944, 25 major carriers and 65 escort carriers were in service, operating more than 36,000 aircraft. When the war ended, these impressive figures had risen to 28 large carriers, 71 smaller carriers (and some aircraft transporters), and more than 41,000 aircraft.

Lexington-class

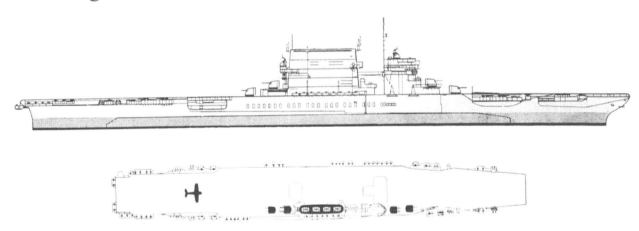

Side and top view of the *Lexington*-class. (U.S. Navy)

Originally, the ships of the *Lexington*-class were laid down in the early 1920s as battle cruisers. The 1922 Washington Naval Treaty limited the displacement for this type of ship, so the six planned ships in this series were not allowed to proceed. However, an exemption in the treaty allowed two of the six cruisers to be completed as aircraft carriers. Construction of the four remaining ships was halted and the unfinished hulls scrapped. In 1925, U.S.S. *Lexington* (CV-2) and U.S.S. *Saratoga* (CV-3) were launched as the first full-scale fleet aircraft carriers. The first carrier, the *Langley* (CV-1), converted from a coal carrier, had served primarily as a test platform for future carrier designs and ended her existence as an aircraft tender when she was sunk early in World War II. The two *Lexington*-class ships were the U.S. Navy's first operational fleet carriers and the largest American aircraft carriers until the completion of U.S.S. *Midway* (CV-41) in 1945.

Commissioned in 1927, both *Lexington* and *Saratoga* were assigned to the Pacific Fleet and participated in numerous fleet exercises in the following years, including in the Atlantic. When Japanese carrier-based aircraft attacked the Pearl Harbor naval base in Hawaii on December 7, 1941, both ships escaped destruction because they were not in port. *Lexington* was en route to the Midway Islands at the time to reinforce the garrison there by delivering aircraft; her sister ship *Saratoga* was at the U.S. West Coast. During a modernization, the

U.S.S. *Saratoga* photographed circa 1927, with a seagoing replica of HMS *Victory*, Admiral Nelson's flagship at the battle of Trafalgar in 1805, in the foreground. (U.S. Navy)

U.S.S. *Saratoga* seen from an aircraft that has just taken off, circa 1928. (U.S. Navy)

Lexington-class received a slightly improved flight deck and, most importantly, more powerful antiaircraft guns. During the naval battle of the Coral Sea, the first naval battle in history fought exclusively among aircraft carriers, *Lexington* received several bomb and torpedo hits on May 8, 1942, and had to be scuttled.

During the war, *Saratoga* participated in the battles for the Solomon Islands and the Gilbert and Marshall Islands, among others. She also supported the British Royal Navy in the Indian Ocean during attacks on the East Indian Territories occupied by Japan. During her service in the invasion of Iwo Jima in early 1945, the carrier suffered heavy damage from kamikaze attacks and, after its repairs, served only as a training ship until the end of the war. During the atomic bomb tests at Bikini Atoll in 1946, *Saratoga* was severely damaged as a target ship and sank. To this day, the wreck is a popular destination for divers (see chapter 5).

The sister ships *Saratoga* (front) and *Lexington* (rear) off the coast of the Hawaiian island of Oahu during the 1930s. Diamond Head is visible in the background. This extinct volcano is the landmark of Hawaii. (U.S. Navy)

U.S.S. *Lexington* under air attack on May 8, 1942 during the battle of the Coral Sea, as photographed from a Japanese aircraft. Heavy black smoke from her stack and white smoke from her bow indicate that the view was taken just after those areas were hit by bombs. The destroyer in the lower left appears to be U.S.S. *Phelps* (DD-360). (U.S. Navy)

A mushroom cloud rises after a heavy explosion on board U.S.S. *Lexington*. This is probably the great explosion from the detonation of torpedo warheads stowed in the starboard side of the hangar, aft, that followed an explosion amidships in the late afternoon. (U.S. Navy)

The heavily damaged *Lexington* shortly before her sinking. The crew leaves the burning ship, which is sunk a short time later by the destroyer *Phelps* with torpedoes. (U.S. Navy)

A Hellcat F6F-3 shortly before takeoff from *Saratoga*'s deck in 1943. (U.S. Navy)

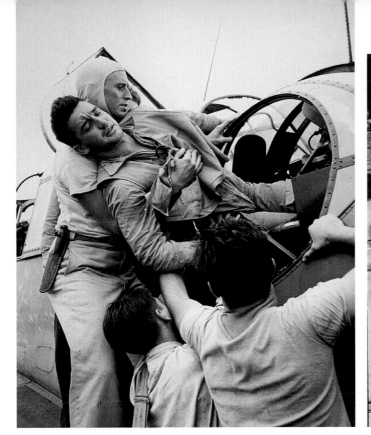

Crew members aboard U.S.S. *Saratoga* lifting an airman out of a TBF Avenger's rear turret after a raid on Rabaul on November 5, 1943. The aircraft and a F6F Hellcat successfully fought off eight attacking Zeroes, downing three. (U.S. Navy)

Jubilant over the success of the task force raid on Rabaul, Cdr. Joseph C. Clifton passes out cigars aboard U.S.S. *Saratoga*. (U.S. National Archives)

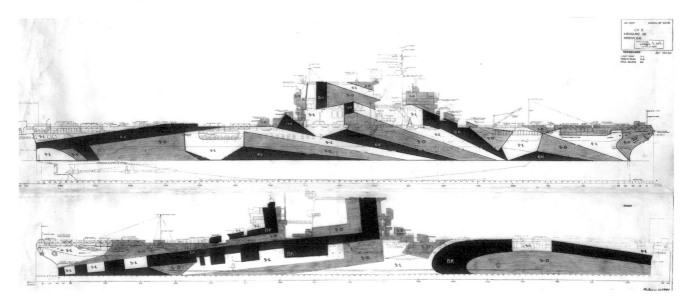

U.S. Navy Camouflage Measure 32, Design 11A: Drawing prepared by the Bureau of Ships for a camouflage scheme intended for U.S.S. *Saratoga* showing the ship's starboard and port sides. She was painted in this camouflage design during her summer 1944 overhaul. (U.S. Navy)

U.S.S. *Saratoga* at war's end. Her large smokestack made it easy to distinguish the *Lexington*-class from other carrier classes. (U.S. Navy)

Operation *Crossroads*' nuclear weapons test, July 26, 1946, at Bikini Atoll: view taken from Eneu Island 10 seconds after the underwater bomb "Baker" was fired. U.S.S. *Saratoga* is visible in the left foreground, being lifted out of the water. She sank later that day. (U.S. Navy)

U.S.S. *Saratoga* sinking in Bikini Atoll lagoon after she was fatally damaged by the "Baker" test. Note its hull number "3" still visible at the front of the flight deck, air escaping from the submerged hull and oil streaming away to starboard. (U.S. Navy)

Lexington-class General Characteristics

Class	*Lexington*
Type	fleet carrier
Name	U.S.S. *Lexington* (CV-2) U.S.S. *Saratoga* (CV-3)
Shipyard	Fore River Shipyard, Quincy, Massachusetts (CV-2) New York Shipbuilding, Camden, New Jersey (CV-3)
Commissioning	December 14, 1927 (CV-2) November 16, 1927 (CV-3)
Standard displacement	36,000 tons (47,700 tons deep load)
Length	888 feet (270.7 m)
Beam	106 feet (32.3 m)
Draft	30 feet 5 in (9.3 m) (deep load)
Propulsion	4 sets turbo-electric transmission
Shafts	4
Shaft horsepower	180,000 shp
Maximum speed	33.3 knots
Armor deck	0.75–2 in (19–51 mm)
Side armor (belt)	5–7 in (127–178 mm)
Armament	4 × twin 8-inch (20.3 cm) guns 12 × single 5-inch (12.7 cm) antiaircraft guns
Aircraft	80-90
Complement	2,800
Fate	*Lexington*: Sunk in Coral Sea, May 8, 1942 *Saratoga*: Sunk as a target ship, July 25, 1946

[Displacement in tons (1 ton = 1.060 kg)]

U.S.S. *Ranger*

After two *Lexington*-class battle cruisers had been converted into aircraft carriers, *Ranger* (CV-4) was the first U.S. carrier to be planned and designed as such. However, with a standard displacement of 14,576 tons, she was only about half the size of the preceding class and strictly adhered to the limitations of the Washington Naval Agreement. After her commissioning in 1934, the *Ranger* made her maiden voyage to South America and then joined the Pacific Fleet. Due to her smaller design compared to the *Lexington*-class, several weaknesses soon became apparent. With a relatively low top speed of 29 knots and limited seaworthiness, *Ranger* had reduced suitability as a fleet carrier for operations along with the other fast fleet carriers in the Pacific. After her transfer to the Atlantic in 1939, she sailed there on patrol and protected convoys. In November 1942, her aircraft supported the capture of Casablanca on the coast of Morocco as part of the Allied invasion of North Africa (Operation *Torch*). Her return to the Pacific in 1944 was followed by service as a training ship. After the war, *Ranger* served for only one more year and was sold for scrapping in Pennsylvania in early 1947.

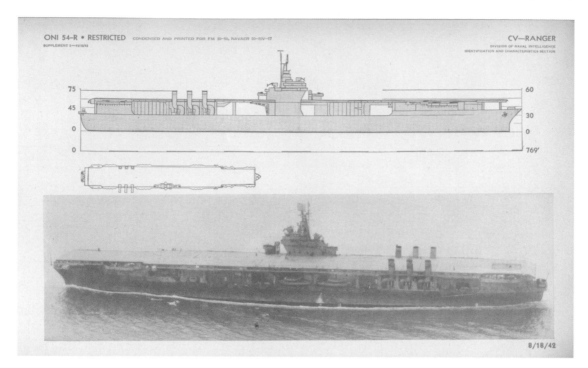

Side and top view of U.S.S. *Ranger*. (U.S. Navy)

U.S.S. *Ranger* in Cuban waters in 1939. Compared to the previous *Lexington*-class, her smaller design earned her the designation "Light Fleet Carrier." (U.S. Navy)

U.S.S. *Ranger* at anchor in 1940. In contrast to the massive smokestack of *Lexington*-class, the new carrier featured six small funnels. These were located on either side of the flight deck aft of the conning tower and were foldable outward. (U.S. National Museum of Naval Aviation)

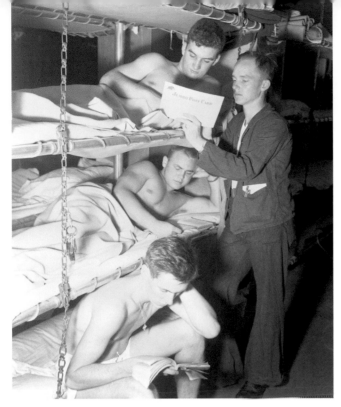

U.S. Navy crewmen relaxing on their bunks in crew quarters aboard a World War II fleet carrier. Compared to smaller ships, such as submarines or destroyers, the living conditions on carriers, battleships or heavy cruisers were quite comfortable as these large ships featured amenities such as mess decks, a hospital, a dentist's office, a barber shop and even a post office. (U.S. Navy)

Ranger-class General Characteristics

Class	*Ranger* (single ship)
Type	Light fleet carrier
Name	U.S.S. *Ranger* (CV-4)
Shipyard	Newport News Shipbuilding, Virginia
Commissioning	February 25, 1933
Standard displacement	14,576 tons (17,577 tons deep load)
Length	769 feet (234.4 m)
Beam	109 feet 5 in (33.4 m)
Draft	22 feet 4.875 in (6.8 m)
Propulsion	2 × steam turbines; 6 × boilers
Shafts	2
Shaft horsepower	53.500 shp
Maximum speed	29 knots
Armor deck	1 in (2.5 cm) (over steering gear)
Side armor (belt)	2 in (5.1 cm)
Armament	8 × 5-inch (12.7 cm) antiaircraft guns 40 × 50 caliber (12.7 mm) machine guns
Aircraft	76–86
Complement	2148
Fate	scrapped in 1947

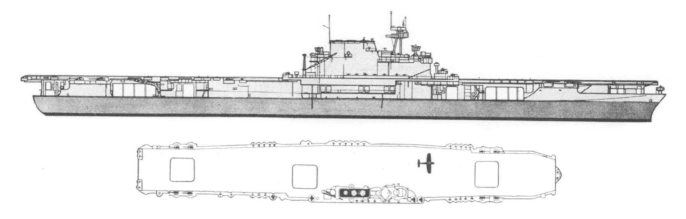

Side and top view of the *Yorktown*-class. (U.S. Navy)

Yorktown-class

After the completion of the *Lexington*-class and the keel laying of U.S.S. *Ranger* in the early 1930s, the U.S. Navy still had 52,000 tons of the 135,000 tons available for the construction of additional aircraft carriers. Therefore, various plans were considered, including the construction of four small carriers resembling *Ranger* or, alternatively, the construction of two large ships like those of the *Lexington*-class. Ultimately, the U.S. Navy decided on two medium-sized fleet carriers, each with a displacement of just under 20,000 tons, and one small carrier of about 14,700 tons. These three ships fully utilized the tonnage limitations of the Washington Naval Treaty, although the third ship, U.S.S. *Wasp* (CV-7), as a single ship, would not be included in this class.

The two medium-sized carriers were named U.S.S. *Yorktown* (CV-5) and U.S.S. *Enterprise* (CV-6) entering service in 1937–1938. When the treaty's terms expired in 1938, the Navy decided to strengthen the new carrier fleet with another full-scale fleet carrier. However, lacking funds for a new design, the third ship, U.S.S. *Hornet* (CV-8), was built on the pattern of the *Yorktown*-class and thus still complied with the restrictions of the long-expired Washington Naval Treaty. Commissioned in October 1941, she and her two sister ships served in the Pacific. Until the Japanese attack on Pearl Harbor, they participated in various fleet maneuvers testing new mission profiles for aircraft carriers as these ships were new and untested in combat. *Yorktown*, *Enterprise*, and *Hornet*, along with *Lexington* and *Saratoga*, would form the backbone of the U.S. Navy during the first half of the Pacific War.

The carriers U.S.S. *Yorktown* (CV-5), right, and U.S.S. *Enterprise* (CV-6) under construction at the Newport News Shipbuilding and Dry Dock Company, Newport News, Virginia, 1935–1936. (U.S. Navy)

The newly commissioned U.S.S. *Yorktown* (CV-5) in fall of 1937. (U.S. Navy)

A SBD Dauntless dive bomber overflying a *Yorktown* class carrier in 1942. The older carrier *Lexington* is in the background. (U.S. Navy)

U.S. Marines manning forward port side 20 mm gun battery aboard U.S.S. *Yorktown* in 1942 (the camera is looking aft). Note the details of gun mountings and shields, rubber non-skid mats on deck and splinter protection on the outboard side of the gun gallery. Aircraft arresting gear is visible on the flight deck, at left. As a result of combat experience, 20 mm gun shields were later modified with angled cut-outs on the inside top of each plate, providing the gunner with better vision to each side of the aiming point. (U.S. Navy)

A 5-inch/38 caliber (12.7 cm) dual-purpose gun mounted on U.S.S. *Yorktown*'s starboard gun platform, looking aft and to starboard, 1937. Note the fuze-setting mechanism on the gun mount's left side and non-skid rubber matting on the deck. (U.S. National Archives)

The 16 B-25 bombers lashed to *Hornet*'s deck. The plan called for them to bomb military targets in Japan and to continue westward to land in China. (U.S. National Archives)

The first B-25 with Jimmy Doolittle at the yoke takes off from the U.S.S. *Hornet*'s deck on April 18, 1942. All 16 aircraft managed the difficult takeoff from the short carrier deck and accomplished their mission to attack several targets in Japan. Fifteen aircraft reached China but all crashed, while the 16th landed in the Soviet Union. This success boosted U.S. morale and proved that Japan was vulnerable despite its initial military successes. However, the consequences were most severely felt in China, where Japanese reprisals caused the deaths of up to 250,000 civilians and 70,000 soldiers (U.S. National Archives)

U.S.S. *Yorktown*'s pilots posing for a group picture. (U.S. Navy)

U.S.S. *Yorktown*, along with U.S.S. *Lexington*, participated in the battle of the Coral Sea in May 1942, suffering heavy damage from bomb hits. However, the carrier was repaired in the record time of only three days at Pearl Harbor, so that it was able to participate in the following engagement, the battle of Midway, in early June 1942. However, *Yorktown* eventually became a victim of the Japanese submarine *I-168* and sank on June 7, 1942, after the battle, following several torpedo hits. In 1998, an expedition led by deep-sea explorer Dr. Robert Ballard discovered *Yorktown*'s wreck at a depth of 5,075 meters in the Pacific.

U.S.S. *Yorktown* in Dry Dock No. 1 at the Pearl Harbor Naval Shipyard, May 29, 1942, receiving urgent repairs for damage received in the battle of the Coral Sea. She left Pearl Harbor the next day to participate in the battle of Midway. (U.S. Navy)

During the battle of Midway, U.S.S. *Yorktown* receiving a hit from a Japanese torpedo bomber on June 4, 1942. (U.S. Navy)

Black smoke pouring from U.S.S. *Yorktown* on June 4, 1942, after she had suffered hits from Japanese dive bombers. (U.S. Navy)

Scene on board U.S.S. *Yorktown*, shortly after being hit by three Japanese bombs. Dense smoke is from fires in her uptakes, caused by a bomb that punctured them and knocked out her boilers. A man with a hammer at right is probably covering a bomb entry hole in the forward elevator. Note arresting gear wires and forward palisade elements on the flight deck; CXAM radar antenna, large national ensign and YE homing beacon antenna atop the foremast; 5-inch (12.7 cm), 50 caliber and 20 mm guns manned and ready at left. The heavy cruiser U.S.S. *Astoria* (CA-34) is visible on the left. (U.S. Navy)

U.S.S. *Yorktown*'s sister ship, *Hornet*, also sank four months later due to Japanese torpedo hits in the battle of the Santa Cruz Islands. After these losses, and until the commissioning of the new *Essex*-class, U.S.S. *Enterprise*, the only survivor of the *Yorktown*-class, was for a time the only operational U.S. aircraft carrier in the Pacific. She participated in nearly every battle in the Pacific (including Midway, Guadalcanal, Gilbert Islands, Leyte and Okinawa) and was the U.S. Navy's most highly decorated warship at the end of the war receiving 20 battle stars, the U. S. Navy Presidential Unit Citation and the U.S. Navy Unit Commendation.

After her decommissioning in 1947, there were efforts to preserve this famous carrier as a museum ship for posterity. However, when these attempts failed, primarily due to financial hurdles, the famous *Enterprise* was scrapped in 1958. In honor of this highly decorated ship, the world's first nuclear-powered carrier, commissioned in 1961, was also christened U.S.S. *Enterprise* (CVN-65). With CVN-65 decommissioned in 2017, a new *Enterprise* (CVN-80) currently under construction is scheduled to enter service in the late 2020s.

U.S.S. *Hornet*, after supporting the capture and defense of Guadalcanal, under attack during the battle of the Santa Cruz Islands on October 27, 1942, where she was irreparably damaged by enemy torpedo and dive bombers. Faced with an approaching Japanese surface force, *Hornet* was abandoned and later torpedoed and sunk by Japanese destroyers. She was in service for a year and six days and was the last U.S. fleet carrier sunk by enemy fire. For these actions, she was awarded four service stars, a citation for the 1942 Doolittle Raid, and her Torpedo Squadron 8 received a Presidential Unit Citation for extraordinary heroism at the battle of Midway. Her wreck was located in late January 2019 resting upright on the ocean floor near the Solomon Islands. (U.S. Navy)

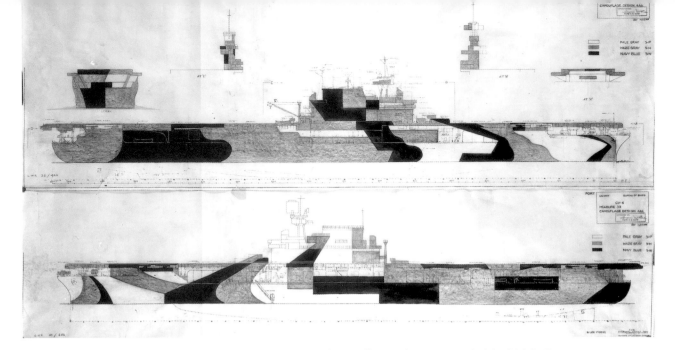

U.S. Navy Camouflage Measure 33, Design 4Ab: Camouflage scheme intended for U.S.S. *Enterprise* in 1944, showing both of the ship's sides, her stern and her superstructure ends. The carrier was painted in this camouflage pattern later in 1944. (U.S. Navy)

U.S.S. *Enterprise* pained in Camouflage Measure 33, Design 4Ab. (U.S. Navy)

A Japanese bomb exploding on the flight deck of U.S.S. *Enterprise*, just aft of the island, during the battle of the Eastern Solomons on August 24, 1942. (U.S. National Archives)

U.S.S. *Enterprise* steaming toward the Panama Canal on October 10, 1945, while en route to New York to participate in Navy Day celebrations following the Japanese surrender a month earlier. While her predecessor U.S.S. *Ranger* had three small funnels on each side of the flight deck, the smokestack aboard *Enterprise* and her two sister ships was combined with the conning tower. (U.S. National Archives)

Insignia of U.S.S. *Enterprise*. (U.S. Navy)

Stern plate of U.S.S. *Enterprise* at Veteran's Memorial Park, River Vale, New Jersey. (Tiberius Wise)

Yorktown-class General Characteristics

Class	*Yorktown*
Type	fleet carrier
Name	U.S.S. *Yorktown* (CV-5) U.S.S. *Enterprise* (CV-6) U.S.S. *Hornet* (CV-8)
Shipyard	Newport News Shipbuilding, Virginia
Commissioning	September 30, 1937 (CV-5) May 12, 1938 (CV-6) October 20, 1941 (CV-8)
Standard displacement	19,800 tons (25,500 tons deep load)
Length	824 ft 9 in (251.38 m)
Beam	109 ft 6 in (33.38 m) width at flight deck
Draft	26 ft (7.9 m)
Propulsion	4 × steam turbines; 9 × boilers
Shafts	4
Shaft horsepower	120.000 shp
Maximum speed	32.5 knots
Armor deck	2.5–4 in (6.4–10.2 cm)
Side armor max.	2.5 in (6.4 cm)
Armament	8 × 5-inch (12.7 cm) guns 4 × quad 1.1-inch (2.8 cm) guns (*Enterprise* upgraded to 40 mm Bofors guns) 24 × 50 caliber (12.7 mm) machine guns (all ships upgraded to 20 mm Oerlikon cannons)
Aircraft	90–96
Complement	2217
Fate	*Yorktown*: Sunk by submarine after battle of Midway, June 6, 1942 *Enterprise*: scrapped 1958–1960 *Hornet*: Sunk off Santa Cruz Islands, October 26, 1942

U.S.S. *Wasp*

America's seventh carrier, *Wasp* (CV-7), was commissioned in 1935 as a single ship with a standard displacement of 14,700 tons. After the keel laying of *Yorktown* and *Enterprise*, the U.S. Navy still had 15,000 tons available for the construction of aircraft carriers according to the terms of the Washington Naval Treaty. Since the design of the previous *Yorktown*-class had proved successful, *Wasp* was constructed as a scaled-down version of that carrier type to take full advantage of the tonnage allowed. After entering service in 1940, the new carrier initially served for two years in the Atlantic, assisting the Royal Navy in transporting aircraft to the Mediterranean island of Malta. With the U.S. Navy having lost *Lexington* at the battle of the Coral Sea and *Yorktown* at Midway, *Wasp* was ordered to the Pacific in June 1942 to reinforce the naval units remaining there.

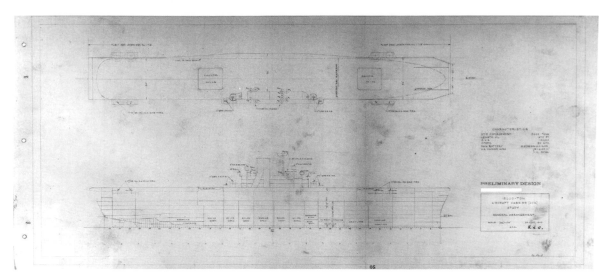

Side and top view of U.S.S. *Wasp*. (U.S. Navy)

There she supported the invasion of Guadalcanal in the Solomons and helped defend the island against possible Japanese attempts to recapture it. On September 15, 1942, *Wasp* was hit by three torpedoes from the Japanese submarine *I-19*, killing 193 men. When fires on board got out of control, the crew had to abandon ship and were picked up by U.S. escort ships. The destroyer U.S.S. *Lansdowne* finally had to sink *Wasp* as she could not be saved.

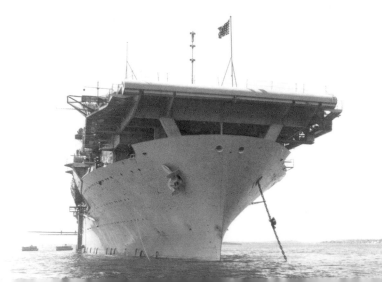

U.S.S. *Wasp* shortly after her commissioning in 1940. Like U.S.S. *Ranger*, she was considered a "*Light* Fleet Carrier." (U.S. Navy)

Close-up of *Wasp*'s bow. The massive structure of aircraft carriers made (and still make) them very sensitive to strong crosswinds. This could lead to accidents when passing through narrow channels. (U.S. Navy)

The burning U.S.S. *Wasp* shortly before her sinking south of Guadalcanal on September 15, 1942. The Japanese submarine *I-19* had sealed the carrier's fate. (U.S. Navy)

Wasp-class General Characteristics

Class	*Wasp* (single ship)
Type	Light fleet carrier
Name	U.S.S. *Wasp* (CV-7)
Shipyard	Fore River Shipyard, Quincy, Massachusetts
Commissioning	April 25, 1940
Standard displacement	14,700 tons (19,7116 tons deep load)
Length	741 feet 3 in (225.9 m)
Beam	109 feet (33.2 m)
Draft	20 feet (6.1 m)
Propulsion	2 × steam turbines; 6 × boilers
Shafts	2
Shaft horsepower	70,000 shp
Maximum speed	29.5 knots
Armor deck	1.25 in (32 mm) deck over steering gear
Side armor max.	3.5 in (89 mm)
Armament	8 × 5-inch (12.7 cm) guns 16 × 1.1-inch (2.8 cm) antiaircraft guns 24 × 50 caliber (12.7 mm) machine guns
Aircraft	80
Complement	2167
Fate	Scuttled off Guadalcanal after Japanese submarine attack, September 15, 1942

Essex-class

The *Essex*-class, which included the *Ticonderoga*-subclass, whose hulls were 52 feet (16 meters) feet longer, consisted of 17 ships by the end of World War II. While seven more were completed by 1950, two carriers were scrapped half-finished. These ships played an important role in the Pacific theater of war beginning in 1943 and they were also used in modernized form in the Korean and Vietnam wars. With 24 ships completed during the war, the *Essex*-class was the most widely built fleet aircraft carrier class.

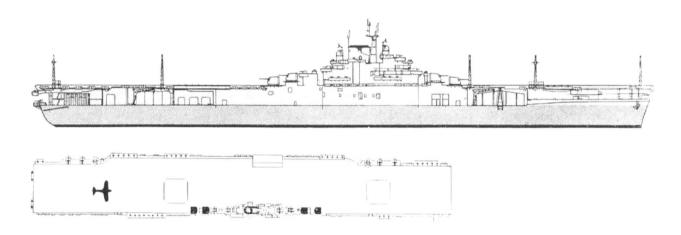

Side and top view of the *Essex*-class in its World War II appearance. (U.S. Navy)

When the displacement limits of the Washington Naval Treaty, ratified 16 years earlier, expired in 1938, the United States, under the Naval Expansion Act, decided to build more aircraft carriers. After the completion of *Hornet*, the last ship of the *Yorktown*-class, the U.S. Navy began planning the successor class. The experiences gained from previous carrier classes were incorporated into the design of the new *Essex*-class in order to create a type of ship that was primarily designed for operations in the vast Pacific. In addition to a greater range of about 17,000 nautical miles, the new carriers were also to be able to accommodate more aircraft. This required an increase of the flight deck's size and hangars below. Since long-distance resupply was difficult, the *Essex*-class was also to be able to carry more spare parts than its predecessors.

After the keel laying of the type ship U.S.S. *Essex* (CV-9), the U.S. Navy authorized three more ships under the Two Oceans Navy Act in May 1940. At that time, the United States considered Japan to become a future adversary, as it was rising economically and militarily. The island nation had been expanding its carrier fleet since the 1920s, had forcibly annexed parts of China and was now expanding in Southeast Asia. The Two-Oceans-Navy Act was intended to increase the size of the U.S. Navy by 70 percent so that naval leaders could have enough ships in the Pacific and Atlantic simultaneously.

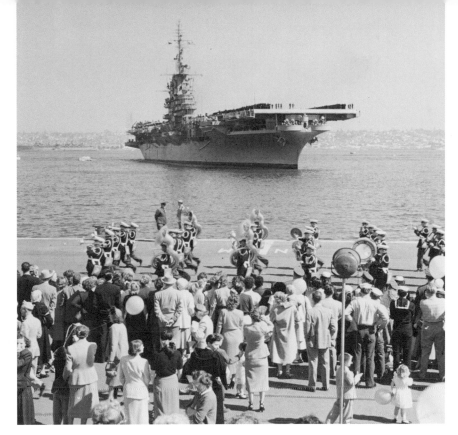

U.S.S. *Essex* in the early 1950s. She participated in several campaigns in the Pacific War, earning the Presidential Unit Citation and 13 battle stars. Decommissioned shortly after the war, she was modernized and recommissioned in the early 1950s as an attack carrier (CVA), eventually becoming an antisubmarine aircraft carrier (CVS). In her second career, she served mainly in the Atlantic, playing a role in the Cuban Missile Crisis. *Essex* also served during the Korean War. She was the primary recovery carrier for the Apollo 7 space mission. Decommissioned for the last time in 1969, the ship was sold for scrap in 1975. (U.S. Navy)

After the defeat of France in the summer of 1940, the U.S. Congress authorized an additional seven *Essex*-class carriers (CV-13 through CV-19). On December 13, 1941, six days after the Japanese attack on Pearl Harbor, two more ships (CV-20 and CV-21) were authorized. The next 10 ships (CV-31 through CV-40) followed in August 1942 and three more (CV-45 through CV-47) in June 1943, at which time the first carriers of the new class appeared as reinforcements in the Pacific theater of war.

In 1945, the final year of the war, U.S. President Franklin D. Roosevelt, however, rejected the construction of an additional six carriers (CV-50 through CV-55) as being unnecessary. During the war, the construction time of an *Essex*-class carrier was between 13 and 20 months. The shipyards were able to achieve this by working three shifts and standardizing components and production processes. Construction of the 26 authorized *Essex/Ticonderoga*-class aircraft carriers took place at five shipyards on the U.S. East Coast:

1. Newport News Shipbuilding in Newport News, Virginia (10 ships)

2. Fore River Shipyard in Quincy, Massachusetts (5 ships)

3. New York Navy Yard in Brooklyn, New York (5 ships)

4. Norfolk Navy Yard in Portsmouth, Virginia (3 ships)

5. Philadelphia Navy Yard, Pennsylvania (3 ships)

Based on operational experience with the first completed carriers (CV-9 through CV-13), U.S. naval architects and engineers made changes to the original design. This included modifying the bow section to prevent damage to the leading edge of the flight deck in high seas and to allow more antiaircraft guns to be placed there. The modified ships were thus 52 feet (16 m) longer than the first *Essex*-class ships. The first was U.S.S. *Ticonderoga* (CV-14) and twelve more carriers followed. For this reason, the lengthened version was called the "long hull" *Ticonderoga*-subclass. Seventeen ships of the *Essex/Ticonderoga* class were completed before the end of the war in August/September of 1945, of which fourteen saw service in the Pacific:

	Name	No.	*	Commissioned	Decommissioned	Shipyard	Fate
1	*Essex*	CV-9	(E)	Dec 31, 1942	Jun 30, 1969	Newport News Shipbuilding, Virginia	scrapped in 1975
2	Yorktown	CV-10	(E)	Apr 15, 1943	Jun 30, 1970	Newport News Shipbuilding, Virginia	Museum ship in Charleston, South Carolina, since 1975
3	*Intrepid*	CV-11	(E)	Aug 16, 1943	Mar 15, 1974	Newport News Shipbuilding, Virginia	Museum ship in New York City since 1982
4	*Hornet*	CV-12	(E)	Nov 29, 1943	Jan 26, 1970	Newport News Shipbuilding, Virginia	Museum ship in Alameda, California, since 1998
5	*Franklin*	CV-13	(E)	Jan 31, 1944	Feb 17, 1947	Newport News Shipbuilding, Virginia	scrapped in 1966
6	*Ticonderoga*	CV-14		May 8, 1944	Nov 16, 1973	Newport News Shipbuilding, Virginia	scrapped in 1974
7	*Randolph*	CV-15		Oct 9, 1944	Nov 16, 1973	Newport News Shipbuilding, Virginia	scrapped in 1974
8	*Lexington*	CV-16	(E)	Feb 17, 1943	Nov 8, 1991	Fore River Shipyard, Quincy, Massachusetts	Museum ship in Corpus Christi, Texas, since 1992
9	*Bunker Hill*	CV-17	(E)	May 25, 1943	Jul 9, 1947	Fore River Shipyard, Quincy, Massachusetts	scrapped in 1973
10	*Wasp*	CV-18	(E)	Nov 24, 1943	Jul 1, 1972	Fore River Shipyard, Quincy, Massachusetts	scrapped in 1973
11	*Hancock*	CV-19		Apr 15, 1944	Jan 30, 1976	Fore River Shipyard, Quincy, Massachusetts	scrapped in 1976
12	*Bennington*	CV-20	(E)	Aug 6, 1944	Jan 15, 1970	New York Navy Yard, Brooklyn, New York	scrapped in 1976
13	*Bon Homme Richard*	CV-31	(E)	Nov 26, 1944	Jul 2, 1971	New York Navy Yard, Brooklyn, New York	scrapped in 1992
14	*Shangri-La*	CV-38		Sep 15, 1944	Jul 30, 1971	Norfolk Navy Yard, Portsmouth, Virginia	scrapped in 1988

*The ships marked with "E" still received the original bow shape according to the design of the type ship U.S.S. *Essex*, all other ships received the modified bow of U.S.S. *Ticonderoga*. From U.S.S. *Boxer* (CV-21) onwards, with the exception of U.S.S. *Oriskany* [CV-34] all new ships received exclusively the "*Ticonderoga*"-bow.

The three carriers U.S.S. *Boxer* (CV-21), U.S.S. *Antietam* (CV-36) and U.S.S. *Lake Champlain* (CV-39) were completed during the war, but did not see direct front-line service. Seven more carriers were completed by 1950, with U.S.S. *Oriskany* (CV-34) being the last to enter service.

U.S.S. *Leyte* (CV-32)

U.S.S. *Kearsarge* (CV-33)

U.S.S. *Oriskany* (E) (CV-34)

U.S.S. *Princeton* (CV-37)

U.S.S. *Tarawa* (CV-40)

U.S.S. *Valley Forge* (CV-45)

U.S.S. *Philippine Sea* (CV-47)

Two other carriers still under construction in 1945, *Reprisal* (CV-35) and *Iwo Jima* (CV-46), remained unfinished and were eventually broken up.

At the beginning of the Pacific War, *Essex*-class carriers operated alone or in groups of two. In case of

A Japanese kamikaze aircraft shortly before hitting the deck of U.S.S. *Essex* off the coast of the Philippines in November 1944. (National Museum of Naval Aviation)

U.S.S. *Essex* hit by the kamikaze off the Philippines. (U.S. Navy)

Close-up of a kamikaze hit on the flight deck of U.S.S. *Essex*. The wooden flight decks of U.S. carriers were not barely armored and therefore very vulnerable to bombs or impacting aircraft. In addition, burning aircraft fuel could spread the fires on board fatally. (National Museum of Naval Aviation)

TBM Avengers and SB2C Helldivers from U.S.S. *Essex* dropping bombs on Hakodate, Japan, in July 1945. (U.S. National Archives)

attack, the ships were supposed to separate from each other and thus force the enemy units to disperse as well. However, this revealed the vulnerability of carriers operating individually, so they were combined into larger battle groups. These "carrier task forces" consisted of three to four or more aircraft carriers, which sometimes included the light carriers of the *Independence*-class, and were escorted by battleships, cruisers, and destroyers. The escort ships formed a screen around the carrier to protect it from air attack. *Essex*-class carriers formed the backbone for Allied offensives in the Pacific War. While American submarines brought Japanese supplies to a virtual standstill by 1945 (and sunk about 100 warships including the carrier *Shinano*), carrier aircraft destroyed almost the entire Japanese surface fleet in major battles such as in Leyte Gulf in 1944 and supported invasions such as at Iwo Jima and Okinawa.

The second U.S.S. *Yorktown* (CV-10), commissioned in 1943, with F6F Hellcat fighters on her flight deck in 1943. The first carrier with this name was sunk the previous year at Midway. CV-10 was called "The Fighting Lady" or "The Lucky Y" coming to fame through the battles for the Marshall Islands, the Mariana Islands and the battle of the Philippine Sea. Her aircraft were also instrumental in the sinking of the Japanese super-battleship *Yamato*, the largest battleship ever built (along with her sister ship *Musashi*). (U.S. Navy)

Although aircraft carriers were the largest navy ships along with battleships, this photo gives an impression of the confinement in the hangar aboard *Yorktown* (CV-10). (U.S. National Archives)

A Japanese torpedo bomber approaching *Yorktown* (CV-10) in 1944, still carrying its torpedo under the fuselage. (National Museum of Naval Aviation)

The bow of U.S.S. *Hornet* (CV-12) showing damage received in a typhoon on June 5, 1945. The flight deck has been bent downwards over the bow. (U.S. Navy)

During the war, no *Essex*-class carrier was lost, neither by enemy action nor accident. However, these powerful but vulnerable ships were very often the target of Japanese air attacks. The U.S.S. *Franklin* was hit hardest in a bombing raid on March 19, 1945, with heavy explosions on board that killed over 700 crewmen. An attack on the U.S.S. *Bunker Hill* on May 11, 1945, killed 372 sailors. Six other aircraft carriers were hit by kamikaze planes during the Pacific War, some of them heavily, U.S.S. *Intrepid* even twice within half a year. In addition, she and U.S.S. *Yorktown* received torpedo hits in 1944, but these did not affect the buoyancy of either ship. U.S.S. *Hornet* and U.S.S. *Bennington* sustained heavy damage to the leading edges of their flight decks in a typhoon on June 5, 1945. These ships had an open space between the flight deck and deck spaces below. This space was often used as emplacements for antiaircraft guns. However, in heavy seas, a lot of seawater would enter the carrier under the flight deck, causing damage and corrosion from the salt water. The introduction of the "hurricane bow" after the war enclosed this opening, thus eliminating the problem and making the ships more seaworthy.

Crews from the repair ship U.S.S. *Ajax* (AR-6) repairing the forward flight deck of U.S.S. *Bennington* (CV-20) at Leyte. On June 5, 1945, the carrier was damaged by Typhoon "Connie" off Okinawa and retired to Leyte, Philippines, for repairs. The ship's aircraft supported the invasion of Iwo Jima and helped sink the Japanese battleship *Yamato*. In 1954, during her Cold War service, a catapult explosion killed 103 crew members. The ship was decommissioned in 1970 and scrapped 24 years later. (U.S. Navy)

Torpedo damage on U.S.S. *Intrepid* (CV-11): During February 1944, a Japanese torpedo bomber scored a hit near her stern five meters below the waterline, jamming her rudder to port and flooding several compartments. Captain Thomas L. Sprague was able to counteract the jammed rudder by running the port side screw at high speed while idling the starboard screw for two days until high winds overpowered the improvised steering. The crew then fashioned a jury-rigged sail out of scrap canvas and hatch covers, allowing *Intrepid* to return to Pearl Harbor for temporary repairs. (U.S. Navy)

Burial at sea for the officers and enlisted men of U.S.S. *Intrepid* (CV-11), who lost their lives when the carrier was hit by Japanese bombs during operations in the Philippines on November 26, 1944. (U.S. Navy)

U.S.S. *Intrepid* (CV-11) burning after a kamikaze hit during the invasion of Okinawa on April 16, 1945. The hit claimed eight lives, however, the damage was repaired within three hours. *Intrepid* was known to the Japanese as a "ghost ship," as she was frequently reported as sunk or badly damaged. She received more hits than any other carrier in the Pacific. (National Museum of Naval Aviation)

The 40 mm Bofors antiaircraft (AA) guns were an effective weapon against Japanese air attacks. During the course of the war, the number of these weapons increased on U.S. Navy ships. The photograph shows a 40 mm quadruple AA gun in action aboard *Hornet* in 1945. (U.S. National Archives)

U.S.S. *Franklin* (CV-13) was severely damaged twice during the Pacific War. In October 1944, two kamikaze aircraft hit her, killing 56 crew members. The photograph shows the carrier on March 19, 1945, after another attack, in which it received two heavy bomb hits causing devastating fires, killing (depending on the source) 724 crew members and injuring another 265. These losses were the heaviest suffered by any U.S. aircraft carrier during World War II. (U.S. Navy)

U.S.S. *Ticonderoga* (CV-14) with list, after she was hit by four kamikaze aircraft off Formosa (present-day Taiwan) on January 21, 1945. (U.S. Navy)

U.S.S. *Ticonderoga* off Formosa (Taiwan). The photograph conveys the perspective of a pilot just before the landing on a moving and swaying aircraft carrier. Her airmen supported the invasion of Iwo Jima and Okinawa and helped sink the *Yamato*. (U.S. Navy)

U.S.S. *Randolph* (CV-15) alongside repair ship U.S.S. *Jason* (ARH-1) at Ulithi Atoll, Caroline Islands, on March 13, 1945, showing damage to her aft flight deck resulting from a kamikaze hit two days earlier. The photograph was taken from a floatplane from the light cruiser U.S.S. *Miami* (CL-89).

Commissioned in October 1944, *Randolph* served in several campaigns in the Pacific, earning three battle stars. Mothballed shortly after the war, she was modernized and recommissioned in the early 1950s as an attack carrier (CVA), and then eventually became an antisubmarine carrier (CVS). In her second career, she operated exclusively in the Atlantic, Mediterranean, and Caribbean. In the early 1960s she served as the recovery ship for two Project Mercury space missions, including John Glenn's historic first orbital flight. Finally decommissioned in 1969, *Randolph* sold for scrap in 1975. (U.S. Navy)

Takeoff from U.S.S. *Lexington* (CV-16) in 1944. Commissioned in February of 1943, she participated in nearly every major operation in the Pacific. Her planes destroyed 372 enemy aircraft in the air, and 475 more on the ground. She destroyed 300,000 tons of enemy cargo and damaged an additional 600,000 tons. The ship's guns shot down 15 planes and assisted in downing five more. The Japanese reported *Lexington* sunk four times but each time she returned to fight again, leading the propagandist "Tokyo Rose" to nickname her "The Blue Ghost." After the war, she operated both in the Atlantic/Mediterranean and the Pacific, but spent most of her time, nearly 30 years, in Pensacola, Florida, as a training carrier (CVT). In 1992, the ship became a floating museum in Corpus Christi, Texas.

A Helldiver just taking off from U.S.S. *Lexington*'s (CV-16) deck, while other aircraft are getting ready for takeoff. The carrier's aircraft had a large part in the sinking of the Japanese battleship *Musashi* (sister ship of *Yamato*), and the aircraft carrier *Zuihō*. (National Museum of Naval Aviation)

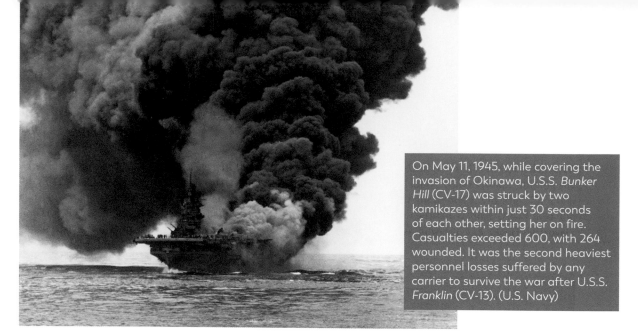

On May 11, 1945, while covering the invasion of Okinawa, U.S.S. *Bunker Hill* (CV-17) was struck by two kamikazes within just 30 seconds of each other, setting her on fire. Casualties exceeded 600, with 264 wounded. It was the second heaviest personnel losses suffered by any carrier to survive the war after U.S.S. *Franklin* (CV-13). (U.S. Navy)

Although U.S.S. *Bunker Hill* was rocked by several explosions and fires spreading inside the ship, she was able to reach Pearl Harbor under her own power. The damage suffered was not completely repaired until shortly after the end of the war, in September 1945. She was never modernized and never saw active service again. *Bunker Hill* and *Franklin* were the only *Essex*-class ships never recommissioned after World War II. She was sold for scrap in 1973 after an effort to save her as a museum ship had failed. (U.S. Navy)

A Helldiver dive-bomber banking to begin its approach to land aboard U.S.S. *Wasp*. (U.S. Navy)

U.S.S. *Wasp* with other U.S. Navy 3rd Fleet carriers at Ulithi Atoll in the Pacific in 1944. From front to rear: *Wasp* (CV-18), *Yorktown* (CV-10), *Hornet* (CV-12), *Hancock* (CV-19) and *Ticonderoga* (CV-14). The ships had received the "Camouflage Measure 33-Design 10a" dazzle paint scheme. (U.S. Navy)

U.S.S. *Hancock* (CV-19) receiving a kamikaze hit during the battle of Okinawa on April 7, 1945. With these attacks, the Japanese Navy, completely outnumbered in numbers and quality, hoped to stop or at least slow down the advancing U.S. forces. Although more than 4,000 Japanese pilots lost their lives carrying out these desperate attacks during the Pacific War, the U.S. advance could not be stopped. (U.S. Navy)

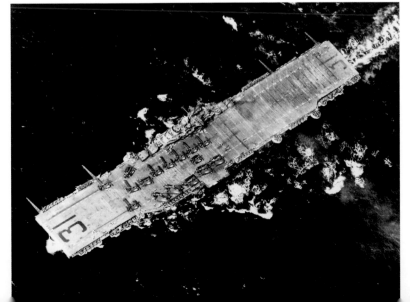

U.S.S. *Bon Homme Richard* (CV-31) photographed in the Central Pacific in 1945. Commissioned in November 1944, she served in the final campaigns of the Pacific War, earning one battle star. Retired shortly after the war, she was recommissioned and operated exclusively in the Pacific, playing a prominent role in the Korean War, for which she earned five battle stars, and the Vietnam War. Finally decommissioned in 1971, the carrier was scrapped 21 years later. (U.S. Navy)

A performance of the ship's orchestra in the *Bon Homme Richard*'s hangar shortly before the end of the war in 1945. (National Museum of Naval Aviation)

Christening of U.S.S. *Shangri-La* (CV-38) on February 24, 1944 by Josephine Doolittle, the wife of James Doolittle, the commander of the famous 1942 "Doolittle Raid," the attack on Tokyo. (U.S. Navy)

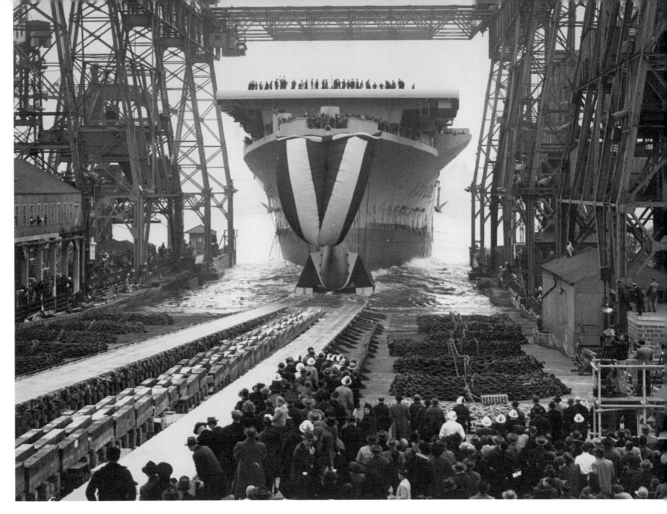

U.S.S. *Shangri-La* sliding into her element. The carrier's construction costs were raised entirely through war bonds and commemorative stamps. Ship launches always took place with great public participation. After her commissioning in September 1944, *Shangri-La*'s aircraft saw action during the battle of Okinawa and bombed land targets on the Japanese home islands as well as warships off the coast and in harbors. (U.S. Navy)

U.S.S. *Lake Champlain* (CV-39) shortly before her commissioning at the Norfolk Naval Shipyard, Virginia, in June 1945. (U.S. Navy)

Lake Champlain at anchor near Norfolk, Virginia, shortly before the end of the war in August 1945. The flight deck is completely filled with aircraft, and the crew is mustered in. After she no longer took an active part in combat missions, she brought back numerous American soldiers from the Pacific to the United States. (U.S. Navy)

A TBM Avenger torpedo aircraft overflying U.S.S. *Antietam* (CV-36) shortly after the end of the war. Although commissioned in January 1945, she did not see combat in World War II. In the early 1950s, after a short period in the reserve fleet, she was re-designated an attack carrier (CVA) and then an antisubmarine warfare carrier (CVS). After the Korean War, *Antietam* spent the rest of her career operating in the Atlantic, Caribbean, and Mediterranean. From 1957 until her deactivation, she was the Navy's training carrier, operating out of Florida. Finally retired in 1963, the ship was scrapped 11 years later. (U.S. Navy)

U.S.S. *Essex* with some of her sister ships, battleships and cruisers mothballed in the reserve fleet in Puget Sound, Washington, after World War II. Many of these ships would serve during the Cold War seeing action in the Korean and Vietnam wars. (U.S. National Archives, 80-G-428458)

Essex-class General Characteristics

Class	*Essex* (incl. *Ticonderoga*-subclass)
Type	Fleet carrier
Standard displacement	27,000 tons (36,380 tons deep load)
Length	short-bow ships: 872 feet (265.8 m) long-bow ships: 888 feet (270.7 m)
Beam	147.5 feet (45.0 m)
Draft	27.5 feet (8.4 m)
Propulsion	8 × geared turbines; 8 × boilers
Shafts	4
Shaft horsepower	150,000 hps
Maximum speed	33 knots
Armor deck	hangar deck: 2.5 in (64 mm) 4th deck: 1.5 in (38 mm)
Side armor	2.5-4 in (64–102 mm)
Armament	12 × 5-inch (12.7 cm) guns 32–72 × 40 mm Bofors guns 55–76 × 20 mm Oerlikon cannons
Aircraft	80–100
Complement	2600

The aircraft director brings a Grumman F4F Wildcat onto the catapult of an escort carrier in 1943. Note the red "Beware of propellers; No smoking" sign on the island of the carrier. (U.S. National Archives)

2
Escort Carriers

During World War II, a small auxiliary aircraft carrier called the "*escort carrier*" supplemented the existing U.S. carrier fleets. The United States built by far the largest number, but Great Britain and Japan also converted existing ships into escort/auxiliary carriers. In the U.S. Navy, they were first designated AVG or ACV (auxiliary carriers) and later classified as CVE (escort carriers). Colloquially, they were also called "baby flattops" or "jeep carriers," because they were far smaller than the existing fleet aircraft carriers of the time.

After the outbreak of war in 1939, the British Royal Navy attempted to better protect its supply convoys from German submarine, E-boat (fast attack boat) and aircraft attacks as well as improve its own air reconnaissance during the battle of the Atlantic. Since the few large fleet carriers were urgently needed in other theaters of war, the Royal Navy opted to convert mostly civilian merchant ships into auxiliary or escort carriers for reasons of time and cost.

In this photo of the escort carrier HMS *Ranee* under construction, the struts on which the flight deck will later be placed are clearly visible. (U.S. Navy)

The technical specifications of this improvised type of ship were based on the requirements of convoy protection. With a displacement of about 10,000 to 16,000 tons, the maximum speed of most ships was between 15–20 knots (28–37 km/h), which was sufficient for protecting slow-moving convoys or participating in submarine-hunting units.

However, escort carriers were too slow to operate with fast warships and large fleet carriers capable of more than 30 knots (55 km/h). In addition, unlike their larger siblings, they had no armor worth mentioning. For this reason, U.S. sailors jokingly called the CVE "combustible, vulnerable, expendable." Even after conversion, the arrangement of bulkheads and watertight compartments still largely corresponded to that of civilian shipping. As a result, escort carriers did not have underwater protection comparable to that of fleet carriers or warships in general either.

Escort carriers could carry 15 to 30 aircraft. Depending on the mission profile, these were mostly fighters, fighter-bombers as well as torpedo bombers. Most of these ships were converted from merchant ships, which usually offered little space for the aircraft. After removal of the original superstructure, the hangar with the flight deck above was added to the upper deck of the ships like a deckhouse. However, this usually shifted the center of gravity upwards, thus requiring further modifications to the hull for stability reasons, but these took up a lot of space. In most cases, the actual hull could not be used for large-scale space utilization, as this hollowing out would have affected stability at sea too much.

The world's first escort carrier, the British HMS *Audacity*, which was converted from the captured German cargo ship *Hannover* in 1941, had no hangar at all, so her aircraft were permanently located on the flight deck exposing them to the elements. The construction of a hangar would have been too costly under the prevailing wartime conditions due to the original nature of the ship's hull. Tankers, on the other hand, were better suited for conversion to escort carriers because the much smaller superstructures were easier to remove and the hull design provided more space for aircraft.

Japan in particular concentrated on converting passenger ships. Although the removal of the superstructure was more complicated, these ships were equipped with more powerful propulsion systems from the outset and therefore usually faster than the escort carriers built from freighters.

U.S.S. *Long Island* (CVE-1) was the U.S. Navy's first escort carrier. Clearly visible is the original hull design of the C-3 cargo liner *Mormacmail*. (U.S. Navy)

At about the same time as the conversion of HMS *Audacity*, the United States built two escort carriers based on merchant ships. The first was commissioned as U.S.S. *Long Island* (CVE-1) by the U.S. Navy in 1941. The sister ship was loaned to the Royal Navy under the U.S. Lend-Lease Act and commissioned as HMS *Archer* (D78) in late 1941. The Lend-Lease Act of 1941 made it possible for the United States, still officially neutral at the time, to supply Great Britain and other countries on loan with materiel essential to the war effort, including warships. U.S.S. *Long Island* and HMS *Archer* were significantly more capable than HMS *Audacity*; in addition to a slightly higher speed, they could carry up to 16 aircraft, while *Audacity* was limited to six to eight.

Based on HMS *Archer*, the construction of four more ships for the Royal Navy followed, later referred to as either the *Archer*- or *Avenger*-class (the second ship after HMS *Archer*). Sometimes *Archer* was also referred to as a single ship, as her four successors differed from her in some details. However, one of the ships, HMS *Charger* (D27), was returned to the United States in March 1942, where it was used as a training ship under the name U.S.S. *Charger* (CVE-30).

The majority of all escort carriers used in World War II were built in the United States. In 1942, American shipyards began building the first 21 *Bogue*-class ships based on cargo ships. The design of this new series benefited from the experience gained with ships already in service, such as U.S.S. *Long Island*. Eleven of these ships were delivered to the Royal Navy as *Attacker*-class under the Lend-Lease Act, while the remaining 10 were commissioned by the U.S. Navy. With a top speed of about 18 knots (33 km/h), these ships could carry up to 24 aircraft. The first 21 ships of this class were followed by another 24 ships. Unlike their predecessors, these were designed from keel laying as escort carriers, but were virtually identical in overall design. Of these modified *Bogue*-class carriers completed by 1944, all but one was transferred to the Royal Navy, where they were designated the *Ameer*- or *Ruler*-class. Almost simultaneously with the construction of the *Bogue*-class,

The *Casablanca*-class, with fifty ships completed, is numerically the largest escort carrier series in history. Some of the ships, such as U.S.S. *Windham Bay* shown here, were still in service in the postwar years as transports and in other roles. (U.S. Navy)

Role of the CVE

The U.S. Navy's escort carriers (CVE's) were used in a variety of roles. They secured convoys against air attack; transported aircraft, personnel, and materiel to bases and to ships in action; engaged submarines; and provided air support for the Allied landings in the Pacific, North Africa, and the French coast. During the naval and air battle at Leyte Gulf in 1944, 18 American escort carriers successfully repelled the attack of the Japanese main battle group for several hours. The U.S. Navy lost escort carriers during the war; two sank off Leyte Gulf, one was sunk by a U-boat, and three others were victims of kamikaze attacks.

the *Sangamon*-class escort carriers based on fleet tankers were built in the United States. These ships could accommodate about 32 aircraft and were capable of 18 knots (33 km/h). After the *Bogue*- and *Sangamon*-classes, American shipyard owner Henry J. Kaiser built the fifty ships of the *Casablanca*-class within a year, the largest series of escort carriers in history (*Bogue*-class: 45 ships). The construction time per ship was unusually short, taking only a few months from keel laying to commissioning. This was achieved by efficient mass production methods that had already been successfully applied to the series construction of the *Liberty* cargo ships.

The first carrier, U.S.S. *Casablanca* (CVE-55), was commissioned by the U.S. Navy on July 8, 1943. The 50th and final ship, U.S.S. *Munda* (CVE-104) followed exactly one year later to the day. The *Casablanca*-class could reach a top speed of about 19 knots (30.5 mph) and carry about 28 aircraft. Although half of the ships were originally to be loaned to the Royal Navy, the U.S. Navy needed all of the ships for itself.

The next series was the *Commencement Bay*-class, which entered service in late 1944 and was considered the most successful escort carrier design compared to its predecessors. With a top speed of around 19 knots (about 35 km/h), this carrier could carry up to 34 aircraft. Of 23 planned ships, only 19 were completed, as construction of the remaining four carriers was halted after the war ended in the Pacific in August 1945. The unfinished hulls were subsequently scrapped. Another series of 12 modified ships was canceled at the same time.

Escort Carriers in World War II

During the war, escort carriers served in a variety of roles, depending on the particular navy as well as the individual area of operations. The Royal Navy used its ships primarily to protect vital transatlantic supply convoys and was supported in this by U.S. Navy units. Carrier-based fighters were used to provide security against land-based enemy reconnaissance planes or bombers, which primarily threatened convoys passing through the Arctic Ocean to the Soviet Union. In antisubmarine warfare, the escort carrier's reconnaissance aircraft could sight individual submarines or entire submarine wolf packs early to guide convoys around them or to engage the boats from the air. In June 1944, this allowed the carrier U.S.S. *Guadalcanal* (CVE-60) to force the German U-boat *U-505* to surface and subsequently capture it intact. The ever-increasing number of British and American escort carriers eventually made a decisive contribution to the Allied victory in the battle of the Atlantic.

Grumman TBF/TBM Avengers flying in formation. This very successful torpedo bomber was carried on numerous U.S. and British escort carriers. (U.S. Navy)

Long Island-class

The two ships of the *Long Island*-class were the first U.S. Navy ships converted from cargo ships to escort carriers. The type ship, U.S.S. *Long Island* (CVE-1), was commissioned in June 1941, while the second one, U.S.S. *Archer* was transferred to the British Royal Navy and renamed HMS *Archer* (BAVG-1). With a length of 495 feet (151 m) and width of 69 feet (21 m), the *Long Island*-class had an operational displacement of about 12,860 tons and was capable of a top speed of 16.5 knots (30.5 km/h). The range was 10,000 nautical miles (19,000 km) at an economic cruising speed of 14 knots (26 km/h). The flight deck was 298 feet (91 m) long. The crew consisted of 970 men.

Postwar Fate of the CVE

The escort carriers loaned to Britain under the Lend-Lease Act were returned to the U.S. after the war. Most of them were sold into civilian hands and, after conversion, continued to serve as merchant ships for many years. British-built carriers also saw service in this role during the postwar period. Most of the U.S. Navy ships were decommissioned shortly after the war and subsequently scrapped. Some carriers mothballed by the Navy were stricken for demolition around 1960. Some *Casablanca*- and *Commencement Bay*-class ships continued to serve as transports, helicopter carriers, or communications ships serving in these roles during the Korean conflict and sporadically during the Vietnam War. The last ships of this type were scrapped in the 1970s, leaving not a single escort carrier in the world today.

The ships could carry about 21 aircraft. These were usually Grumman F4F Wildcat fighters (to fight enemy aircraft) and Douglas TBD torpedo bombers (later replaced by Grumman TBF Avengers), which were mainly used against sea targets. A 5-inch (12.7 cm) cannon and two 3-inch (7.6 cm) cannons were primarily used for self-defense against air attacks. Before the United States entered the war in December of 1941, U.S.S. *Long Island* had served as a testing platform, so that the knowledge gained with her was incorporated into the designs of subsequent escort carrier classes. HMS *Archer* became the prototype or type ship of the *Archer*-class named after her, all of which were delivered to the Royal Navy. During World War II, U.S.S. *Long Island* took part in the battles for the island of Guadalcanal in the Pacific in 1942, but was also used as an aircraft transport and training carrier. After the war, the ship was sold and, following a conversion, served as a cargo and training ship. In 1977, it was scrapped in Belgium.

Aerial view of U.S.S. *Long Island* as an aircraft transport. (U. S. National Archives)

Long Island-class General Characteristics

Class	*Long Island* (2 ships completed)
Shipyard	Sun Shipbuilding & Drydock Co., Chester, Pennsylvania
Commissioning	June 2, 1941
Standard displacement	10,220 tons (12,860 tons full load)
Length	495 feet (151 m)
Beam	69 feet (21 m)
Draft	25 feet 8 in (7.82 m)
Propulsion	4 × Diesel (total of 8,500 shp)
Shafts	1
Maximum speed	16.5 knots (30.5 km/h)
Range	10,000 nm (19,000 km)
Crew	970
Aircraft	21
Complement	1 × 5-inch (12.7 cm) gun 2 × 3-inch (7.6 cm) guns
Fate	scrapped in Belgium in 1977

Bogue-class

In the early stages of World War II, the successful operations of German U-boats against transatlantic supply convoys vital to the war effort posed an increasingly existential threat to Great Britain. Under the Lend-Lease Act, passed in 1941, the United States, still neutral at the time, was able to lend the British extensive aid in the form of materiel and weapons. As a result, 31 of the 45 *Bogue*-class escort carriers built at American shipyards were loaned to the Royal Navy. The remaining 14 ships saw service in the U.S. Navy. This class of carriers was created beginning in 1941 from converted "*MARAD-C3*" ships that had been developed in the United States as fast-to-build production cargo ships. Unlike previous escort carrier designs, this new series was better through-designed, as engineers benefited from experience with ships already in service. The *Bogue*-class consisted of two groups. These were almost identical, but the second batch was slightly improved and equipped with reinforced antiaircraft armament in the form of additional 40 mm as well as 20 mm guns. The ships of the first group delivered to the Royal Navy were named the *Attacker*-class. The ships of the second batch for the Royal Navy were designated the *Ameer-/Ruler*-classes.

The ships had an overall length of 496 feet (151.2 m), and the maximum width (flight deck) was 112 feet (34 m). The flight deck was connected to the hangar below by two elevators. The operational displacement when fully loaded was about 14,200 tons. Two boilers generated steam pressure for a turbine that transmitted its 8,500-horsepower output to a single propeller. Top speed was about 18 knots (33 km/h), making these ships too slow for operations with the larger fleet carriers.

The U.S. Navy ships received Allis-Chalmers turbines and had an enormous range (varying depending on the source) of up to 26,300 nautical miles (48,700 km) at a cruising speed of 15 knots. The Royal Navy ships received "General Electric" turbines but had a range of only 14,000 nm (26,000 km). Armament originally

Fate of the *Bogue*-class

At the end of the war, the carriers loaned to Britain were returned to the United States, where they were decommissioned along with the American ships. Most of the carriers were subsequently converted back to civilian cargo ships and continued to serve as such for many years until they were scrapped. U.S.S. *Croatan* (CVE-25) still served in the Vietnam War as a transport for helicopters and military equipment. With 45 completed ships, the *Bogue*-class was numerically the second largest series of escort carriers in history after the *Casablanca*-class (50 ships). No ship of the *Bogue*-class was preserved for posterity.

included two 5-inch guns on either side at the stern and was supplemented by several 40 mm and 20 mm guns for antiaircraft defense.

The ships could carry up to 28 aircraft, but there were usually only about 24 aircraft aboard. The U.S. Navy carriers usually carried a combination of Grumman F4F Wildcats (fighters) and Grumman TBF/TBM Avengers (torpedo bombers, submarine hunters), as well as other aircraft models. The ships in Royal Navy service also received American Grumman F4F Wildcats, which were called "Martlet" by the British. They were joined by Hawker Sea Hurricanes (fighters) and Fairey Swordfish (torpedo bombers and submarine hunters). The ships' crew comprised 850 to 890 men.

The American and British ships of the *Bogue*-class were used in virtually all theaters during World War II, serving in convoy duty, as submarine hunters, supporting various landing operations, and transporting aircraft and materiel. Of this class, only one ship, the U.S. Navy's U.S.S. *Block Island* (CVE-21), was lost in combat.

Bogue-class General Characteristics

Class	*Bogue* (45 ships completed)
Shipyard	Seattle-Tacoma Shipbuilding, Washington Ingalls Shipbuilding, Mississippi Western Pipe & Steel, California
Commissioning	1942–1944
Standard displacement	8,390 tons (13,980 tons)
Length	495 ft 8 in (151.08 m)
Beam	112 feet (34 m)
Draft	26 ft (7.9 m)
Propulsion	1 × turbine; 2 × boilers (total 8,500 shp)
Shafts	1
Maximum speed	18 knots (33 km/h)
Range	up to 26,300 nm (48,700 km)
Complement	850–890
Aircraft	24–28
Armament	2 × 5-inch (12.7 cm guns) various 40 mm and 20 mm AA guns
Fate	44 ships scrapped, 1 sunk (U.S.S. *Block Island*, CVE-21).

This photo of the U.S.S. *Bogue* taken in February 1945 near the Bermuda Islands shows the intricate details of the hull as well as the conning tower, the so-called "island." (U.S. Navy)

U.S.S. *Bogue*

U.S.S. *Bogue* (CVE-9) remained in service with the U.S. Navy and became one of the most successful U-boat hunter-killers of the war. Between May 1943 and the end of the war in Europe, she and escort ships sank eleven German and two Japanese submarines. After being decommissioned in 1946, she remained in reserve until being scrapped in Japan in 1960.

Aerial view of the German U-boat *U-569*, taken by an aircraft of U.S.S. *Bogue* on May 22, 1943, in the North Atlantic. After two TBM Avenger bombers of the carrier damaged the submarine with depth charges, the German crew scuttled it. From the 46 crew members, 25 were rescued. (U.S. Navy)

After the crash landing of an Avenger on U.S.S. *Bogue*, the crew tries to get the damaged aircraft back into a straight position. Under the wing (at that time new) rockets can be seen, which were used to fight submarines. (U.S. National Archives)

U.S.S. *Card*

U.S.S. *Card* (CVE-11) served in the U.S. Navy from early 1943, initially deploying as a troop and aircraft transport for North Africa. Beginning in the summer of 1943, she participated very successfully in the hunt for German U-boats as part of a "Hunter-Killer Group" and helped sink a total of eleven boats. however, after being decommissioned in 1946, U.S.S. *Card* was reactivated in 1958 as an aircraft transport. During the Vietnam War, she carried troops and materiel and was damaged by explosive ordnance by North Vietnamese combat divers in 1964 but was able to be repaired. The ship was decommissioned in 1970 and scrapped the following year.

U.S.S. *Card* entering Norfolk Harbor, Virgina, in March 1943. (U.S. Navy)

An Avenger on approach to land on U.S.S. *Card*. Landing on the flight deck, which was only about 500 feet long, was difficult even for experienced pilots, as it sometimes moved or "rolled back and forth" a lot due to the swell. The Grumman TBF/TBM Avenger was the U.S. standard torpedo bomber in World War II and was also delivered to the Royal Navy as well as to the Royal New Zealand Air Force. (U.S. Navy)

U.S.S. *Copahee*

After entering service, the U.S.S. *Copahee* (CVE-12) served primarily as a troop and aircraft transport for U.S. bases in the Pacific beginning in fall of 1942. She also brought captured Japanese aircraft, engines and parts to the United States for testing and evaluation. U.S.S. *Copahee* was decommissioned in late 1945 and scrapped in 1969.

A F4F Corsair warming up its engine on the U.S.S. *Copahee*'s flight deck. This fighter aircraft proved to be very successful in combat against Japanese aircraft and as a fighter-bomber against ground targets. This aircraft type was also used by the Royal Navy and the Royal New Zealand Air Force. (U.S. Navy)

U.S.S. *Core*

After her commissioning in the U.S. Navy in late 1942, U.S.S. *Core* (CVE-13) first served as a training carrier for pilots, but later saw action as part of a "Hunter-Killer-Group" in the Atlantic. She and her escort ships sank seven German U-boats. Decommissioned in 1946, *Core* was reactivated in the 1950s. In 1961, she carried helicopter pilots and personnel to South Vietnam to support the government there. After being decommissioned for a second time in 1970, she was scrapped the following year.

U.S.S. *Core* in the Atlantic hunting German U-boats. (U.S. Navy)

U.S.S. *Nassau*

After entering service in the U.S. Navy in late 1942, U.S.S. *Nassau* (CVE-16) served exclusively in the Pacific. There she transported aircraft and troops to various U.S. bases and used her aircraft to support landing operations at the Aleutian Islands, Tarawa, the Marshall Islands, Palau and the Philippines. Shortly after the war, *Nassau* was decommissioned and scrapped in Japan in 1961.

The island on U.S.S. *Nassau's* starboard side, where the bridge and the air-traffic control are located. Compared to a larger aircraft carrier such as U.S.S. *Essex*, this superstructure aboard an escort carrier was quite small. A larger structure would have taken up too much space on the flight deck and also shifted too much weight to the starboard side affecting the ship's stability, especially in heavy seas. (U.S. Navy)

This photograph shows U.S.S. *Nassau's* bow section during loading at Mare Island, California, in April 1944. (U.S. Navy)

U.S.S. *Altamaha*

After U.S.S. *Altamaha* (CVE-18) was commissioned into the U.S. Navy in late 1942, she initially served as a supply ship for American bases in the Pacific and for pilot training. While there, she also visited Australia and delivered aircraft to India. In February 1944, an airship landed on her deck in San Diego Harbor, California. Two months later, *Altamaha* served in antisubmarine warfare in the Pacific and was damaged by a typhoon in December. After the war, she was transferred to the reserve fleet and scrapped in Japan in 1961.

A Grumman F6F Hellcat fighter aircraft taking off from U.S.S. *Altamaha*. The Hellcat was the Wildcat's successor and was also used by the Royal Navy. Initially, the British designation was Gannet but later switched back to Hellcat. Too much smoke from the ship's funnel (left) could sometimes make visibility poor, thus making landings more difficult. (U.S. Navy)

U.S.S. *Barnes*

Commissioned into the U.S. Navy in the spring of 1943, U.S.S. *Barnes* (CVE 20) served mainly as a transport in the Pacific and trained carrier pilots. Her aircraft also supported U.S. attacks on Japanese-occupied Tarawa Atoll and the Gilbert Islands in the Pacific. The ship was decommissioned in 1946 and scrapped in 1959/60.

This photo of U.S.S. *Barnes* impressively shows the transport capacity of escort carriers. On the front section of the flight deck, Lockheed P-38 Lightning fighters are visible. These were used as interceptors, fighter-bombers and reconnaissance aircraft. On the remaining deck, numerous Republic P-47 Thunderbolt fighters can be seen, which were mainly used as fighter-bombers to fight ground targets and as escorts. (U.S. Navy)

U.S.S. *Block Island*

After entering service in the U.S. Navy in the spring of 1943, U.S.S. *Block Island* (CVE-21) initially delivered aircraft to Belfast, Ireland. She then carried out four missions as part of a "Hunter Killer Group," sinking the German U-boats *U-220* and *U-1059* and assisted in the destruction of four more boats. On May 29, 1944, however, U.S.S. *Block Island* was so badly damaged by torpedoes from the German U-boat *U-549* near the Canary Islands that she had to be sunk by her escort ships. A short time later, however, U.S. escort destroyers were able to sink *U-549*.

Recovery of a TBF Avenger that missed the deck of U.S.S. *Block Island* on approach to land. (U.S. Navy)

U.S.S. *Breton*

Commissioned into the U.S. Navy in the spring of 1943, U.S.S. *Breton* (CVE-23) served exclusively as a carrier in the "Carrier Transport Squadron." She carried troops, aircraft and materiel to fleet units engaged in combat and to bases in the Pacific. In this capacity, she participated in the battle of the Philippine Sea in June 1944 and the capture of Okinawa in April of 1945. The following year, she was decommissioned and scrapped in 1973.

U.S.S. *Breton*'s massive stern. Platforms mounted to the hull house the 5-inch (12.7 cm) guns, which could be used against ships and aircraft. (U.S. Navy)

U.S.S. *Croatan*

After entering service in the U.S. Navy in the spring of 1943, U.S.S. *Croatan* (CVE-25) initially served as the core of a Hunter-Killer-Group to hunt German U-boats. By the end of the year, she transported aircraft and personnel to North Africa. In 1944, she and her escort ships were able to destroy four U-boats, and two more the following year. She was initially decommissioned at the end of the war, but then reactivated as an aircraft transport and used as an experimental ship by NASA in 1964. The following year, U.S.S. *Croatan* carried helicopters to Vietnam. Her decommissioning took place in 1970, and she was scrapped a year later.

U.S.S. *Croatan* photographed from a boat in coastal waters. (U.S. National Archives)

U.S.S. *Prince William*

After an abbreviated shakedown cruise, U.S.S. *Prince William* (CVE 31, not to be confused with CVE-19) was sent to the Pacific in the summer of 1943 delivering aircraft and troops to the forces there. Beginning in the spring of 1944, she was used for pilot training and shortly thereafter carried aircraft and personnel to North Africa. After being used again as a training carrier, she served as a transport between Hawaii and the U.S. East Coast from summer 1945 until the end of the war. Decommissioned in 1946, she was finally scrapped in Japan in 1961.

U.S.S. *Prince William* primarily served as a transport. (U.S. Navy)

Bogue-class, First Group

Original name (U.S. Navy)	Active service in U.S. Navy	New Name (Royal Navy)	Active service in Royal Navy
U.S.S. *Altamaha* (CVE-6)	-	HMS *Battler* (D18)	Oct 31, 1942–Feb 12, 1946
U.S.S. *Barnes* (CVE-7)	-	HMS *Attacker* (D02)	Sep 30, 1942–Jan 5, 1946
U.S.S. *Block Island* (CVE-8)	-	HMS *Hunter* (D80)	Jan 9, 1943–Dec 29, 1945
U.S.S. *Bogue* (CVE-9)	Apr 9, 1943–Nov 30, 1946	-	-
U.S.S. *Breton* (CVE-10)	-	HMS *Chaser* (D32)	Apr 9, 1943–May 12, 1946
U.S.S. *Card* (CVE-11)	Nov 8, 1942–May 3, 1946	-	-
U.S.S. *Copahee* (CVE-12)	Feb 15, 1942–Jul 5, 1946	-	-
U.S.S. *Core* (CVE-13)	Dec 10, 1942–Oct 4, 1946	-	-
U.S.S. *Croatan* (CVE-14)	-	HMS *Fencer* (D64)	Mar 1, 1943–Dec 11, 1946
U.S.S. *Hamlin* (CVE-15)	-	HMS *Stalker* (D91)	Dec 21, 1942–Dec 29, 1945
U.S.S. *Nassau* (CVE-16)	Aug 20, 1942–Oct 28, 1946	-	-
U.S.S. *St. George* (CVE-17)	-	HMS *Pursuer* (D73)	Jun 1, 1943–Feb 12, 1946
U.S.S. *Altamaha* (CVE-18)	Sep 15, 1942–Sep 27, 1946	-	-
U.S.S. *Prince William* (CVE-19)	-	HMS *Striker* (D12)	Apr 29, 1943–Feb 12, 1946
U.S.S. *Barnes* (CVE-20)	Feb 20, 1943–Aug 29, 1946	-	-
U.S.S. *Block Island* (CVE-21)	Mar 8, 1943–May 29, 1944 (sunk by German U-boat *U-549*)	-	-
no name (CVE-22)	-	HMS *Searcher* (D40)	Apr 7, 1943–Nov 29, 1945
U.S.S. *Breton* (CVE-23)	Apr 12, 1943–Aug 20, 1946	-	-
no name (CVE-24)	-	HMS *Ravager* (D70)	Apr 25, 1943–Feb 26, 1946
U.S.S. *Croatan* (CVE-25)	Apr 28, 1943–May 20, 1946	-	-
no name (BAVG-6)	-	HMS *Tracker* (D24)	Jan 31, 1943–Nov 29, 1945

Modified *Bogue*-class, Second Group

(The ships in Royal Navy service were designated as the *Ameer/Ruler*-class)

Original name (U.S. Navy)	Active service in U.S. Navy	New name (Royal Navy)	Active service in Royal Navy
U.S.S. *Prince William* (CVE-31)	Apr 9, 1943– Aug 29, 1946	-	-
U.S.S. *Chatham* (CVE-32)	-	HMS *Slinger* (D26)	Aug 11, 1943–Feb 27, 1946
U.S.S. *Glacier* (CVE-33)	-	HMS *Atheling* (D51)	Oct 28, 1943–Dec 13, 1946
U.S.S. *Pybus* (CVE-34)	-	HMS *Emperor* (D98)	Aug 6, 1943–Feb 12, 1946
U.S.S. *Baffins* (CVE-35)	-	HMS *Ameer* (D01)	Jul 20, 1943–Jan 17, 1946
U.S.S. *Bolinas* (CVE-36)	-	HMS *Begum*(D38)	Aug 12, 1943–Jan 4, 1946
U.S.S. *Bastian* (CVE-37)	-	HMS *Trumpeter* (D09)	Aug 4, 1943–Apr 6, 1946
U.S.S. *Carnegie* (CVE-38)	-	HMS *Empress*(D42)	Aug 12, 1943–Feb 4, 1946
U.S.S. *Cordova*(CVE-39)	-	HMS *Khedive* (D62)	Aug 25, 1943–Jan 26, 1946
U.S.S. *Delgada* (CVE-40)	-	HMS *Speaker* (D90)	Nov 20, 1943–Jul 17, 1946
U.S.S. *Edisto* (CVE-41)	-	HMS *Nabob* (D77)	Sep 7, 1943–Sep 30, 1944
U.S.S. *Estero* (CVE-42)	-	HMS Premier (D23)	Nov 3, 1943–Apr 2, 1946
U.S.S. *Jamaica* (CVE-43)	-	HMS *Shah* (D21)	Sep 27, 1943–Dec 6, 1945
U.S.S. *Keweenaw* (CVE-44)	-	HMS *Patroller* (D07)	Oct 22, 1943–Dec 13, 1946
U.S.S. *Prince*(CVE-45)	-	HMS *Rajah* (D10)	Jan 17, 1944–Dec 13, 1946
U.S.S. *Niantic*(CVE-46)	-	HMS *Ranee* (D03)	Nov 8, 1943–Nov 21, 1946
U.S.S. *Perdido* (CVE-47)	-	HMS *Trouncer* (D85)	Jan 31, 1944–Mar 3, 1946
U.S.S. *Sunset*(CVE-48)	-	HMS *Thane* (D48)	Nov 19, 1943–Nov 15, 1945
U.S.S. *St. Andrews* (CVE-49)	-	HMS *Queen* (D19)	Dec 7, 1943–Oct 31, 1946
U.S.S. *St. Joseph* (CVE-50)	-	HMS *Ruler* (D72)	Aug 22, 1943–Jan 29, 1946
U.S.S. *St. Simon* (CVE-51)	-	HMS Arbiter (D31)	Dec 31, 1943–Mar 3, 1946
U.S.S. *Vermillion* (CVE-52)	-	HMS *Smiter* (D55)	Jan 20, 1944–Apr 6, 1946
U.S.S. *Willapa*(CVE-53)	-	HMS *Puncher* (D79)	Feb 5, 1944–Jan 16, 1946
U.S.S. *Winjah* (CVE-54)	-	HMS *Reaper* (D82)	Feb 18, 1944–May 20, 1946

Sangamon-class

The four ships of the *Sangamon*-class were originally completed as civilian oil tankers of the *MARAD-T3-S2-A1* type in 1939–1940. However, the U.S. Navy acquired the ships shortly thereafter and initially placed them into service as *Cimarron*-class naval tankers. At that time, the 45 *Bogue*-class escort carriers were under construction, which were built on the hulls of *MARAD-C3* cargo ships. Due to a shortage of other "C3" hulls, it was decided to resort to four of the *Cimarron*-class. Although the *Sangamon*-class, built from tanker hulls, proved to be a better escort carrier type than the *Bogue*-class, converted from freighters, no more tankers were converted because the U.S. Navy also had a great need for fleet tankers. The experience gained with the *Sangamon*-class served as the development basis for the subsequent *Commencement Bay*-class. In service, the *Sangamon*-class proved to be robust and stable even in heavy seas.

With an overall length of app. 555 feet (169 m), the flight deck covered almost the entire hull. The maximum width (flight deck) was 115 feet (35 m). Two aircraft elevators connected the flight deck with the hangar below. The operational displacement was 24,250 tons. Four steam boilers powered two propulsion turbines transmitting their total power of 13,500 hp to two propellers. The top speed of 18 knots (33 km/h) made the *Sangamon*-class, like its predecessors, too slow to operate with large fleet carriers. At a cruising speed of 15 knots, the ships had an enormous range of 24,000 nautical miles (44,400 km). The crew consisted of 860 to 1,080 men. Armament included two 5-inch (12.7 cm) guns and several 40 mm and 20 mm antiaircraft guns. The *Sangamon*-class could carry between 25 and 32 aircraft, depending on the type. On board were mostly a combination of Grumman F4F Wildcat fighters, Grumman TBF/TBM Avenger bombers, and Douglas SBD Dauntless dive bombers.

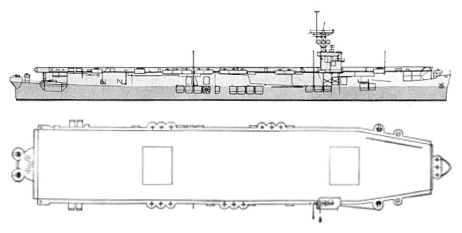

Side and top views of the *Sangamon*-class from a U.S. Navy recognition book. (U.S. Navy)

A *Sangamon*-class carrier is hit by a kamikaze aircraft while in Leyte Gulf, Philippines, October 1944. (U.S. Navy)

The U.S.S. *Sangamon*'s flight deck lined up with Douglas SBD Dauntless dive bombers. Due to its successful operation mainly in the Pacific, this aircraft became one of the most famous of World War II. (U.S. Navy)

U.S.S. *Sangamon*

Originally laid down in 1939 as the civilian tanker *Esso Trenton*, the ship was acquired by the U.S. Navy in October 1940 as a fleet tanker and renamed U.S.S. *Sangamon* (AO-28). After her conversion and subsequent commissioning as an escort carrier (ACV-26, later CVE-26) in August 1942, her aircraft provided air support during the Allied landings in North Africa two months later. Beginning in 1943, U.S.S. *Sangamon* protected supply convoys in the Pacific and participated in attacks on the Gilbert Islands, the Marshall Islands, the Marianas, and Leyte (Philippines). On January 25, 1944, one of her aircraft missed the arresting cables during landing and crashed into the aircraft standing on the flight deck. This caused a fire killing nine crewmen. During the invasion of Leyte, the carrier was hit by an aerial bomb on October 20, 1944, but it penetrated the ship's side to the outside and exploded in the water about 270 yards alongside the ship. On May 4, 1945, a hit by a kamikaze aircraft near Okinawa caused heavy fires on board, but they were brought under control. Eleven crewmen died in this incident, and 25 were reported missing. Repairs took place at Norfolk, Virginia. Decommissioned in October 1945, the ship was sold into civilian hands to serve as a merchant vessel for the next several years. Scrapping took place in Japan in 1960.

U.S.S. *Suwannee*

U.S.S. *Suwannee* (CVE-27) was also a civilian tanker named *Markay* before being converted into an escort carrier in the fall of 1942. Shortly thereafter, her aircraft provided air support during the Allied invasion of North Africa, sinking a French submarine in the process. In the Pacific, the carrier protected supply convoys from 1943 and took part in the battles for the Gilbert Islands, the Marshall Islands and the Philippines, among others. On June 19, 1944, one of its aircraft sank the Japanese submarine *I-184* in the Philippine Sea. On October 25, a kamikaze aircraft in Leyte Gulf punctured U.S.S. *Suwannee*'s flight deck killing several crewmen. After her repair, she did not see any further combat, but assisted in the occupation of Japan after its surrender. In 1947 the ship was decommissioned and 15 years later scrapped in Bilbao, Spain.

U.S.S. *Suwannee* after the kamikaze attack from October 25, 1944. Parts of the A6M5 Zero's Nakajima Sakae 21, 14-cylinder radial engine were found in the vicinity of the hit. (U.S. Navy)

U.S.S. *Chenango*

After the civilian tanker *Esso New Orleans* was acquired by the U.S. Navy in 1941 and renamed U.S.S. *Chenango* (ACV-28, later CVE-28), she was commissioned as an escort carrier in September 1942. After supporting the invasion of North Africa, she was severely damaged by a hurricane in the Atlantic in November 1942. After her repairs, U.S.S. *Chenango* escorted supply ships in the Pacific during the invasion of the Solomon Islands and supported U.S. Marines during their landing operations. In the invasions of the Gilbert and Marshall Islands, the carrier helped provide cover for landing forces and participated in the fighting

Bow view of U.S.S. *Chenango*. After the end of the war, she returned 1,900 former Allied prisoners of war and 1,500 civilians held captive by the Japanese to their homelands. (U.S. National Archives)

for the Philippines in Leyte Gulf. During the landing on Okinawa in the spring of 1945, U.S.S. *Chenango*'s aircraft again provided air support. In 1946, she was decommissioned and scrapped 14 years later.

U.S.S. *Santee*

Like her three sister ships, *Esso Seakay* was acquired by the U.S. Navy and after a short use as the naval tanker U.S.S. *Santee* (AO-29), she was converted to an escort carrier (ACV-29, later CVE-29). Shortly after commissioning in August 1942, one of her aircraft lost a bomb during takeoff, which exploded on the flight deck. However, this accident caused only minor damage, allowing the carrier to participate in the invasion of North Africa in the fall as planned. In 1943, U.S.S. *Santee* searched for German U-boats in the Atlantic and transported aircraft. In November 1943, she escorted the new battleship U.S.S. *Iowa* (BB-61) back to the United States with President Franklin D. Roosevelt on board, who was on his way back from his conferences in Cairo and Tehran. In the following year, U.S.S. *Santee* ferried aircraft in the Pacific and protected tankers supplying naval forces engaged in combat. On October 25, 1944, a kamikaze aircraft in Leyte Gulf punctured the flight deck and damaged the hangar below. Just minutes later, the ship also received a torpedo hit from a Japanese submarine. Despite water flooding in and a six-degree list, the ship was held and later repaired. In the spring of 1945, her aircraft provided air support in the invasion of Okinawa, the last major battle of World War II. In 1946, the carrier was decommissioned and scrapped 13 years later.

In this starboard photograph of U.S.S. *Santee*, the smoke from the smokestack is clearly visible. It was placed at the stern to keep the smoke as far away from the flight deck as possible. Nevertheless, it sometimes obscured the view of the stern for landing pilots when the wind blew it in the ship's direction. A fence-like arresting device was installed at the bow, which was used when landing aircraft could not catch the arresting steel wire ropes on deck or had defective tailhooks. (U.S. Naval History and Heritage Command)

U.S.S. *Santee* in her former life as a tanker (AO-29). (U.S. Navy)

Sangamon-class General Characteristics

Class	*Sangamon* (4 ships completed)
Shipyard	Federal Shipbuilding and Drydock Co., New Jersey (*Sangamon / Suwannee*) Sun Shipbuilding & Drydock Co., Pennsylvania (*Chenango / Santee*)
Commissioning	*Sangamon*: Aug 25, 1944 *Suwannee*: Sep 24, 1942 *Chenango*: Sep 19, 1942 *Santee*: Sep 24, 1942
Standard displacement	11,400 tons (24,275 tons)
Length	553 feet (169 m)
Beam	114 ft (35 m)
Draft	32 ft (9.8 m)
Propulsion	2 × turbines; 2 × boilers (total of 13,500 shp)
Shafts	2
Maximum speed	18 knots (33 km/h)
Complement	1080
Aircraft	25–32
Armament	2 × 5-inch (12.7 cm) gun Various 40 mm and 20 mm AA guns
Fate	All ships scrapped 1959–1962

Propulsion

Propulsion

Because of the wartime shortage of turbines, the *Casablanca*-class was fitted with two Skinner Unaflow reciprocating engines supplied with steam by four boilers. The total power of 9,000 hp was transmitted to two propellers. The maximum speed was 19 knots (30.5 km/h). At a cruising speed of 15 knots, the range was app. 10,200 nautical miles (18,900 kilometers).

Casablanca-class

The loss of several aircraft carriers or their repair-related overhaul in 1942 and the increasing threat to supply convoys to the British Isles from the growing German U-boat fleet made the construction of new aircraft carriers imperative. Industrialist Henry J. Kaiser laid out a plan for his shipyard in Vancouver, Washington, to build 50 escort carriers within a year. This goal was to be achieved using the same mass production methods that had proven successful in building *Liberty* transport ships. After Kaiser was awarded the contract, the keel of the first ship, U.S.S. *Casablanca* (CVE-55), was laid on November 3, 1942. Just eight months later, it was commissioned by the U.S. Navy on July 8, 1943. The last unit of the class, U.S.S. *Munda* (CVE-104,) entered service on July 8, 1944, exactly one year after the first ship. Eventually, the total construction time for each carrier was reduced to only three months by optimizing work procedures over time. The initial plan to loan 25 of the 50 carriers to the Royal Navy was dropped because the U.S. Navy needed them itself.

With a maximum beam of 108 feet or 33 meters (flight deck), the overall length was 513 feet (156.2 m), with the flight deck covering almost the entire hull. The flight deck, which was connected by two elevators to the hangar deck below, had an air-powered catapult on the port side for accelerated aircraft takeoff. However, the aircraft could also take off by themselves, depending on the type. For landings, there were several arresting steel wire rope systems as well as three barriers made of rubber bands that could bring the landing aircraft to a stop if they missed the arresting wires.

The *Casablanca*-class could carry up to 28 aircraft. Mostly these were sixteen F4F Wildcat fighters and twelve TBF/TBM-Avenger torpedo bombers for antisubmarine warfare. However, some of the ship also carried SBD Dauntless dive bombers and used them against surface ships and land targets, among others. Like all escort carriers, these vessels carried only light antiaircraft armament, consisting of one 5-inch (12.7 cm) gun and about forty 40 mm guns and about twenty 20 mm guns. The crew consisted of 910 men.

Although these vessels were originally designed and built as escort ships for transatlantic supply convoys, they saw service in all theaters during World War II including the Pacific, where their aircraft supported attacks on Japanese island positions and warships, and provided air support for numerous Allied landings, such as those in the Philippines, Iwo Jima and Okinawa. In the Pacific, these ships also escorted supply convoys, hunted submarines, transported aircraft, personnel, and materiel to Pacific bases, and provided supplies to fleet units engaged in combat. Some ships also served as training carriers for pilots and crews. One of the most significant engagements of the *Casablanca*-class in the re-conquest of the Philippines in October 1944 was the battle off Samar in Leyte Gulf. Here, a convoy of six escort carriers and its escort ships held off a numerically superior Japanese naval force and forced it to turn back. A total of five carriers were lost during the war.

Postwar Fate

After the end of the war, most of the ships were decommissioned, partly for cost reasons and partly because the propulsion systems were considered obsolete and the maximum speed of 19 knots was not considered sufficient for future tasks. During the Korean War (1950-53), however, some ships were reactivated and used primarily as aircraft transports. In 1955, U.S.S. *Thetis Bay* (CVE-90) was converted into the U.S. Navy's first assault helicopter aircraft carrier (later amphibious assault ship) and served in that role until 1964. By the mid-1960s, all *Casablancas* had been scrapped.

Casablanca-class General Characteristics

Class	*Casablanca* (50 ships completed)
Shipyard	Kaiser Shipyards, Washington
Commissioning	1943–1944
Standard displacement	8,188 tons (10,902 tons full load)
Length	513 feet (156.2 m)
Beam	108 feet (33 m)
Draft	20 ft 9 in (6.32 m)
Propulsion	4 × boilers 2 × reciprocating engines (total 13,500 shp)
Shafts	2
Maximum speed	19 knots (30.5 km/h)
Range	10,200 nm (18,900 km)
Complement	ca. 910
Crew	28
Aircraft	2 × 5-inch (12.7 cm) gun Various 40 mm and 20 mm AA guns
Complement	45 ships scrapped until mid-1960s; 5 ships sunk during WWII.

U.S.S. *Casablanca*

After entering service in July 1943, U.S.S. *Casablanca* (CVE-55) repeatedly served as a training carrier for ship and air crew and transported troops and materiel to bases and theaters of war in the Pacific. These included Hawaii, Guam, Samar, Manus, and Palau. After being decommissioned in 1946, the carrier was scrapped in Pennsylvania the following year.

U.S.S. *Casablanca* at anchor in the Pacific. These ships had virtually no armor; there was only some light splinter protection. (U.S. Navy)

Crew members returning to U.S.S. *Casablanca* after their shore leave otherwise known as "liberty." (U.S. National Archives)

U.S.S. *Liscome Bay*

Commissioned in August 1943, U.S.S. *Liscome Bay* participated in the successful attack on the Gilbert Islands in the Pacific, with her aircraft attacking Japanese airfields and fortifications. After capturing the islands, however, the ship was torpedoed by the Japanese submarine *I-175* on November 24, 1943 and sank with the loss of 644 crewmen. Only 272 men were rescued by escort ships.

Burial at sea of two crew members of U.S.S. *Liscome Bay* who died from their injuries despite being rescued when their sink sank. (U.S. National Archives)

U.S.S. *Anzio*

Commissioned in August 1943, U.S.S. *Anzio* (CVE-57), which was originally named *Coral Sea*, participated in the conquest of the Gilbert Islands, carried aircraft as well as materiel, and saw action in the battles for New Guinea, the Marianas, and Okinawa. The carrier was decommissioned in 1946 and scrapped in 1959/60.

U.S.S. *Anzio*'s flight deck with aircraft tied down during heavy seas. (U.S. Navy)

U.S.S. *Corregidor*

Commissioned in August of 1943, U.S.S. *Corregidor*'s (CVE-58) aircraft provided air support during the invasion of Kwajalein (Marshall Islands) in the Pacific early the following year. Later, the carrier joined the attacks on the Marianas (Saipan and Guam), served as a training carrier and hunted Japanese submarines. Although retired in 1946, the ship was reactivated as an aircraft transport during the Korean War in 1951 and the Lebanon Crisis in 1958. U.S.S. *Corregidor* was decommissioned the same year and scrapped shortly afterwards.

A F6F Hellcat on the flight deck aboard U.S.S. *Corregidor* after landing. (U.S. Navy)

U.S.S. *Mission Bay*

Commissioned in September 1943, U.S.S. *Mission Bay* (CVE-59) protected supply convoys and hunted submarines in the Atlantic. In early 1944, she transported aircraft and personnel to India and shortly thereafter escorted the cruiser U.S.S. *Quincy* coming from Gibraltar back to the United States; on board this ship was President Franklin D. Roosevelt on his way back from the Yalta Conference. After further operations against German U-boats in the Atlantic, the ship ended the war as a training carrier. After being decommissioned, it was finally scrapped in Japan in 1959/60.

Starboard view of U.S.S. *Mission Bay* entering coastal waters. (U.S. Navy)

U.S.S. *Guadalcanal*

U.S.S. *Guadalcanal* (CVE-60), commissioned in September 1943, had her greatest success when she was able to force the German U-boat *U-505* to surrender off the coast of West Africa on June 4, 1944. In the process, the "Enigma" encryption machine on board fell into American hands. *U-505*'s capture was the first capture of a foreign vessel by an U.S. ship since 1815, when the sloop U.S.S. *Peacock* had taken possession of the British ship HMS *Nautilus*. With three more German U-boats sunk, U.S.S. *Guadalcanal* was the most successful submarine hunter of the *Casablanca*-class. After being decommissioned in 1946, the ship was scrapped in Japan in 1959/60.

The German *U-505* after surrendering to U.S.S. *Guadalcanal*. Today, this Type IXC U-boat is a world-class exhibit at the Museum of Science and Industry, Chicago. (U.S. Navy)

U.S.S. *Guadalcanal* photographed from shore in 1945. (U.S. Navy)

U.S.S. *Manila Bay*

After entering service in October 1943, U.S.S. *Manila Bay* (CVE-61) saw action in numerous campaigns in the Pacific—the Marshall Islands, New Guinea, Leyte Gulf and the Philippines. On January 5, 1945, a Japanese kamikaze aircraft hit U.S.S. *Manila Bay*'s flight deck in the Mindanao Sea off the Philippines killing fourteen crew members and causing fires on the flight deck and the hangar deck below. However, the ship was operational again after a short time. After being decommissioned in 1946, it was scrapped in Japan in 1959.

Aircraft aboard U.S.S. *Manila Bay* during warm-up before takeoff. (U.S. Navy)

U.S.S. *Natoma Bay*

Commissioned in October 1943, U.S.S. *Natoma Bay* (CVE-62) served in several theaters in the Pacific, where her aircraft helped sink several Japanese ships. During the fighting at Okinawa, the carrier was hit by a kamikaze aircraft on June 7, 1945, which tore a hole in the deck near the bow, killing one crewman and injuring others. *Natoma Bay* was decommissioned in 1946 and scrapped in Japan in 1959.

This photograph of U.S.S. *Natoma Bay* with Avenger (front) and Wildcat (rear) aircraft illustrates the space savings that could be achieved by retractable wings. (U.S. Navy)

U.S.S. *St. Lo*

Commissioned in October 1943, U.S.S. *St. Lo* (CVE-63, originally U.S.S. *Midway*) initially served as a transport and was then ordered to the Pacific in the summer of 1944 to support the fleet. On October 25, during the fighting at Leyte Gulf, the carrier was hit by a kamikaze aircraft, which penetrated the flight deck, and exploded in the hangar below, where aircraft were being refueled. A large fire broke out and after half an hour the ship sank with the loss of 143 lives (different figures depending on the source).

U.S.S. *St. Lo* exploding after being hit by a kamikaze aircraft. The carrier sank a short time later. (U.S. Navy)

U.S.S. *Tripoli*

Commissioned in October 1943, U.S.S. *Tripoli* (CVE-64) served primarily in the Atlantic disrupting the refueling of German U-boats in the open sea. On April 19, 1944, her aircraft attacked *U-513* unsuccessfully, which was eventually sunk by an American PBM Mariner flying boat off the coast of Brazil. In the further course of the war, U.S.S. *Tripoli* took part in the hunt for other submarines in the North Atlantic. After Japan's surrender in September 1945, the carrier brought American soldiers home from the Pacific. In the postwar period, the ship was converted into a transport and supplied U.S. troops in Europe. It was decommissioned in 1958 and scrapped in Japan two years later.

U.S.S. *Tripoli* during the mid-1950s, while transporting Republic F-84 Thunderjet fighters on her flight deck. (U.S. Navy)

The lack of armor protection made ships like U.S.S. *Wake Island* very vulnerable to kamikaze attacks. (U.S. Navy)

U.S.S. *Wake Island*

Commissioned in November 1943, U.S.S. *Wake Island* (CVE-65) initially transported aircraft to India, and then became part of a "Hunter Killer Group" in the Atlantic, where she sank *U-543* in July 1944. A few months later, the carrier saw action in the Pacific in the recapture of the Philippines, as well as in the invasion of Iwo Jima in 1945. During a mission en route to Okinawa in March 1945, a kamikaze aircraft crashed into the sea so close to the ship that its wreckage and shrapnel penetrated the ship's side and caused flooding. After her repair, U.S.S. *Wake Island* served as an aircraft and troop transport. The ship was scrapped shortly after being decommissioned in Baltimore in 1946.

U.S.S. *White Plains*

Commissioned in November 1943, U.S.S. *White Plains* (CVE-66) participated in various operations in the Pacific until she was hit by a kamikaze aircraft in Leyte Gulf on October 25, 1944. After repairs, the ship served as an aircraft transport. It was decommissioned in 1946 and scrapped in 1958/59 in Baltimore.

A Japanese kamikaze aircraft attacking U.S.S. *White Plains* (CVE-66) but narrowly missing the carrier in Leyte Gulf on October 25, 1944. On the same day, the sister ship U.S.S. *St. Lo* was sunk by a kamikaze attack. (U.S. Navy)

U.S.S. *Solomons*

Commissioned in November 1943, U.S.S. *Solomons* (CVE-67) first transported aircraft to Brazil and was then used to hunt submarines in the Atlantic. In the process, she sank her only German U-Boat off the Brazilian coast. In the fall of 1944, she transported aircraft and personnel to Casablanca, Morocco and then served as a training carrier until the end of the war. In 1946, U.S.S. *Solomons* was decommissioned and subsequently scrapped.

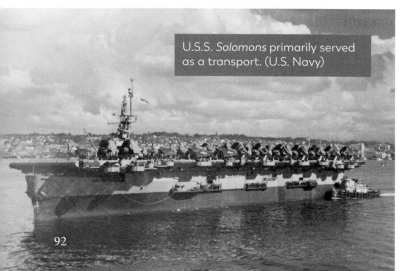

U.S.S. *Solomons* primarily served as a transport. (U.S. Navy)

A TBF/TBM Avenger crashing while trying to land on U.S.S. *Solomons*. (U.S. Navy)

U.S.S. *Kalinin Bay*

Commissioned in November 1943, U.S.S. *Kalinin Bay* (CVE-68) first saw action in the battles for the Gilbert and Marshall Islands and the Marianas. On October 25, 1944, during fighting in Leyte Gulf, several kamikaze aircraft attacked her. Although two could be shot down, the other two hit the ship and caused heavy damage. However, as these did not cause U.S.S. *Kalinin Bay* to sink, she was able to be repaired in San Diego. In 1946, the ship was decommissioned and subsequently scrapped.

The shell fragments pictured here are from the bomb the Japanese aircraft was carrying to attack U.S.S. *Kalinin Bay*. (U.S. Navy)

A scale model of U.S.S. *Kalinin Bay* with the color scheme giving an impression of the camouflage effect. This should have made it difficult for enemy pilots to locate or identify the carrier from high altitude. The blue-gray color should have let the ship optically merge with the open sea. (U.S. Navy)

U.S.S. *Kasaan Bay*

After entering service in December 1943, U.S.S. *Kasaan Bay* (CVE-69) initially carried aircraft to Casablanca, hunted submarines in the Mediterranean, and supported Allied cargo operations to southern France beginning in 1944. In early 1945, the carrier moved to the Pacific transporting aircraft to Pearl Harbor, Guam and Ulithi Atoll. Finally, U.S.S. *Kasaan Bay* escorted Allied supply convoys between the Marshall Islands and the Marianas. In 1946, the ship was decommissioned and scrapped 14 years later.

Crew members aboard U.S.S. *Kasaan Bay* arranging a F6F Hellcat aircraft on the flight deck to save space. (U.S. Navy)

U.S.S. *Fanshaw Bay*

Commissioned in December 1943, U.S.S. *Fanshaw Bay* (CVE-70) served exclusively in the Pacific. There on June 15, 1944, shortly before the invasion of Saipan, she received a heavy bomb hit detonating on the aft deck elevator, killing fourteen men and injuring another 23. Despite water flooding in, the ship was held and brought to Pearl Harbor for repairs. She saw action in Leyte Gulf and off Okinawa in 1945. U.S.S. *Fanshaw Bay* was decommissioned the following year and scrapped in 1959.

Crew members aboard U.S.S. *Fanshaw Bay* carrying bombs across the flight deck to various aircraft. Depending on the bomb type, these often weighed several hundred pounds, so they had to be moved by a small cart. (U.S. Navy)

U.S.S. *Kitkun Bay*

Commissioned in December 1943, U.S.S. *Kitkun Bay* (CVE-71) saw her first action in May 1944, when her aircraft attacked Japanese strongholds in the Marianas. The ship then took part in the fighting in Leyte Gulf, during which she was hit by a kamikaze aircraft in October 1944. The following month, in the Strait of Surigao (Philippines), she received another kamikaze hit causing water flooding, which could be brought under control. In all, seventeen crewmen died in both attacks. After the war, the carrier was decommissioned and scrapped in 1947.

Avengers parked on the flight deck of U.S.S. *Kitkun Bay* with their wings folded. In order to "park" the aircraft safely, they were lashed to the flight deck. (U.S. Navy)

U.S.S. *Tulagi*

Commissioned in December 1943, U.S.S. *Tulagi* (CVE-72) transported aircraft to Casablanca and participated in the Allied invasion of France, with her aircraft bombing German positions. After transferring to the Pacific,

she participated in the invasion of Luzon (Philippines) in early 1945 attacking Japanese strongholds. In the process, her battle group was attacked by kamikaze aircraft, which sank several U.S. Navy ships. In the spring of 1945, U.S.S. *Tulagi* patrolled Okinawan waters for submarines. After the war, she was decommissioned and scrapped shortly thereafter.

A Hellcat crashing on U.S.S. *Tulagi*'s flight deck after a failed landing attempt. While the pilot survived this accident, debris flying around often posed a real danger for the flight deck personnel. (U.S. Navy)

U.S.S. *Gambier Bay* under fire shortly before her sinking. (U.S. Navy)

U.S.S. *Gambier Bay*

Commissioned in December 1943, U.S.S. *Gambier Bay* (CVE-73) participated in missions beginning in the summer of 1944 for the later conquest of the Marianas. During the subsequent fighting in Leyte Gulf, her and other carriers' aircraft flew air strikes against superior enemy forces and were able to sink three cruisers and severely damage another. In the process, however, U.S.S. *Gambier Bay* came under direct artillery fire from Japanese cruisers and the battleship *Yamato*, which in the meantime had closed to within a very short range. The carrier was finally sunk on the morning of October 25, 1944, along with three escort ships, but most crew members were rescued.

U.S.S. *Nehenta Bay*

Commissioned in December 1943, U.S.S. *Nehenta Bay* (CVE-74) initially saw antisubmarine warfare service in the Marianas (Guam and Saipan) and was damaged by a typhoon in August 1944. After repair and a brief service as a training carrier, she secured the airspace during the invasion of Okinawa beginning in May 1945. Decommissioned in 1946, *Nehenta Bay* was scrapped 14 years later.

An Avenger from U.S.S. *Nehenta Bay* in airspace over Tinian Island (Marianas) during the U.S. invasion in July 1944. (U.S. Navy)

U.S.S. *Hoggatt Bay*

Commissioned in January 1945, U.S.S. *Hoggatt Bay* (CVE-75) initially saw action in the Pacific as part of a "Hunter Killer Group" and helped sink three Japanese submarines. During the fighting for the Philippines, her aircraft supported the landing in the Gulf of Lingayen in early 1945. Here, U.S.S. *Hoggatt Bay* had to repel numerous kamikaze attacks. Her last major deployment, beginning in May 1945, was in support of the invasion of Okinawa. Decommissioned in 1946, the ship was scrapped 14 years later.

Crew members aboard U.S.S. *Hoggatt Bay* attempting to push an Avenger, which flipped over during landing, to one of the aircraft elevators. (U.S. Navy)

U.S.S. *Kadashan Bay*

U.S.S. *Kadashan Bay* (CVE-76), commissioned in January 1944, participated in the invasion of Palau in September 1944 as well as the fighting for the Philippines in Leyte Gulf. There she was hit by a kamikaze aircraft on January 8, 1945, and after making temporary repairs locally, had to be sent to San Francisco for final repairs. For the rest of the war, U.S.S. *Kadashan Bay* was to serve as a supply carrier, but the Japanese surrender in August/September 1945 made such missions unnecessary. In 1946, she was decommissioned and scrapped 13 years later.

U.S.S. *Kadashan Bay* with a load of medium bombers. (U.S. Navy)

U.S.S. *Marcus Island*

Commissioned in January 1944, U.S.S. *Marcus Island* (CVE-77) took part in the fighting in Leyte Gulf in October 1944 and helped sink and damage several Japanese warships. In December, her aircraft destroyed two small Japanese naval units near the coast in Lingayen Gulf. In 1945, the carrier participated in operations against the Nansei Islands (Ryukyu Islands) south of Japan and in the invasion of Okinawa. Decommissioned after the war, it was scrapped in 1960.

An Avenger from U.S.S. *Marcus Island* after its ditching in the sea. As can be seen in the picture, the two crew members survived. After crashing or making a forced landing in hostile waters, it was often American submarines that rescued naval aviators, including George H. W. Bush, who would become President of the United States in 1989. (U.S. Navy)

U.S.S. *Savo Island*

Commissioned in February 1944, U.S.S. *Savo Island* (CVE-78) secured American naval units with her aircraft during the fighting in Leyte Gulf and the subsequent invasion, beginning in September. In the spring of 1945, she supported landing forces at Okinawa and then ferried aircraft from San Diego to Pearl Harbor, Hawaii. At the end of the war, U.S.S. *Savo Island* participated in the occupation of Japan. The ship was decommissioned in 1946 and scrapped in Hong Kong in 1960.

U.S.S. *Savo Island* in the Pacific Ocean. The open bow under the flight deck limited the seaworthiness of these ships. (U.S. Navy)

U.S.S. *Ommaney Bay*

Commissioned in February 1944, U.S.S. *Ommaney Bay* (CVE-79) initially supported the invasion of Leyte with air strikes against Japanese land positions and ships beginning in the fall of 1944. A short time later, she met her fate: On January 4, 1945, she was hit by a kamikaze aircraft in the Surigao Strait near the Philippines, whose two bombs detonated inside the ship. Because of the fires that had now broken out on board and the danger that the ship's ammunition might explode, the carrier was evacuated and eventually sunk by an escort ship. 93 crew members and two men on an escort destroyer lost their lives.

U.S.S. *Ommaney Bay*, painted in camouflage, prior to entering dry dock in November 1944. (U.S. Navy)

U.S.S. *Petrof Bay*

Commissioned in February 1944, U.S.S. *Petrof Bay* (CVE-80), initially served as an aircraft transport in the Pacific and participated in the attacks on Truk Atoll (Chuuk Atoll) in May 1944 and in the battles for Palau in September. During the fighting in Leyte Gulf, her aircraft damaged Japanese battleships including *Yamato*. On this occasion, the carrier narrowly escaped a torpedo hit from a Japanese submarine. In October, her aircraft damaged a cruiser and sank a destroyer in the Visayas Sea near the Philippines. During the invasions of Iwo Jima and Okinawa in 1945, U.S.S. *Petrof Bay*'s aircraft provided air support and searched the sea for submarines. Decommissioned in 1946, the ship was scrapped in Antwerp, Belgium, 13 years later.

U.S.S. *Petrof Bay* painted in Camouflage Measure 33, Design 10A in June 1944. (U.S. Navy)

U.S.S. *Rudyerd Bay* along with the fleet tanker U.S.S. *Severn* (in front). Supply ships like this ensured that warships could stay in the area of operations for a long time. (U.S. Navy)

U.S.S. *Rudyerd Bay*

Commissioned in February 1944, U.S.S. *Rudyerd Bay* (CVE-81) primarily protected American and Allied warships and supply ships during various operations and landings in the Pacific (including the Marianas, Iwo Jima, Okinawa). Decommissioned in 1946, the carrier was scrapped in Italy 14 years later.

U.S.S. *Saginaw Bay*

Commissioned in March 1944, U.S.S. *Saginaw Bay* (CVE-82) supported the invasions of Palau, Leyte, Iwo Jima and Okinawa. In 1946, the ship was retired and scrapped in Rotterdam in 1959.

An Avenger landing aboard U.S.S. *Saginaw Bay*. The arresting steel wire ropes on deck and the aircraft's tailhook can be seen clearly. When landing, the pilot had to catch one of several steel wire cables to stop his aircraft. If he failed to do so, he had to take off again and attempt a new landing approach. Sometimes the aircraft would drift off to the sides, fall overboard, or hit the island (bridge). (U.S. Navy)

The U.S. destroyer escort U.S.S. *Crowley* (DE-303) transferring a sick crewman to the escort carrier U.S.S. *Sargent Bay* in the Pacific, January 15, 1945. (U.S. Navy)

U.S.S. *Sargent Bay*

Commissioned in March 1944, U.S.S. *Sargent Bay* (CVE-83) initially escorted supply convoys to New Guinea in the Pacific. In 1945, her aircraft provided air support during the invasions of Iwo Jima and Okinawa. Decommissioned the following year, the ship was scrapped at Antwerp in 1959.

U.S.S. *Shamrock Bay*

Commissioned in March 1944, U.S.S. *Shamrock Bay* (CVE-84) initially transported aircraft and personnel to Casablanca. After transferring to the Pacific, she was hit by a kamikaze aircraft in the Gulf of Lingayen near the Philippines. The damage sustained meant that not all of her airborne aircraft could land on her, so they had to be picked up by other carriers. During the invasions of Iwo Jima and Okinawa, she protected the supply fleet. Decommissioned in 1946, the carrier was scrapped in Hong Kong in 1959.

U.S.S. *Shamrock Bay* underway off Norfolk, Virginia in November 1944. She is painted in camouflage Measure 33, Design 10A. The 28 aircraft of Composite Squadron 42 (VC-42), 16 FM-2 Wildcats and 12 TBM-3 Avengers, are tied down between the ship's two elevators, as it sails from Norfolk towards the Panama Canal, which she reached six days later. (U.S. Navy)

U.S.S. *Shipley Bay* as an aircraft transport in the Pacific. (U.S. Navy)

U.S.S. *Shipley Bay*

Commissioned in March 1944, U.S.S. *Shipley Bay* (CVE-85) transported a total of 496 aircraft to various theaters in the Pacific on several missions. She also supplied the fleet carriers engaged in combat operations with aircraft, personnel, and materiel. Beginning in April 1945, her aircraft attacked Japanese positions on Okinawa as part of the invasion. When the war ended, she lay in San Diego for overhaul. Decommissioned in 1946, U.S.S. *Shipley Bay* was scrapped 13 years later.

U.S.S. *Sitkoh Bay*

Commissioned in March 1944, U.S.S. *Sitkoh Bay* (CVE-86) served primarily as an aircraft transport, supplying American forces in various theaters in the Pacific. Decommissioned in 1946, the ship was reactivated four years later to support U.N. forces in Korea as a transport. In 1951, U.S.S. *Sitkoh Bay* delivered aircraft to French forces in Indochina (present-day Vietnam). In 1960, the carrier was finally retired and scrapped in Japan the following year.

This aerial view of U.S.S. *Sitkoh Bay* (CVE-86) illustrates how important escort carriers were as aircraft transports, as they could carry up to 75 aircraft (in their hangar and on the flight deck combined), depending on the type of aircraft. (U.S. Navy)

Plank Owner's certificate presented to Mrs. Evelyn Kendall, wife of Rear Admiral H. S. Kendall, and sponsor of U.S.S. *Steamer Bay*. (U.S. Navy)

U.S.S. *Steamer Bay*

After entering service in April 1944, U.S.S. *Steamer Bay* (CVE-87) served as an aircraft transport in the Pacific and provided air support along with other escort carriers during the landings in the Gulf of Lingayen, at Iwo Jima and at Okinawa in 1945. Decommissioned in 1947, the ship was scrapped at Portland, Oregon, in 1959.

U.S.S. *Cape Esperance*

Commissioned in April 1944, U.S.S. *Cape Esperance* (CVE-88, originally U.S.S. *Tananek Bay*) served almost exclusively as an aircraft transport in the Pacific. The aircraft she delivered were used primarily by carrier battle groups in Leyte Gulf (invasion of the Philippines) and in the battles for Iwo Jima and Okinawa. Decommissioned in 1946, U.S.S. *Cape Esperance* was reactivated four years later and delivered aircraft to Japan for use in the Korean War, but also to Europe and to Pakistan. In 1959, the carrier was decommissioned for the second time and shortly thereafter scrapped in Japan.

U.S.S. *Cape Esperance* was one of the longest-serving ships of her class. This photo shows her as the utility carrier U.S.N.S. *Cape Esperance* (T-CVU-88) at Pearl Harbor, Hawaii, with a cargo of aircraft during the mid-1950s. Visible planes include Douglas AD Skyraiders, McDonnell F2H Banshees, and North American F-100 Super Sabres. The tug U.S.S. *Neoga* is alongside. (U.S. Navy)

More than 2,500 carrier pilots were trained on U.S.S. *Takanis Bay* during World War II. (U.S. Navy)

U.S.S. *Takanis Bay*

Commissioned in April 1944, U.S.S. *Takanis Bay* (CVE-89) served almost exclusively as a training carrier. After the war, she helped bring American troops from the Pacific home to the United States. After being decommissioned in 1946, she was scrapped in Japan 14 years later.

U.S.S. *Thetis Bay*

Commissioned in April 1944, U.S.S. *Thetis Bay* (CVE-90) delivered aircraft to carriers engaged in combat until the end of the war. Her decommissioning in 1946 was followed by reactivation in 1955 as the U.S. Navy's first attack helicopter carrier known later as "assault helicopter aircraft carrier," and finally as "amphibious assault ship." The ship was now intended to provide helicopter support to the U.S. Navy and Marine Corps during operations. These aircraft were also intended to transport troops from the carrier to shore. During her second career, U.S.S. *Thetis Bay* was also part of the U.S. naval task force during the 1962 Cuban Missile Crisis in the Atlantic. Two years later, she was decommissioned for the second time and subsequently scrapped.

This aerial photo of U.S.S. *Thetis Bay* shows that larger aircraft types such as PBY Catalina flying boats could be carried on the flight decks of escort carriers. (U.S. Navy)

U.S.S. *Makassar Strait* (in the foreground) along with two of her sister ships in the reserve fleet at Tacoma, Washington, in 1951. After the war, many escort carriers were scrapped, while others were mothballed for several more years until reactivation or final scrapping. (U.S. Navy)

U.S.S. *Makassar Strait*

Commissioned in April 1944, U.S.S. *Makassar Strait* (CVE-91) initially served as a training carrier. Beginning in the spring of 1945, she protected supply ships in the fighting near the Nansei Islands (Ryukyu Islands) south of Japan and later participated in the bombardment of Japanese positions there. In total, more than 15,000 landings took place on U.S.S. *Makassar Strait*. After further service as a training carrier and transport for returning soldiers, the ship was decommissioned in 1946. Beginning in 1958, U.S.S. *Makassar Strait* was used as a target ship, but ran aground under tow near San Nicholas Island, California in 1961, where the hull broke apart. The wreck was demolished on site in subsequent years.

Aerial view of the wrecked ex-U.S.S. *Makassar Strait* near San Nicholas Island, California, in 1963. (U.S. Navy)

U.S.S. *Windham Bay*

Commissioned in May 1944, U.S.S. *Windham Bay* (CVE-92) initially transported aircraft and materiel to the Pacific as well as captured Japanese aircraft to Hawaii. During the battles for Iwo Jima and Okinawa, she supported the fleet carriers' operations. In June 1945, she and other ships were caught in a severe typhoon and sustained heavy damage. Repair work at San Diego lasted until the end of the war. Mothballed in 1946, she was reactivated in 1950 to supply the fleet primarily with aircraft and materiel during the Korean War. In 1959, U.S.S. *Windham Bay* was finally decommissioned and scrapped in Japan two years later.

U.S.S. *Windham Bay* transporting jet fighters in the late 1950s. (U.S. Navy)

An Avenger takes off from U.S.S. *Makin Island*. The ship's antiaircraft guns are visible to the left. (U.S. Navy)

U.S.S. *Makin Island*

Commissioned in May 1944, U.S.S. *Makin Island* (CVE-93) provided air support for U.S. naval forces in Leyte Gulf beginning in November. In 1945, her aircraft supported the landings on Iwo Jima and Okinawa as U.S. forces overcame Japanese resistance. She later served as an escort for minesweeping operations in the South China Sea. Decommissioned in 1946, the carrier was scrapped the following year.

U.S.S. *Lunga Point*

Commissioned in May 1944, U.S.S. *Lunga Point*'s aircraft initially secured supply vessels and warships during the fighting in Leyte Gulf. During the invasions of Iwo Jima and Okinawa, the ship was subjected to numerous air attacks by kamikaze aircraft but remained virtually undamaged. The carrier was decommissioned in 1946 and scrapped in Japan in 1960.

U.S.S. *Lunga Point* (CVE-94) in heavy seas. The aircraft on the flight deck were exposed to the elements with almost no protection, so they often had to be wrapped in foil before shipment. (U.S. Navy)

A damaged U.S. Marine Corps F4U Corsair being taken off U.S.S. *Bismarck Sea* in California. Escort carriers not only carried new aircraft to theatres of war, but also transported damaged aircraft back to the United States for repair. (U.S. Navy)

U.S.S. *Bismarck Sea*

Commissioned in May 1944, U.S.S. *Bismarck Sea* (CVE-95) was given only a short operational life: After participating in the invasion of the Gulf of Lingayen (Philippines), she was hit by two kamikaze aircraft off Iwo Jima on February 21, 1945. Since the hits caused the shipboard fire extinguishing system to fail, the fires could not be brought under control and the carrier had to be abandoned. Out of 923 crew members, 318 men were killed.

U.S.S. *Salamaua*

Commissioned in May 1944, U.S.S. *Salamaua* (CVE-96) initially transported supplies and aircraft to Hawaii and New Guinea, provided air support to supply convoys in Leyte Gulf beginning in October, and participated in the Luzon (Philippines) landings. Here, her aircraft bombed Japanese coastal defenses and provided cover for landing ships. On January 13, 1945, the carrier was severely damaged by the impact of a kamikaze aircraft. After her repairs, U.S.S. *Salamaua* took part in the invasion of Okinawa and was again damaged by a typhoon in June. Shortly after the Japanese surrender, she sailed to Tokyo Bay, where her aircraft monitored the Allied occupation. Decommissioned in 1946, the ship was scrapped shortly thereafter.

When U.S.S. *Salamaua* was hit by a kamikaze aircraft on January 13, 1945, 15 crewmen were killed and 80 were injured. (U.S. Navy)

U.S.S. *Hollandia* leaving a port as seen from the port side. (U.S. Navy)

U.S.S. *Hollandia*

Commissioned in June 1944, U.S.S. *Hollandia* (CVE-97) primarily carried aircraft, personnel, and materiel to various Pacific bases and theaters of war. In April 1945, her aircraft provided air support to invading forces at Okinawa. Decommissioned in 1946, she was scrapped 14 years later at Portland, Oregon.

U.S.S. *Kwajalein*

Commissioned in June 1944, the U.S.S. *Kwajalein* (CVE-98) almost exclusively served as a transport for aircraft, personnel and materiel, supplying various bases in the Pacific. In addition, she delivered aircraft to fleet carriers engaged in combat in the battles for the Philippines, Formosa (present-day Taiwan), and off the coast of China. Decommissioned in 1946, the carrier was finally scrapped in Japan 14 years later.

U.S.S. *Kwajalein* underway with six OS2U Kingfisher floatplanes parked on her flight deck in June 1944. Many escort carriers were named after Pacific islands or historic or more recent battles fought by the United States. (U.S. Navy)

U.S.S. *Admiralty Islands* with both deck elevators lowered. (U.S. Navy)

U.S.S. *Admiralty Islands*

Commissioned in June 1944, U.S.S. *Admiralty Islands* (CVE-99) transported aircraft, personnel and materiel, and served as a training carrier. On July 20, 1945, a fire occurred on board when a landing aircraft crashed. This resulted in the death of one crew member. The carrier was decommissioned in 1946 and scrapped the following year.

U.S.S. *Bougainville*

Commissioned in June 1944, U.S.S. *Bougainville* (CVE-100) initially transported aircraft to the Marshall and Admiralty Islands and the Marianas. In 1945, she supplied aircraft, pilots and materiel to the fleet carriers engaged in combat at Iwo Jima and later at Okinawa. U.S.S. *Bougainville* was decommissioned in 1946 and scrapped in 1960.

This photograph impressively shows the cargo capacity of the U.S.S. *Bougainville* as there are about 60 aircraft on the flight deck. (U.S. Navy)

U.S.S. *Matanikau*

Commissioned in June 1944, U.S.S. *Matanikau* (CVE-101) exclusively served as a transport for aircraft, personnel and materiel, and as a training carrier. After the war, she supported the occupation of Japan and brought American soldiers back home to the United States. Decommissioned in 1946, she was scrapped in Japan 14 years later.

U.S.S. *Matanikau* with an empty flight deck after delivering her load of aircraft. (U.S. Navy)

U.S.S. *Attu*

Commissioned in June 1944, U.S.S. *Attu* (CVE-102) served primarily as a supply ship for bases in the Pacific as well as for the fighting fleet. In the summer of 1945, she was damaged by a typhoon and repaired in San Diego. After the war ended, like many of her sister ships, she brought American servicemen back home to the United States. Decommissioned in 1946, U.S.S. *Attu* was scrapped in Baltimore two years later.

U.S.S. *Attu* steaming on a parallel course with a supply ship, exchanging personnel via a cable system. The flight deck is crowded with numerous F4U Corsairs. (U.S. Navy)

U.S.S. *Roi*

Commissioned in July 1944, U.S.S. *Roi* (CVE-103) initially transported aircraft and materiel to the Pacific like many of her sister ships. Shortly before the end of the war, she served as a supply ship for fleet carriers during the bombardment of the Japanese islands. After Japan's surrender, U.S.S. *Roi* returned American troops back home to the United States as part of Operation *Magic Carpet*. Shortly after her decommissioning in 1946, she was scrapped.

U.S.S. *Roi* at anchor at the end of the war in late summer 1945. (U.S. Navy)

U.S.S. *Munda*

Commissioned in July 1944, U.S.S. *Munda* (CVE-104) was the 50th and final unit of the *Casablanca*-class, numerically the largest aircraft carrier class in history. The ship served exclusively as a transport for bases and ships in the Pacific and was decommissioned in 1946 and scrapped in Japan in 1960. No ship of this class has been preserved for posterity.

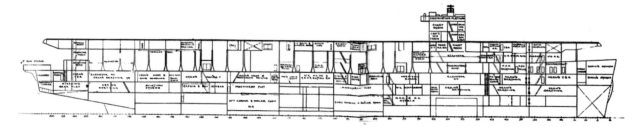

Inboard profile of U.S.S. *Munda*. She saw less than two years of active service. (U.S. Navy)

Casablanca-class	Active service in World War II
U.S.S. *Casablanca* (CVE-55)	Jul 8, 1943–Jun 10, 1946
U.S.S. *Liscome Bay* (CVE-56)	Aug 7, 1943–Nov 24, 1943 (sunk by Jap. submarine *I-175*)
U.S.S. *Anzio* (CVE-57)	Aug 27, 1943–Aug 5, 1946
U.S.S. *Corregidor* (CVE-58)	Aug 31, 1943–Jul 20, 1946
U.S.S. *Mission Bay* (CVE-59)	Sep 13, 1943–Feb 21, 1947
U.S.S. *Guadalcanal* (CVE-60)	Sep 25, 1943–Jul 15, 1946
U.S.S. *Manila Bay* (CVE-61)	Oct 5, 1943–Jul 31, 1946
U.S.S. *Natoma Bay* (CVE-62)	Oct 14, 1943–May 20, 1946
U.S.S. *St. Lo* (CVE-63)	Oct 23, 1943–Oct 25, 1944 (sunk by Jap. kamikaze)
U.S.S. *Tripoli* (CVE-64)	Oct 31, 1943–May 22, 1946
U.S.S. *Wake Island* (CVE-65)	Nov 7, 1943–Apr 5, 1946
U.S.S. *White Plains* (CVE-66)	Nov 15, 1943–Jul 10, 1946
U.S.S. *Solomons* (CVE-67)	Nov 21, 1943–May 15, 1946
U.S.S. *Kalinin Bay* (CVE-68)	Nov 27, 1943–May 15, 1946
U.S.S. *Kasaan Bay* (CVE-69)	Dec 4, 1943–Jul 6, 1946
U.S.S. *Fanshaw Bay* (CVE-70)	Dec 9, 1943–Aug 14, 1946
U.S.S. *Kitkun Bay* (CVE-71)	Dec 15, 1943–Apr 19, 1946
U.S.S. *Tulagi* (CVE-72)	Nov 15, 1943–Apr 30, 1946
U.S.S. *Gambier Bay* (CVE-73)	Dec 28, 1943–Oct 25, 1944 (sunk by Jap. naval forces)
U.S.S. *Nehenta Bay* (CVE-74)	Jan 3, 1944–Apr 15, 1946
U.S.S. *Hoggatt Bay* (CVE-75)	Jan 11, 1944–Jul 20, 1946
U.S.S. *Kadashan Bay* (CVE-76)	Jan 18, 1944–Jun 14, 1946
U.S.S. *Marcus Island* (CVE-77)	Jan 26, 1944–Dec 12, 1946
U.S.S. *Savo Island* (CVE-78)	Feb 3, 1944–Dec 12, 1946
U.S.S. *Ommaney Bay* (CVE-79)	Feb 11, 1944–Jan 4, 1945 (hit by kamikaze aircraft and scuttled)
U.S.S. *Petrof Bay* (CVE-80)	Feb 18, 1944–Jul 31, 1946
U.S.S. *Rudyerd Bay* (CVE-81)	Feb 25, 1944–Jun 11, 1946
U.S.S. *Saginaw Bay* (CVE-82)	Mar 2, 1944–Jun 19, 1944
U.S.S. *Sargent Bay* (CVE-83)	Mar 9, 1944–Jul 23, 1946

U.S.S. *Shamrock Bay* (CVE-84)	Mar 15, 1944–Jul 6, 1946
U.S.S. *Shipley Bay* (CVE-85)	Mar 21, 1944–Jun 28, 1946
U.S.S. *Sitkoh Bay* (CVE-86)	Mar 28, 194–Nov 30, 1946
U.S.S. *Steamer Bay* (CVE-87)	Apr 4, 1944–Jun 1, 1946
U.S.S. *Cape Esperance* (CVE-88)	Apr 8, 1944–Aug 22, 1946
U.S.S. *Takanis Bay* (CVE-89)	Apr 15, 1944–May 1, 1946
U.S.S. *Thetis Bay* (CVE-90)	Apr 21, 1944–Aug 7, 1946
U.S.S. *Makassar Strait* (CVE-91)	Apr 27, 1944–Aug 9, 1946
U.S.S. *Windham Bay* (CVE-92)	May 3, 1944–Jan 17, 1947
U.S.S. *Makin Island* (CVE-93)	May 9, 1944–Apr 19, 1946
U.S.S. *Lunga Point* (CVE-94)	May 14, 1944–Nov 24, 1946
U.S.S. *Bismarck Sea* (CVE-95)	May 20, 1944–Feb 21, 1945 (sunk by Jap. kamikaze)
U.S.S. *Salamaua* (CVE-96)	May 26, 1944–May 9, 1946
U.S.S. *Hollandia* (CVE-97)	Jun 1, 1944–Jan 17, 1947
U.S.S. *Kwajalein* (CVE-98)	May 4, 1944–Aug 16, 1946
U.S.S. *Admiralty Islands* (CVE-99)	Jun 13, 1944–Apr 26, 1946
U.S.S. *Bougainville* (CVE-100)	Jun 18, 1944–Nov 3, 1946
U.S.S. *Matanikau* (CVE-101)	Jun 24, 1944–Oct 11, 1946
U.S.S. *Attu* (CVE-102)	Jun 30, 1944–Jun 8, 1946
U.S.S. *Roi* (CVE-103)	Jul 6, 1944–May 9, 1946
U.S.S. *Munda* (CVE-104)	Jun 8, 1944–Sep 13, 1946

Commencement Bay-class

Since the *Sangamon*-class was considered a successful escort carrier type primarily because of its robust construction, many of its design elements found their way into the design of the subsequent *Commencement Bay*-class. Unlike their predecessors, these new ships were not created from existing tankers or cargo ships. The U.S. Navy went to the drawing board to design an escort carrier whose hull form was derived from "T3" tankers and adapted to the design requirements of a carrier. For this reason, the *Commencement Bay*-class was considered the most successful series of escort carriers. The design also took into account the possibility of using this series as supply carriers for smaller naval units. Therefore, this class was constructed with very large bunker spaces for fuel and could, for example, refuel destroyers during ongoing operations at sea.

The ships had an overall length of app. 558 feet (169.9 m), a maximum beam of 75 feet or 22.9 meters (flight deck), and a draft of 28 feet (8.5 m). The full displacement was about 21,400 tons. Propulsion consisted

Service and Fate

Nineteen of the 33 planned ships were completed, but only a few saw active service in World War II. In subsequent years, most of the ships in the class were converted to helicopter carriers, submarine-hunting aircraft carriers, or training ships for crews and pilots. Some also participated in the Korean War in these roles. Because the *Commencement Bay*-class was too small to operate the heavy jets designed in the 1950s and 1960s, the remaining ships were retired by about 1960 and eventually scrapped.

of two geared turbines supplied with steam pressure from four boilers. The total power output of 16,000 hp was transmitted to two propellers and allowed a top speed of 19 knots (35 km/h). The range was app. 10,000 nautical miles (19,000 km) steaming at an economic cruising speed of 15 knots (27.7 km/h). The crew consisted of about 1,066 men. Onboard armament consisted of two 5-inch (12.7 cm) guns and numerous 40 mm and 20 mm antiaircraft guns. The Commencement Bay-class could carry up to 34 aircraft. On board were mostly a combination of Grumman F4F Wildcats (fighters), Grumman TBF/TBM Avengers (torpedo bombers, antisubmarine aircraft) and other models.

Commencement Bay-class General Characteristics

Class	*Commencement Bay* (19 ships completed)
Shipyard	Todd Pacific Shipyards (diverse locations) Seattle-Tacoma Shipbuilding Corporation, Washington
Commissioning	1944–1946
Standard displacement	10,900 tons (24,100 tons full load)
Length	558 feet (169.9 m)
Beam	75 feet (22.9 m)
Draft	30 ft 8 in (9.35 m)
Propulsion	4 × boilers 2 × turbines (16,000 shp)
Shafts	2
Maximum speed	19 knots (35 km/h)
Range	10,000 nm (19,000 km)
Complement	1066
Crew	34
Aircraft	2 × 5-inch (12.7 cm gun) Various 40 mm and 20 mm AA guns
Complement	All ships scrapped until the 1960s

Port view of U.S.S. *Commencement Bay*. Her hull form was derived from "*T3*" tankers. (U.S. Navy)

U.S.S. *Commencement Bay*

Commissioned in November of 1944, U.S.S. *Commencement Bay* (CVE-105) was the type ship of the class. She did not see any combat and was instead used as a training carrier for pilots and crews. Decommissioned in 1946, she was scrapped in 1971.

U.S.S. *Block Island*

Commissioned in December 1944, U.S.S. *Block Island* (CVE-106, not to be confused with CVE-21, sunk in 1944) saw action only shortly before the end of the war, including the invasions of Okinawa and Borneo. In 1946, the ship was transferred to the reserve fleet and served as a training ship for the U.S. Naval Academy at Annapolis, Maryland, for the next four years. After her reactivation in 1951, she served three more years as a submarine-hunting carrier and was finally scrapped in Japan in 1960.

U.S.S. *Block Island* in 1952 as a submarine-hunting carrier. (U.S. Navy)

An Avenger flipping over while landing on U.S.S. *Gilbert Islands*. (U.S. Navy)

U.S.S. *Gilbert Islands*

Commissioned in February 1945, U.S.S. *Gilbert Islands* (CVE-107) saw her first combat action during the invasion of Okinawa, when her aircraft attacked Japanese positions and airfields in May. Shortly thereafter, her pilots provided air support during the invasion of Borneo. Although decommissioned in 1946, she was reactivated five years later, serving as a transport and training carrier, and as a floating communications center during the Vietnam War under the name U.S.S. *Annapolis* (AGMR-1). Finally decommissioned in 1976, she was scrapped three years later.

U.S.S. *Kula Gulf*

Commissioned in May 1945, U.S.S. *Kula Gulf* (CVE-108) did not see combat duty as the war ended while she was en route to the Pacific. Beginning in September, she patrolled off the coast of China, ferrying aircraft and bringing American servicemen back home to the United States. After five years in reserve, U.S.S. *Kula Gulf* was reactivated for the Korean War in 1951 and later served in the Vietnam War. Finally decommissioned in 1969, the ship was scrapped two years later.

U.S.S. *Kula Gulf* at sea with several Corsairs parked on her flight deck. (U.S. Navy)

U.S.S. *Cape Gloucester*

Commissioned in March 1945, U.S.S. *Cape Gloucester* (CVE-109) was deployed to the waters around Okinawa that summer to protect minesweepers from kamikaze attacks. Thereafter, her aircraft flew raids against Japanese positions in occupied China and provided aerial reconnaissance, shooting down several enemy aircraft. After the war, she transported former Australian, New Zealand, British and Dutch prisoners of war from Japan or formerly Japanese-occupied territories to Okinawa, now controlled by the United States, from where the men were brought home. In 1946, U.S.S. *Cape Gloucester* was decommissioned and finally scrapped in 1971.

U.S.S. *Salerno Bay*

Commissioned in May 1945, U.S.S. *Salerno Bay* (CVE-110) did not see any active service during World War II and was instead used as a training carrier and transport, among other roles. Decommissioned in 1947, the ship was reactivated four years later for the Korean War as a training ship, but did not see any action in that conflict either. Finally retired in 1954, U.S.S. *Salerno Bay* was scrapped in Bilbao, Spain, six years later.

Close-up of U.S.S. *Salerno Bay*'s bow section showing how the flight deck's leading edge was installed atop the ship's bow. Five Avenger torpedo bombers are parked on the flight deck. (U.S. Navy)

U.S.S. *Vella Gulf* in the Pacific in 1945. (U.S. Navy)

U.S.S. *Vella Gulf*

Commissioned in April 1945, U.S.S. *Vella Gulf* (CVE-111) participated in attacks on the islands of Rota and Pagan in the Marianas in July. When she was at anchor at Apra Harbor, Guam, in August 1945 and it was announced that Japan was about to surrender, the crew of U.S.S. *Vella Gulf* and other ships celebrated the news with fireworks. Decommissioned in 1946, the carrier was scrapped in 1971.

U.S.S. *Siboney*

Commissioned in May 1945, U.S.S. *Siboney* (CVE-112) was en route to Hawaii to supply Pearl Harbor with aircraft, personnel and materiel when Japan surrendered. Subsequently, the carrier participated in the unsuccessful search for Rear Admiral William D. Sample, who was listed as missing in action with his aircraft and crew. After two brief decommissionings in the late 1940s, U.S.S. *Siboney* served as a training and test ship during the Korean War. She was finally retired in 1956 and scrapped 15 years later.

A rare 1949 color photograph showing an Avenger crashing into U.S.S. *Siboney*'s island (bridge) after a failed landing attempt. (U.S. Navy)

An Avenger preparing for takeoff from U.S.S. *Siboney* in 1949. (U.S. Navy)

115

U.S.S. *Puget Sound* shortly after the war. (U.S. Navy)

U.S.S. *Puget Sound*

Commissioned in June 1945, U.S.S. *Puget Sound* (CVE-113) did not see any combat action during the war, but participated in the occupation of Japan starting in October, helping to remove sea mines and returning American soldiers back home to the United States. After just over two years of active service, the ship was decommissioned in 1946 and scrapped in Hong Kong in 1962.

U.S.S. *Rendova*

U.S.S. *Rendova* (CVE-114) was not commissioned until October 1945, several weeks after the Japanese surrender. In the following years, she served primarily as a training carrier and transport. During the Korean War, she provided air support for U.S. and allied forces. Decommissioned in 1955, the carrier was scrapped in 1971.

U.S.S. *Rendova* entering Gibraltar harbor in April 1948, with a deck load of aircraft, including AT-6 training planes to be delivered to the Turkish Air Force. Photographed from the fleet carrier U.S.S. *Valley Forge* (CV-45), which was then on her around-the-world cruise. Note Grumman F8F Bearcat fighters in the foreground. (U.S. National Archives)

U.S.S. *Bairoko* saw service as one of the few American escort carriers in the Korean War. (U.S. Navy)

U.S.S. *Bairoko*

Commissioned in July 1945, U.S.S. *Bairoko* (CVE-115), did not see any combat action in World War II either. She later took part in maneuvers, served as a training carrier and later during the Korean War. In 1954, she was part of the support fleet during the hydrogen bomb tests at Bikini Atoll. Decommissioned the following year, the ship was scrapped in Hong Kong six years later.

An Avenger overflying U.S.S. *Badoeng Strait* during the late 1940s. (U.S. Navy)

U.S.S. *Badoeng Strait*

U.S.S. *Badoeng Strait* (CVE-116) was not commissioned until November 1945, so she did not see any combat action until the Korean War. There she used her aircraft for antisubmarine warfare or to bombard enemy positions on land, among other missions. The ship was decommissioned in 1957 and scrapped in 1972.

U.S.S. *Saidor*

U.S.S. *Saidor* (CVE-117) was commissioned on September 4, 1945—two days after Japan's official surrender. In 1946, the carrier was used as a floating photo laboratory during the atomic bomb tests as part of Operation *Crossroads* at Bikini Atoll, as thousands of photographs of the tests had to be developed and evaluated in just a few days. Decommissioned in 1947, the ship was scrapped in 1970.

U.S.S. *Saidor* during sea trials in 1945. (U.S. Navy)

U.S.S. *Sicily* transporting automobiles and aircraft in 1953/54. (U.S. Navy)

U.S.S. *Sicily*

U.S.S. *Sicily* (CVE-118) was not commissioned until February 1946, six months after the end of the war. During the Korean War, her aircraft provided air support to ground forces and covered the retreat of American forces from Changjin Reservoir (Chosin Reservoir) to Hungnam, among other duties. In 1954, the ship was decommissioned and scrapped in 1961.

U.S.S. *Point Cruz*

Commissioned in October 1945, U.S.S. *Point Cruz* (CVE-119) initially transported aircraft to the Pacific until she was first transferred to the reserve in mid-1947. After being reactivated for service in Korea and Vietnam, the ship was decommissioned in 1969 and scrapped two years later.

U.S.S. *Point Cruz* as a helicopter carrier in 1955. (U.S. Navy)

U.S.S. *Mindoro* with one of her deck elevators lowered and several Sikorsky helicopters on her flight deck for submarine hunting in 1954. (U.S. Navy)

U.S.S. *Mindoro*

Commissioned in December 1945, U.S.S. *Mindoro* (CVE-120) served primarily as a training ship for naval aviators and helped develop antisubmarine techniques. She also participated in some fleet maneuvers in the Atlantic, Caribbean, as well as the Mediterranean. After being decommissioned in 1955, the ship was scrapped in Hong Kong five years later.

U.S.S. *Rabaul*

U.S.S. *Rabaul* (CVE-121) was launched in June 1945—too late to see active service in World War II. Many of her sister ships didn't participate in that conflict either. Although transferred to the U.S. Navy in August 1946, U.S.S. *Rabaul* never saw active service and was immediately mothballed. The ship was scrapped in 1973.

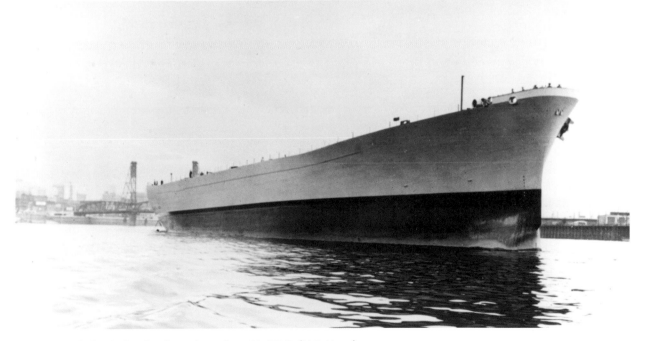

U.S.S. *Rabaul* after her launch on June 14, 1945. (U.S. Navy)

U.S.S. *Palau* as an aircraft transport in the postwar period. (U.S. Navy)

U.S.S. *Palau*

Commissioned in January 1946, U.S.S. *Palau* (CVE-122) served primarily as a training ship and aircraft transport during her short active career. Retired in 1954, she was scrapped six years later.

U.S.S. *Tinian*

Launched in September 1945, U.S.S. *Tinian* (CVE-123) was never commissioned and transferred to the reserve fleet immediately after her completion. Although reclassified first as a helicopter carrier and then as an aircraft transport, she was never activated and finally scrapped in 1971. The keels of four more *Commencement*-class carriers were laid, but their construction was stopped in the early stages and the material already used was demolished.

The never commissioned U.S.S. *Tinian* photographed from the starboard side. (U.S. Navy)

Commencement Bay-class	Active service in World War II
U.S.S. _Commencement Bay_ (CVE-105)	Nov 27, 1944–Nov 30, 1946
U.S.S. _Block Island_ (CVE-106)	Dec 30, 1944–May 28, 1946
U.S.S. _Gilbert Islands_ (CVE-107)	Feb 5, 1945–May 21, 1946
U.S.S. _Kula Gulf_ (CVE-108)	May 12, 1945–Jul 3, 1946
U.S.S. _Cape Gloucester_ (CVE-109)	Mar 5, 1945–Nov 5, 1946
U.S.S. _Salerno Bay_ (CVE-110)	May 19, 1945–Oct 4, 1947
U.S.S. _Vella Gulf_ (CVE-111)	Apr 9, 1945–Aug 9, 1946
U.S.S. _Siboney_ (CVE-112)	May 14, 1945–Dec 6, 1949
U.S.S. _Puget Sound_ (CVE-113)	Jun 5, 1944–Oct 18, 1946
U.S.S. _Rendova_ (CVE-114)	Oct 22, 1945–Jan 27, 1950
U.S.S. _Bairoko_ (CVE-115)	Jun 16, 1945–Apr 14, 1950
U.S.S. _Badoeng Strait_ (CVE-116)	Nov 14, 1945–Apr 20, 1946
U.S.S. _Saidor_ (CVE-117)	Nov 4, 1945–Sep 12, 1947
U.S.S. _Sicily_ (CVE-118)	Feb 27, 1946–Jul 5, 1954
U.S.S. _Point Cruz_ (CVE-119)	Oct 16, 1945–Jun 30, 1947
U.S.S. _Mindoro_ (CVE-120)	Dec 4, 1945–Aug 4, 1955
U.S.S. _Rabaul_ (CVE-121)	never commissioned
U.S.S. _Palau_ (CVE-122)	Jan 15, 1946–Jun 15, 1954
U.S.S. _Tinian_ (CVE-123)	never commissioned
U.S.S. _Bastogne_ (CVE-124)	canceled
U.S.S. _Eniwetok_ (CVE-125)	canceled
U.S.S. _Lingayen_ (CVE-126)	canceled
U.S.S. _Okinawa_ (CVE-127)	canceled
CVE-128 to CVE-139	no name assigned, canceled before keel laying

3
Light Carriers

Independence-class

In 1941, even before the Japanese attack on Pearl Harbor, it had become clear to President Roosevelt that the tensions between the United States and Japan would soon lead to an armed conflict. Although the U.S. Navy had numerous ships, including several fleet carriers, either under construction or planned, no new carriers were expected to become available before 1943/44. This situation led to the idea to convert some of the many cruisers then under construction to carriers. Although studies from October 1941 concluded that aircraft carriers converted from cruiser hulls would be less capable, they were available much sooner. After the attack on Pearl Harbor on December 7, 1941, the need for more carriers became urgent. Despite efforts to accelerate the construction of the *Essex*-class fleet carriers, these large ships could not be completed in time to replace the losses of U.S.S. *Lexington* (CV-2) in Coral Sea (May 1942), U.S.S. *Yorktown* (CV-5) at Midway (June 1942), U.S.S. *Hornet* (CV-8) near the Solomon Islands, and U.S.S. *Wasp*

Born from Cruisers

Since the *Independence*-class was based on a light cruiser, they were fast ships capable of 31.5 knots (58 km/h) and therefore about twelve knots faster than the *Casablancas*, thus allowing them to keep up and operate with the fleet carrier task groups.

(CV-7) at Guadalcanal (September 1942). By fall of 1942, the available U.S. carriers had been reduced to U.S.S. *Enterprise* (CV-6) and U.S.S. *Saratoga* (CV-3) in the Pacific and U.S.S. *Ranger* (CV-4) in the Atlantic. Therefore, as early as spring of 1942, the U.S. Navy reordered nine *Cleveland*-class light cruisers then under construction at the New York Shipbuilding Corporation shipyard, Camden, New Jersey, to be converted into light carriers of the *Independence*-class.

The resulting design had a relatively small island as well as a short (550 feet; 168 m) and narrow flight deck (109 feet; 33 m) leading to a high aircraft accident rate. Moreover, the small hangar deck caused a significant increase in the carrier's topside weight, thus significantly limiting its seaworthiness, in particular when facing typhoons in the Pacific. In order to reduce this enormous weakness at least to a certain degree, blisters were added to the original cruiser hull, increasing the original beam by 5 feet (1.5 m) to 71 feet and 6 inches (21.8 m). For comparison, the *Essex*-class fleet carriers had a flight deck up to 862 feet (262.7 m) long and about 147 feet (45 m) wide, while the *Casablanca*-class escort carriers, which entered service at the same time as the *Independence*-class, had an even shorter flight deck measuring just about 500 feet (152 m) in length and up to 108 feet (33 m) in width.

The *Independence*-class carried 30 to 34 aircraft, which was a little more than the 28 of the *Casablancas* but only one third of that of the *Essex*-class. The air group originally consisted of nine fighters, nine scout bombers, and nine torpedo bombers, but later revised to about two dozen fighters and nine torpedo bombers. All in all, the *Independence*-class light carriers were limited-capability ships, whose principal virtue was near-term availability.

Initially classified as "aircraft carriers" (CV), all were re-designated "light aircraft carriers" (CVL) in July 1943 while four ships were still under construction (CVL-27–CVL-30). Commissioned along with the first eight of the *Essex*-class fleet carriers in the course of 1943, the nine *Independence*-class light carriers became a vital component of the Fast Carrier Task Force, which carried the U.S. offensive across the Pacific from November 1943 until the end of the war in August 1945. Despite their design weaknesses, the ships of the *Independence*-class made their contribution to the victories in numerous battles against the Japanese Navy in the Pacific. This was also accomplished by well-trained ship crews and capable aircraft flown by well-trained pilots and crews.

Postwar Service

After the end of World War II, U.S.S. *Independence* (CVL-22), along with the fleet carrier U.S.S. *Saratoga* (CV-3), was expended as target ships in the Operation *Crossroads* atomic tests at Bikini Atoll in 1946. After laying up her remaining seven sister ships in 1947, the U.S. Navy returned five of them to service in 1948–53, two with the French Navy. While two ships served as training carriers, U.S.S. *Bataan* (CVL-29) was called to action with U.S. Marine Corps air groups. In the early 1950s, she and U.S.S. *Cabot* (CVL-28) were modernized receiving antisubmarine warfare equipment and modified funnels. After the final decommissioning and scrapping of six of the remaining ships, only U.S.S. *Cabot*, sold to Spain and renamed *Dédalo*, survived in active service until 1989. Eventually, she, too, was scrapped in 1999–2003 leaving no survivor of the *Independence*-class.

U.S.S. *Independence*

Commissioned in January 1943, U.S.S. *Independence* (CV/CVL-22) took part in the attacks on Rabaul and Tarawa before being torpedoed by Japanese aircraft, necessitating repairs in San Francisco from January to July 1944. After repairs, she launched strikes against targets in Luzon and Okinawa. U.S.S. *Independence* was part of the carrier group that sank the remnants of the Japanese fleet in the battle of Leyte Gulf and several other warships in the Surigao Strait. After the war, the surplus carrier was expended in the Operation *Crossroads* atomic tests at Bikini Atoll in July 1946. After surviving both tests with little damage, she was used as a radiation research hulk for several years afterward and finally sunk as a target in January 1951. In 2009, deep sea archaeologists located the relatively intact wreck of U.S.S. *Independence* in 2,600 feet (790 m) of water in Monterey Bay, California.

The new light carrier U.S.S. *Independence* in San Francisco Bay in July 1943. Note that she still carries Douglas SBD Dauntless dive bombers. Before entering combat, the air group would only consist of Grumman F6F Hellcat fighters and TBF Avenger torpedo bombers. (U.S. Naval History and Heritage Command)

Correspondents aboard an LCU viewing the badly damaged U.S.S. *Independence* on July 3, 1946, two days after the first atomic test "Able." This was the unengaged side of the ship. She was moored far enough away from the second atomic detonation point "Baker" to avoid further physical damage but was severely contaminated. (U.S. Navy)

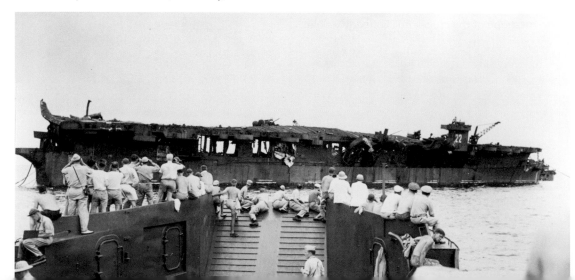

Light Carriers in Battle

Along with seven fleet carriers, eight battleships and numerous other warships, eight light carriers participated in the decisive battle of the Philippine Sea in June 1944, which effectively ended Japan's carrier air power with losses totaling three carriers (out of nine), approximately 400 carrier aircraft, and around 200 land-based aircraft. In this engagement, the eight light carriers provided 40 percent of the Fast Carrier Task Force's fighters and 36 percent of the torpedo bombers. In total, the U.S. was able to operate about 900 aircraft against the 450 carrier-based and 300 land-based Japanese aircraft.

U.S.S. *Princeton*

Commissioned in February 1943, U.S.S. *Princeton* (CV/CVL-23) operated with the fast fleet carrier task forces participating in various U.S. invasions of Japanese-held islands in the Pacific. In the battle of the Philippine Sea in June of 1944, her aircraft contributed 30 kills and her antiaircraft guns another three, plus one assist, to the devastating toll inflicted on Japan's naval air power. During the battle of Leyte Gulf, U.S.S. *Princeton* (in Task Group 38.3) cruised off Luzon and sent her aircraft against airfields there to prevent Japanese land-based aircraft attacks on Allied ships massed in the Gulf. On October 24, 1944, she was hit by a bomb dropped by a Yokosuka D4Y dive bomber striking her between the elevators, punching through the wooden flight deck and hangar before exploding. Despite little structural damage, a fire broke out and quickly spread owing to burning gasoline, and caused further explosions. When it became clear that U.S.S. *Princeton* could not be saved, the light cruiser U.S.S. *Reno* (CL-96) had to scuttle her by firing torpedoes at the burning hulk.

U.S.S. *Princeton* being prepared for launching, at the New York Shipbuilding Yard, Camden, New Jersey, on October 16, 1942. She was launched two days later. The shape of the cruiser hull is clearly visible. (U.S. Navy)

Stern view of U.S.S. *Princeton*. The cruiser hull and machinery enabled the light carrier to reach a maximum speed of 31.5 knots. (U.S. Navy)

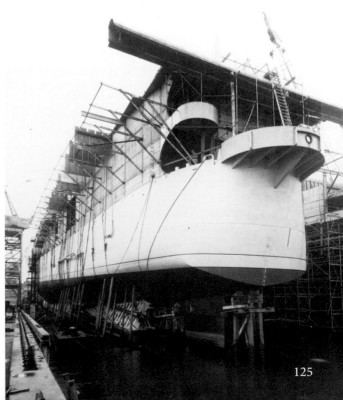

U.S.S. *Princeton* afire in the morning of October 24, 1944, soon after she was hit by a Japanese bomb during operations off the Philippines. This view shows smoke rising from the ship's second large explosion, as the light cruiser U.S.S. *Reno* (CL-96) steams by in the foreground. (U.S. National Archives)

View of U.S.S. *Princeton*'s aft port side and flight deck, seen from the light cruiser U.S.S. *Birmingham* (CL-62) as she came alongside to help fight fires during the afternoon of October 24, 1944. Note the aircraft elevator blown out of position and turned upside down, and the flight deck buckled by the hangar deck explosions that followed the Japanese bomb hit. The protection of the *Independence*-class was modest, and munitions often had to be stowed at the hangar level, a factor that contributed greatly to the U.S.S. *Princeton*'s loss. (U.S. National Archives)

U.S.S. *Belleau Wood* (CV/CVL-24)

Commissioned in March 1943, U.S.S. *Belleau Wood* operated with various task forces throughout the war. During the battle of the Philippine Sea, her aircraft sank the Japanese carrier *Hiyō*. After participating in the battle of Leyte Gulf, while patrolling east of Leyte on October 30, 1944, she shot down a Japanese kamikaze aircraft which fell on her flight deck aft, causing fires setting off ammunition and killing 92 crewmen. By most accounts the last Japanese aircraft shot down in World War II was a Yokosuka D4Y3 dive bomber which was destroyed by Clarence A. Moore, an F6F Hellcat pilot of "The Flying Meat-Axe" VF-31 from U.S.S. *Belleau Wood*. Decommissioned in 1947, the carrier was transferred to the French Navy and renamed *Bois Belleau* in June 1951. After serving in the First Indochina War (which would later become the Vietnam War), the ship was returned to the U.S. Navy for scrapping in September 1960.

A photo sequence showing a Japanese Mitsubishi A6M kamikaze barely missing U.S.S. *Belleau Wood* on April 6, 1945. The aircraft hit the water about 100 feet (30 m) from the starboard side abaft the stacks. Shrapnel from a bomb hit the ship and the aircraft's propeller hit the flight deck. (U.S. Navy)

Bow view of U.S.S. *Cowpens* off the Mare Island Naval Shipyard, California, on May 12, 1945. The bulky flight deck construction made the ships of the *Independence*-class top heavy, thus significantly limiting their seaworthiness, in particular when facing typhoons in the Pacific. (U.S. Navy)

Stern view of U.S.S. *Cowpens*. The light carriers of the *Independence*-class were unsatisfactory ships for aviation with their narrow, short decks and slender, high-sheer hulls. The names of the ships of the *Independence*-class followed the U.S. Navy's policy of naming aircraft carriers after historic navy ships or historic battles: The battle of Cowpens in 1781 was a significant engagement during the American Revolutionary War. (U.S. Navy)

U.S.S. *Cowpens*

Commissioned in May of 1943, U.S.S. *Cowpens* (CV/CVL-25) participated in various U.S. invasions of Japanese-held islands in the Pacific. In the battle of the Philippine Sea in June of 1944, her aircraft accounted for a portion of the huge tally of Japanese aircraft shot down. During the decisive phase of the battle of Leyte Gulf on November 25-26, U.S.S. *Cowpens* provided combat air patrols for the U.S. Navy ships pursuing the fleeing remnant of the Japanese combat fleet. During the disastrous typhoon "Cobra" on December 18, 1944, the carrier lost one man from her crew, several aircraft and some equipment. After participating in the Okinawa invasion and the attacks on the Japanese homeland, the carrier returned troops back home from the Pacific during Operation *Magic Carpet* from November 1945 to late January 1946, Decommissioned one year later, the ship was scrapped starting in November 1959.

U.S.S. *Cowpens* during her refit at the Mare Island Navy Yard, San Francisco, in May 1945, which included the installation of new radar systems. The heavy cruiser U.S.S. *Chester* (CA-27) is in the background. Note the small radar fitted director forward. (U.S. National Archives)

U.S.S. *Cowpen's* pilots and crewmen looking at bombs that have been inscribed with messages for Japanese targets on Wake Island in October of 1943, just before the raids. (U.S. National Archives)

Ships of Task Force 50 en route to the Gilberts and Marshalls to support the invasions of Makin and Tarawa, in November 1943. Ships are (l-r): battleship U.S.S. *Alabama* (BB-60); her sister ship U.S.S. *Indiana* (BB-58), in the distance, camouflaged; and U.S.S. *Monterey* (CVL-26). Light carriers had enough speed to take part in fleet actions with the larger fleet carriers and fast battleships while escort carriers did not. (National Archives)

U.S.S. *Monterey*

Commissioned in June 1943, U.S.S. *Monterey* (CV/CVL-26) operated with Task Force 58 (TF 58) during raids in the Caroline Islands, Mariana Islands, northern New Guinea, and the Bonin Islands from February to July 1944. During this time, she also fought in the battle of the Philippine Sea on June 19-20 and later supported landings at Leyte (Philippines) in October. In December, she was hit by typhoon "Cobra," which lasted two days and tore loose some aircraft from their cables, causing several fires on the hangar deck. During the storm, future U.S. President Gerald R. Ford, who served on board the ship, was almost swept overboard. Eventually, the crew was able to contain the fire. After her overhaul, U.S.S. *Monterey* supported the TF 58's landings at Okinawa from May to June 1945, then joined TF 38 for the final strikes against the Japanese homeland from July to August for Operation *Magic Carpet*. Retired in 1947, she was reactivated as a training carrier during the Korean War three years later. Decommissioned again in January 1956, U.S.S. *Monterey* was re-designated as an aircraft transport (AVT-2) in 1959. The ship was finally stricken 11 years later.

A Grumman F6F Hellcat fighter on the flight deck elevator aboard U.S.S. *Monterey* in June 1944. *Monterey*'s aircraft sank five enemy warships, and damaged others. Moreover, she was responsible for the destruction of thousands of tons of Japanese shipping, hundreds of aircraft, and vital industrial complexes. (U.S. Navy)

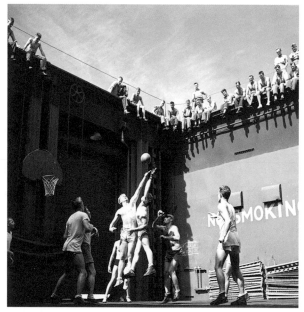

Crewmen in the U.S.S. *Monterey*'s forward elevator well playing basketball in mid-1944. Jumper at left is Gerald R. Ford, who would serve as the 38th U.S. president from 1974–1977. (U.S. Navy)

Task Group 38.3 entering Ulithi anchorage after strikes in the Philippines Islands, on December 12, 1944. The light carrier U.S.S. *Langley* is in lead, followed by the fleet carrier U.S.S. *Ticonderoga* (CV-14), fast battleships and cruisers. (U.S. National Archives)

U.S.S. *Langley*

Commissioned in August of 1943, U.S.S. *Langley* (CVL-27) participated in various assaults and invasions in the Pacific with TF 38 before supporting the landings on Leyte. Japan's efforts to stop the U.S. advance included a counterattack by most available major fleet units, Operation *Sho-Go*. On October 24, 1944, U.S.S. *Langley*'s aircraft participated in the battle of the Sibuyan Sea. Aircraft of TF 38 attacked the Japanese Center Force, as it steamed toward the San Bernardino Strait and the U.S. beachhead at Tacloban. The Japanese units temporarily retired. The following day, TF 38 intercepted the Japanese aircraft carriers. In the ensuing battle off Cape Engaño, Japan lost four carriers, two battleships, four heavy cruisers, one light cruiser, and five destroyers. U.S.S. *Langley*'s aircraft assisted in the destruction of the carriers *Zuihō* and *Zuikaku*, the latter being the only surviving carrier of the six that had attacked Pearl Harbor in 1941. In the war's final year, she participated in the Iwo Jima and Okinawa landings as well in the attacks on the Japanese homeland and finally in Operation *Magic Carpet*. Decommissioned in 1947, the ship was transferred to France and renamed *La Fayette* four years later. After being returned to the U.S. Navy, the carrier was stricken in March of 1963 and scrapped at Baltimore the following year.

A F6F Hellcat fighter aborting a landing on U.S.S. *Langley* on October 10, 1944. Task Force 38 carriers hit Japanese targets in the Okinawa area on that day. (U.S. Navy)

U.S.S. *Langley* rolling heavily during the typhoon "Connie" in June 1945. (U.S. Navy)

U.S.S. *Cabot* underway en route to the Japanese-held Wake Island in July 1945, which she and the battleship U.S.S. *Pennsylvania* (BB-38) attacked on August 1. (U.S. Navy)

U.S.S. *Cabot*

Commissioned in July of 1943, U.S.S. *Cabot* (CVL-28) joined TF 58 and participated in the invasion of the Marshall Islands. She launched sorties in the battle of the Philippine Sea, which hopelessly crippled Japanese naval aviation, and her aircraft pounded Japanese bases on Iwo Jima, Pagan, Rota, Guam, Yap and Ulithi. On November 26, 1944, while patrolling off Luzon (Philippines), she was hit by two kamikaze aircraft, killing 62 crewmen. Then her aircraft attacked the Japanese homeland and the Bonins to suppress opposition to the invasion of Iwo Jima. Continued strikes against Okinawa in March of 1945 prepared for the subsequent invasion.

Retired in February 1947, U.S.S. *Cabot* was reactivated and modernized as an antisubmarine warfare (ASW) carrier the following year. After her transfer to the reserve fleet in January 1955, she was modernized and transferred to Spain as *Dédalo* in 1967. After striking her from the U.S. Naval Vessel Register, she was eventually sold to Spain in 1972. After her final retirement in 1989, the plan to preserve this last former U.S. light carrier as a floating museum failed. The ship was scrapped at Brownsville, Texas, from 1999–2003.

Aerial port bow view of the Spanish aircraft carrier *Dédalo* (the former U.S.S. *Cabot*) underway in 1988. (U.S. Dept. of Defense)

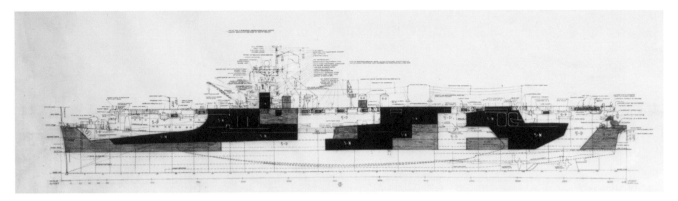

Camouflage scheme intended for light aircraft carriers of the *Independence*-class (1944) showing the ship's port side. (U.S. Navy)

U.S.S. *Bataan*

Commissioned in November 1943, U.S.S. *Bataan* (CVL-29) joined TF 58 along with the fleet carrier U.S.S. *Hornet* (CV-12) and her sister ships U.S.S. *Belleau Wood* and U.S.S. *Cowpens* supporting various operations in the Pacific, including the invasion of the Mariana Islands, the battle of the Philippine Sea, Okinawa and the attacks on the Japanese homeland. Retired in 1946, the ship was reactivated as an antisubmarine warfare (ASW) carrier in 1950. After serving during the Korean War in various roles, including with the U.S. Marine Corps air groups, U.S.S. *Bataan* was decommissioned for the final time four years later and stricken for scrapping in 1959.

U.S.S. *Bataan* painted in "Measure 32 Design 8A camouflage" pattern intended to make it more difficult for the enemy to identify the ship type, its shape and the distance to it. (U.S. Navy)

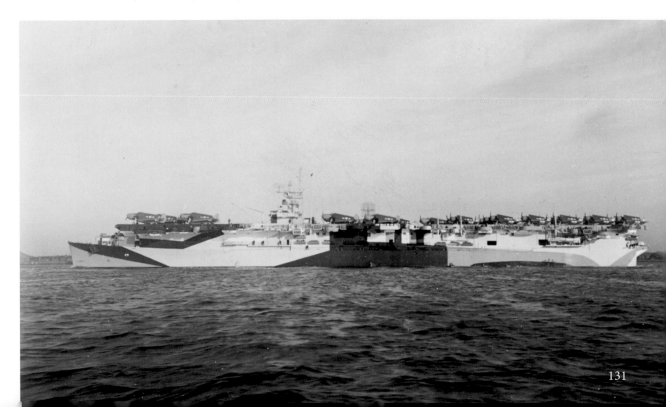

Lieutenant George H.W. Bush in his Grumman TBM Avenger aboard U.S.S. *San Jacinto* in 1944. (U.S. Navy)

U.S.S. *San Jacinto*

Commissioned in November of 1943, U.S.S. *San Jacinto* (CVL-30) participated in various operations before fighting in the battle of the Philippine Sea in June of 1944. On September 2, while piloting a TBF Avenger torpedo bomber, future U.S. President George H. W. Bush was hit by antiaircraft fire while attacking Japanese positions on the island of Chichijima south of Japan. Lieutenant Bush completed his bombing run, then guided his crippled aircraft out to sea. While two other crew members were lost, Bush parachuted into the sea and was rescued by the submarine U.S.S. *Finback*. U.S.S. *San Jacinto* supported the strikes against Okinawa and operated aircraft equipped with cameras to get information essential for future invasion plans. During the invasion of Leyte in the central Philippines on October 20, the carrier provided close air support and narrowly escaped various kamikaze attacks during strikes against the Japanese homeland. Decommissioned in 1947, U.S.S. *San Jacinto* was sold for scrap 14 years later.

Former President George H.W. Bush (in office 1989–1993 as the 41st president) looking at a display of his former ship, the U.S.S. *San Jacinto*, in the tribute room of the aircraft carrier that bears his name, U.S.S. *George H.W. Bush* (CVN-77). Bush and his wife, Barbara, visited the carrier in July of 2010 watching flight operations, touring the ship and visiting with the crew. (U.S. Navy)

Independence-class General Characteristics

Class	Independence
Type	Light carrier
Shipyard	New York Shipbuilding Corp., Camden, New Jersey
Standard displacement	11,000 tons (15.100 tons deep load)
Length	622 feet 6 in (190 m)
Beam	71 feet 6 in (21.8 m)
Draft	26 feet (7.9 m)
Propulsion	4 × steam turbines; 4 × boilers
Shafts	4
Shaft horsepower	100.000 hps
Maximum speed	31.5 knots
Armament	26 × 40 mm AA guns 55–76 × 20 mm AA cannons
Aircraft	34
Complement	1460

	Name	No.	Commissioned	Decommissioned	Fate
1	*Independence*	CV/CVL-22	Jan 14, 1943	Aug 28, 1946	Scuttled in 1951.
2	*Princeton*	CV/CVL-23	Feb 25, 1943	n/a	Scuttled after air attack on October 24, 1944.
3	*Belleau Wood*	CV/CVL-24	Mar 31, 1943	Jan 13, 1947	Transferred to France in 1953. Scrapped in 1960
4	*Cowpens*	CV/CVL-25	May 28, 1943	Jan 13, 1947	Scrapped in Portland in 1960.
5	*Monterey*	CV/CVL-26	Jun 17, 1943	Jan 16, 1956	Scrapped in Philadelphia in 1971.
6	*Langley*	CVL-27	Aug 31, 1943	Feb 11, 1947	Transferred to France in 1951. Scrapped in 1964.
7	*Cabot*	CVL-28	Jul 24, 1943	Jan 21, 1955	Transferred to Span in 1967. Scrapped in Texas, 1999–2003.
8	*Bataan*	CVL-29	Nov 17, 1943	Apr 9, 1954	Scrapped in San Francisco in 1961.
9	*San Jacinto*	CVL-30	Sep 26, 1943	Mar 1, 1947	Scrapped in Los Angeles in 1971.

U.S.S. *Saipan* underway in the mid-1950s. On deck are Douglas AD-5 Skyraiders of Marine Attack Squadron VMA-333 "Fighting Shamrocks." (U.S. Navy)

Saipan-class

The *Saipan*-class aircraft carriers were a class of two light carriers *Saipan* (CVL-48) and *Wright* (CVL-49) laid down during the war. Like the previous *Independence*-class, they were based on cruiser hulls, but were built from the keel up as carriers, and were based on heavy rather than light cruiser hulls. Completed too late for war service, they first served as carriers before U.S.S. *Wright* was converted into a command ship and U.S.S. *Saipan* into a major communications relay ship in the late 1950s. Decommissioned in 1970, both ships were scrapped 10 years later.

The light carrier U.S.S. *Wright* (CVL-49; left) and the fleet carrier U.S.S. *Leyte* (CV-32; right) moored at Naval Air Station Quonset Point, Rhode Island, in 1950. While the former could carry some 42 aircraft, the latter had space for up to 100. Both ships did not see action in World War II. Note the difference in size, in particular the width of the flight deck which made U.S.S. *Leyte* and her *Essex*-class sister ships a much safer platform for takeoffs and especially for landings. (U.S. Navy)

Because the F4U Corsair was such a well-designed and successful fighter aircraft during World War II, it continued to serve into the 1950s. This photo shows a F4U-4 Corsair (BuNo. 96871) of Fighter Squadron 24 (VF-24) aboard the carrier U.S.S. *Philippine Sea* (CV-47) for a deployment to the Western Pacific and Korea in 1951. (U.S. Navy)

4

Carrier Aircraft

When the first airplanes took to the skies at the beginning of the 20th century, it did not take long before the idea arose of having these machines take off from a ship. During 1910–1911, Eugene B. Ely proved that ships were suitable for both aircraft takeoffs and landings. During World War I, carrier-based aircraft saw action for the first time (as described in chapter 1). Inspired by these successes, air power strategists wanted to take this new weapon to the next level.

The target ship ex-SMS *Ostfriesland* shortly before she was sunk by aircraft-dropped bombs on July 21, 1921. (U.S. Navy)

Donald E. Runyon, fighter pilot of the U.S.S. *Enterprise*'s Squadron 6 (VF-6) on September 10, 1942, during the Guadalcanal campaign. His Grumman F4F-4 Wildcat is decorated with a tombstone containing 41 "meatballs," each representing a Japanese plane claimed by the squadron. Runyon was one of the leading F4F aces, credited with shooting down eight Japanese aircraft while flying Wildcats. (U.S. Navy)

The End of the Battleship Era

During World War II, carrier-based aircraft were used on a large scale for the first time. These were to play a critical role, especially during major naval battles in the Pacific and in hunting submarines in the Atlantic. During this epic conflict, the battleship, which had been considered supreme for decades, repeatedly fell victim to carrier-based (and in some cases land-based) aircraft. It was therefore both sensational and terrifying that in May 1941 a Royal Navy Swordfish biplane was able to disable the state-of-the-art German battleship *Bismarck* by placing a torpedo in her steering gear. In the Japanese attack on the U.S. naval base at Pearl Harbor (Hawaii) in December 1941, the use of 350 carrier aircraft showed that even an entire fleet could be destroyed or at least crippled from the air. The precedent for this type of warfare had been demonstrated the previous year by the successful attack by British carrier pilots on Italian battleships in Taranto Harbor.

Towards the end of the war, even the two largest battleships ever built, the Japanese *Yamato* and *Musashi*, were sunk by bombs and torpedoes from American carrier aircraft on the high seas. This and other sinking successes made the carrier the most powerful surface warship of the war. This type of ship, still relatively new at the time, thus supplanted the battleship as the dominant weapon at sea. Some of the largest engagements at sea, including the battle of Midway in 1942 and the air and sea battle in Leyte Gulf in 1944, were decided by the use of carriers and their aircraft. The long range of carrier-based reconnaissance aircraft also made it possible to observe the movements of enemy naval forces or troops on land.

Amphibious Landings

Carrier-based aircraft were also successfully used in Allied amphibious landing operations in the Pacific and in North Africa. Before troops could go ashore, massive attacks by fighters and bombers weakened enemy resistance on land. However, battleships were also successfully employed in this effort. These shelled enemy positions with their precise artillery in coordination with the attacks by aircraft. The extent of the threat posed by carrier aircraft to the enemy was confirmed by the Japanese armed forces, which deployed thousands of so-called "kamikaze" aircraft from 1944 onward to stop the advancing U.S. carrier fleets. The Japanese pilots were supposed to crash themselves on the enemy carriers in a suicide mission in order to sink them or at least prevent them from launching their own aircraft.

Testing a new Weapon

In the summer of 1921, the U.S. military used the former German battleship SMS *Ostfriesland*, which had been awarded to the United States as a war prize, as a target ship for testing aerial bombs. The defenseless ship, bobbing in the sea and marked with conspicuous markings, finally sank after several hits. During these bombardments, *Ostfriesland* was unable to defend herself, nor were any attempts made to seal the leaks caused by close hits. Nevertheless, this high-profile demonstration showed that more advanced aircraft (land and carrier-based) would become an existential threat to warships in the future.

In Profile:
Douglas TBD Devastator

Douglas TBD-1 Devastator (BuNo. 0308) from U.S. torpedo squadron VT-8, aircraft carrier U.S.S. Hornet (CV-8), circa May 1942. This aircraft was lost on June 4, 1942 during the battle of Midway with its crew LT(jg) Jeff Davis Woodson and Otway David Creasy, Jr., ARM2c.

Douglas TBD Devastator

(torpedo bomber and horizontal bomber)

When the U.S. Navy needed a new carrier-based torpedo and horizontal bomber in 1934, several American aircraft manufacturers began design work. Among these was the Douglas Aircraft Company, whose prototype XTBD-1 made its first test flight in April 1935. Other bombers developed at that time included the Northrop BT-1 (later known as the SBD Dauntless), the Brewster SBA and the Vought SB2U Vindicator. After the start of series production, the first aircraft designated "TBD" (Torpedo Bomber Douglas) were delivered to the U.S. Navy starting in the summer of 1937, some of which formed the torpedo squadron of the carrier U.S.S. *Saratoga*.

Subsequently, six more carriers were equipped with the TBD. The U.S. Navy did not give its aircraft memorable names until late 1941. Thus, the simple designation TBD became TBD Devastator.

The monoplane was innovative in many respects and was considered the world's most capable torpedo bomber when it was introduced. It was also the first all-metal naval aircraft to feature hydraulically folding wings and an enclosed "greenhouse" cockpit. The semi-folding landing gear was designed so that the low-wing aircraft could also make so-called "belly landings" in an emergency without causing too much damage to the fuselage. On-board armament consisted of a fixed, forward-firing 30 caliber (7.62 mm) machine gun (which was later replaced by a 50

A Douglas TBD-1 Devastator during a flight over land. (U.S. Navy)

View into the cockpit of a just completed TBD-1 Devastator. (U.S. Navy)

The TBD Devastator and some other aircraft types were powered by a Pratt & Whitney R-1830 radial engine. Images like this one taken at manufacturer Douglas were intended to encourage the female population of the United States to actively contribute their share to American war production. (U.S. Library of Congress)

Three Devastators in formation flight over land in 1938. When the Pacific War began in 1941, this aircraft type was obsolete. Despite successful sorties during the battle of the Coral Sea in May 1942, Devastator squadrons suffered a 90 percent loss rate in the battle of Midway a month later. As a result, the U.S. Navy decided to withdraw this type from front-line service. (U.S. Naval Aviation Museum)

A TBD Devastator dropping a torpedo. In order for the torpedo to run in the predetermined direction, the airplane had to fly straight ahead as slowly as 100 knots (180 km/h) for some time before dropping it for stabilization. In doing so, however, it was very vulnerable to fire from enemy ships or aircraft. (U.S. Navy)

A Devastator carrying two 500 lb (227 kg) bombs. (U.S. Navy)

caliber (12.7 mm version)) and a second movable one in the rear cockpit. The aircraft could carry either one torpedo under the fuselage or various types of bombs (100 lb to 1,000 lb / 45 kg to 454 kg) in a bomb bay or under the wings.

The crew consisted of the pilot in the front, the bombardier in the center, and the radio operator in the rear, who also operated the second machine gun. The Devastator was equipped with the "Norden Bombsight," a very innovative and accurate bomb sight at the time. The aircraft was powered by a radial piston engine of the type Pratt & Whitney R-1830-64 Double Wasp with 850 to 900 hp (depending on the source), enabling it to reach a speed of app. 178 knots (331 km/h) as well as a service ceiling of 19,500 feet (5,900 meters) The aircraft had a range of 716 miles (622 nm; 1,152 km) with 1,000 lb (450 kg) of bombs.

In 1940, it became clear that the once innovative aircraft was now obsolete in comparison to foreign counterparts such as the Japanese torpedo and horizontal bomber Nakajima B5N Kate. Moreover, its low speed, limited maneuverability and lack of significant armor and self-sealing fuel tanks made the aircraft a "sitting duck" for the new Japanese fighter Mitsubishi A6M Zero. Of the 130 Devastators built, about 100 were still active in 1940/41, while the rest had already been decommissioned through wear and tear. At that time, the American aircraft industry was already working on successors such as the Grumman TBF Avenger, which, however, would not become available until mid-1942. Until then, the Devastator had to serve as the standard torpedo bomber on U.S. aircraft carriers.

Battle of the Coral Sea

During the battle of the Coral Sea in May 1942, in which for the first time only aircraft carriers fought against each other through their aircraft, Devastator pilots made a major contribution to the sinking of the Japanese carrier *Shōhō*. The sinking succeeded, although some torpedoes dropped by the aircraft malfunctioned.

During battle of Midway in June 1942, 41 Devastators from the U.S. carriers *Hornet*, *Enterprise* and *Yorktown* attacked the four enemy Japanese aircraft carriers *Akagi*, *Kaga*, *Hiryū*, and *Sōryū*. Here the torpedo bombers flying without much fighter protection were all but four were shot down by Mitsubishi A6M Zeros and antiaircraft fire without causing any damage to the enemy.

A Devastator during maintenance. Note the painted remark on the fuselage. (U.S. Navy)

Devastator aircraft with wings folded aboard the carrier U.S.S. *Ranger* in 1942. (U.S. Navy)

In the end, the U.S. Navy was able to destroy all four Japanese carriers because, among others, SBD Dauntless dive bombers were able to fly very successful attacks, while the Japanese fighters were busy with the defense against the Devastators or were distracted by them. After Midway, the remaining Devastators were withdrawn from front-line service and used mainly as instructional aircraft for mechanics until their final retirement in 1944. Although no intact example exists today, the crash sites of some Devastators are known. Therefore, there are considerations to salvage one aircraft that had to ditch off Miami in 1943 due to lack of fuel and sank there.

Douglas TBD-1 Devastator General Characteristics

Length	35 ft 0 in (10.67 m)
Wingspan	50 ft 0 in (15.24 m)
Height	15 ft 1 in (4.60 m)
Powerplant	1 × Pratt & Whitney R-1830-64 Double Wasp radial piston engine (850–900 hp, varies depending on source)
Maximum speed	178 knots (206 mph; 331 km/h)
Range	716 miles (622 nm; 1,152 km)
Crew	3
Service ceiling	19,500 feet (5,900 m)
Empty weight	5,600 lb (2,540 kg)
Gross weight	9,289 lb (4,213 kg)
Armament	2 × 30 caliber (7.62 mm) MGs 1 × torpedo or 1 × 1,000 lb (454 kg) bomb or 2 × 500 lb (227 kg) bombs or 12 × 100 lb (45 kg) bombs

In Profile:
Vought SB2U Vindicator

The only known Vindicator in existence is a SB2U-2 variant (BuNo. 1383), in the National Museum of Naval Aviation at NAS Pensacola, Florida. This aircraft was ditched in Lake Michigan while conducting training operations from the training aircraft carrier U.S.S. *Wolverine* (IX-64) during World War II. After locating the aircraft at a depth of 130 feet (40 m), it was raised in the 1990s, restored and is now on display in the museum.

Vought SB2U Vindicator

(dive bomber and reconnaissance aircraft)

In the mid-1930s, the U.S. Navy required the development of a new carrier-based dive bomber that could also be used as a reconnaissance aircraft. The tender required the participating manufacturers to submit two designs each for a monoplane and a biplane. Finally, the manufacturer Vought was awarded the construction contracts for the prototypes, which were both delivered in April 1936. The comparative tests showed the clear superiority of the monoplane designated XSB2U-1, on the basis of which the first carrier-based aircraft of this type was ordered in 1936 as a dive bomber and reconnaissance aircraft. Since the U.S. Navy ordered several monoplanes at that time, such as the fighter Brewster F2A Buffalo and the torpedo bomber Douglas TBD Devastator, a change from the classic biplane to the more effective monoplane became apparent.

The Vought SB2U-1 Vindicator was a low-wing monoplane with retractable landing gear and folding wings. The aircraft was made almost entirely of metal, with only the rear fuselage section covered with fabric. The adjustable propeller could be used as a brake during dive bombing from high altitude, but in practice fell short of expectations. The armament included a fixed, forward-firing 30 caliber (7.62 mm) machine gun in the right wing and another

A Vindicator prototype during wind tunnel testing in 1937. (NACA/NASA)

A Vindicator approaching the carrier U.S.S. *Saratoga* in 1938. This type of aircraft also saw service in the navies of Great Britain and France. (U.S. Navy)

movable one in the rear of the cockpit. As a bomb load, the Vindicator could carry a 1,000 lb (454 kg) bomb in a trapezoidal rack below the fuselage, which ensured that when the bomb was released it did not accidentally fall into the propeller. Alternatively, additional small bombs could be mounted under the wings.

After delivery of the first aircraft to the Navy in 1937/38, the design was slightly modified twice. The last variant, SB2U-3, received auxiliary tanks under the wings to increase the range up to about 1,120 miles (970 nm; 1,800 km; varies depending on source). Propulsion was provided by an 825 hp Pratt & Whitney R-1535-96 radial engine, enabling the Vindicator to reach a top speed of app. 220 knots (404 km/h) and a service ceiling of 23,000 feet (7,000 m). Light armor protection was also added, but the aircraft did not receive self-sealing tanks. The previous armament was replaced by two 50 caliber (12.7 mm) machine guns.

Between 1937 and 1943, Vindicators were used on the carriers *Lexington*, *Saratoga*, *Ranger* and *Wasp*. In addition, they also served with the U.S. Marine Corps. During the battle of Midway in June 1942, Vindicator and SBD Dauntless dive bombers unsuccessfully attacked the Japanese battleship *Haruna*, but later managed to sink the cruiser *Mikuma*. During these missions, some Vindicators were shot down. After that, the aircraft type was withdrawn from front-line service and used only for training purposes.

In 1940, the French Navy ordered about 40 Vindicators for two carrier-based squadrons. However, the ship designated for this purpose, the *Bearn*, was deemed too slow. The squadrons then deployed ashore suffered heavy losses during fighting against German forces that same year. After France's surrender, the few remaining aircraft were decommissioned. The British Royal

An SB2U-2 Vindicator on an elevator aboard the carrier U.S.S. *Wasp* in 1940. (U.S. Navy)

Land-based Vindicator destroyed during the Japanese aerial attack on Pearl Harbor and U.S. military bases on Oahu on December 7, 1941. Note the construction of the fuselage. (U.S. National Park Service)

Navy now took over the 50 Vindicators, which had also been ordered by France but which could not be delivered anymore. The British gave them the designation Chesapeake MK I. As such, they were to attack German U-boats from an escort carrier during transatlantic supply convoys. In practice, however, the relatively heavy bomber proved to be underpowered for this kind of mission, so it was replaced by the Fairey Swordfish in the fall of 1941. From then on, the Chesapeake MK I served only as a training aircraft and in other support roles.

The Vindicator crew consisted of the pilot and the navigator/observer, who also operated the rear machine gun. (U.S. Navy)

Preserving a Vindicator

About 260 Vindicators were built, only one known example still survives. This one had crashed into Lake Michigan in 1943 while approaching the training carrier U.S.S. *Wolverine*. It was restored after its recovery in 1990.

The last known surviving SB2U-2 Vindicator (Bureau Number 1383), now on display at the National Museum of Naval Aviation, Florida. (U.S. National Museum of Naval Aviation)

Vought SB2U-3 Vindicator General Characteristics

Length	33 ft 11 3⁄4 in (10.36 m)
Wingspan	41 ft 10 7⁄8 in (12.80 m)
Height	14 ft 3 in (4.34 m)
Powerplant	1 × Pratt & Whitney R-1535-96 Twin Wasp Junior radial engine (825 hp)
Maximum speed	220 knots (250 mph; 404 km/h)
Range	1,120 miles (970 nm; 1,800 km; varies depending on source)
Crew	2
Service ceiling	23,000 feet (7,000 m)
Empty weight	5,634 lb (2,556 kg)
Gross weight	9,421 lb (4,273 kg)
Armament	2 × 30 caliber (7.62 mm) MGs later 2 x 50 caliber (12.7 mm MGs) 1 × 1,000 lb (454 kg) bomb or 2 × 500 lb (227 kg) bombs

In Profile:
Douglas SBD Dauntless

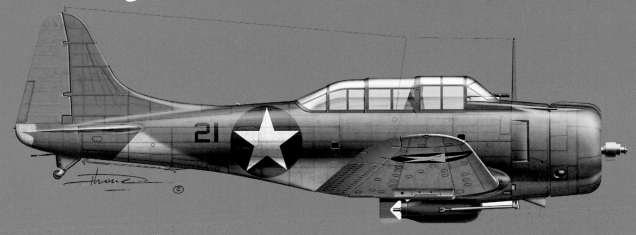

This Douglas SBD-3 Dauntless (BuNo 06583) was accepted on August 24, 1942 and served with a number of U.S. Marine Corps units, but it did not go overseas. Transferred to the navy, the aircraft was lost in Lake Michigan in the fall of 1943 in a flight accident during carrier qualifications. In 1991, the aircraft was raised by A & T Recovery at the request of the National Museum of Naval Aviation (NMNA). It is now on display at the National Museum of the U.S. Marine Corps.

Douglas SBD Dauntless

(dive bomber and reconnaissance aircraft)

The development of the Douglas SBD Dauntless goes back to a 1934 U.S. Navy tender for a new carrier-based dive bomber and reconnaissance aircraft. Initially, the manufacturer Northrop, built a prototype that made its maiden flight in 1935 as the XBT-1. After the acquisition of Northrop by the Douglas Aircraft Company (1937) and further development of the prototype, the aircraft was given the final name Douglas SBD Dauntless.

The SBD Dauntless was an all-metal, low-wing monoplane that could be used primarily as a dive bomber, but also as a reconnaissance aircraft due to its long range. The wings had perforated dive brakes on the underside for speed control during dive. Folding wings were not used for stability reasons. However, the aircraft's landing gear was retractable. After series production began in 1940, the U.S. Navy, the U.S. Marine

An SBD Dauntless over Wake Island in 1943. (U.S. Navy)

A Dauntless landing on the carrier U.S.S. *Ranger*. Clearly visible are the arresting gear's steel wire ropes laid across the aircraft landing area, designed to be caught by an aircraft's tailhook. During a normal arresting, the tailhook engaged the wire and the aircraft would be stopped. Otherwise, accidents could occur if the landing aircraft crashed into the aircraft standing on the front flight deck. The introduction of the angled flight deck eliminated most of this risk, since the landing aircraft now could now come to a stop next to the aircraft taking off. (U.S. Navy)

Battle of Midway

After its first successful deployment during the battle of the Coral Sea in May 1942, the SBD Dauntless played an outstanding role in the sinking of the four Japanese aircraft carriers *Akagi*, *Kaga*, *Hiryū*, and *Sōryū* during the battle of Midway in June. Dauntless bombers swooped down on the enemy ships and dropped their bombs just before pulling up.

Corps and the USAAF (U.S. Army Air Forces) ordered modified versions of the new dive bomber. As the war progressed, the forces of Free France also received the SBD Dauntless for use against the Axis powers. Other bombers were delivered to New Zealand and Mexico. In addition, the British Royal Navy received some aircraft for testing.

The early Dauntless variants did not yet have self-sealing fuel tanks or effective armor; these were not available until the SBD-3 version (1941). The last and most powerful type was the SBD-6 introduced in 1944 with a 1,350 hp Wright R-1820-66 Cyclone radial engine. This gave the Dauntless a top speed of 220 knots (410 km/h) as well as a service ceiling of 25,530 feet (7,780 m). The range was 1,115 miles (969 nm; 1,794 km, depending on the source even more).

The relatively powerful armament included two forward-firing fixed 50 caliber (12.7 mm) machine guns in the forward fuselage section and two movable 30 caliber (7.62 mm) machine guns in the rear cockpit. The Dauntless could carry a 1,600 lb (726 kg) bomb under its fuselage. As with the Vindicator, a special dropping device was designed to prevent the bomb from falling into the propeller during a dive attack. A 325 lb

Five SBD-5 Dauntless dive bombers and four Grumman F4F-4 Wildcat fighters (right) on the flight deck of the escort carrier U.S.S. *Santee* (CVE-29) during Operation *Torch*, the Allied invasion of French North Africa, in November 1942. (U.S. Library of Congress)

A gunner loading his weapon in the cockpit of an SBD Dauntless at Marine Corps Bombardier and Air Gunners School at Marine Corps Air Station, El Centro, California. (U.S. Navy)

Two SBD Dauntless training aircraft in California in 1943. (U.S. Navy)

A SBD-5 Dauntless of Bombing Squadron VB-16 flying an antisubmarine patrol low over the battleship U.S.S. *Washington* (BB-56) en route to the invasion of the Gilbert Islands on November 12, 1943. Visible in the background is U.S.S. *Lexington* (CV-16), the aircraft's home carrier. Note the depth charge carried by the SBD. (U.S. Navy)

Land-based SBD-5 Dauntless operating from a Pacific island. (U.S. Navy)

(147 kg) bomb could be additionally or alternatively mounted under each wing. The crew consisted of the pilot and the radio operator/gunner, who also operated the rear machine gun. By the time of the attack on Pearl Harbor in December 1941, four fleet carriers operated SBD Dauntless squadrons.

During the battles for the Solomon Islands in 1942, land- and carrier-based Dauntless pilots inflicted heavy losses on Japanese warships and their supply vessels. In addition, the bomber saw action in the Allied landings in North Africa in November 1942 and in the hunt for German naval forces in Norwegian waters. After the battle of the Philippine Sea in the Pacific in 1944, the very successful SBD Dauntless was mostly replaced by its successor, the Curtiss SB2C Helldiver. However, this new aircraft was less popular with the crews than the Dauntless, which was considered more reliable and less vulnerable to enemy fire. Until the end of the war, it was still used primarily for antisubmarine warfare, after which it was withdrawn from service.

Despite its rather low top speed of only 220 knots, the SBD Dauntless was one of the most successful aircraft of the Pacific War, sinking more enemy ships than any other Allied bomber. This included six Japanese aircraft carriers as well as numerous larger warships and freighters. For this reason, the SBD Dauntless was nicknamed "Slow But Deadly" in reference to its "SBD" designation. A total of 5,936 aircraft were built by 1944. Today, several surviving or restored examples can still be found in various museums.

Douglas SBD-6 Dauntless General Characteristics

Length	33 ft 1.25 in (10.09 m)
Wingspan	41 ft 6.375 in (12.66 m)
Height	13 ft 7 in (4.14 m)
Powerplant	1 × Wright R-1820-66 Cyclone radial piston engine (1,350 hp)
Maximum speed	220 knots (255 mph; 410 km/h)
Range	1,115 miles (969 nm; 1,794 km, depending on the source)
Crew	2
Service ceiling	25,530 feet (7,780 m)
Empty weight	6,404 lb (2,905 kg)
Gross weight	9,359 lb (4,245 kg)
Armament	2 × 50 caliber (12.7 mm) MGs 2 × 30 caliber (7.62 mm) MGs 1 × 1,600 lb (726 kg) bomb and 2 × 325 lb (147 kg) bombs Various rockets (experimental)

In Profile:
Curtiss SB2C Helldiver

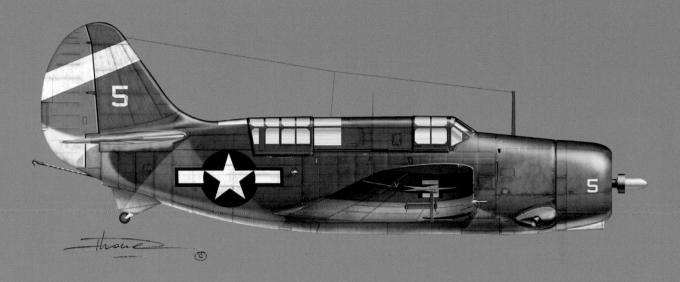

A Curtiss SB2C Helldiver in tricolor scheme and tail markings for Bombing Squadron 80 (VB-80), which operated off the aircraft carrier U.S.S. *Hancock* (CV-19), in February 1945. This aircraft is the SB2C-5, BuNo. 83589. Today, it is flying with the Commemorative Air Force, based in Graham, Texas.

Curtiss SB2C Helldiver

(dive bomber and reconnaissance aircraft)

In the late 1930s, the development of a successor for the obsolete carrier-based biplane dive bomber known as the Curtiss SBC Helldiver began. The new aircraft was also intended to replace the SBD Dauntless in the long run. After the prototype's maiden flight in 1940, series production was delayed, so that the first aircraft, designated Curtiss SB2C Helldiver, were not delivered to the armed forces until late 1942. 978 of the first variant SB2C-1 were delivered to the U.S. Navy, about 900 aircraft went to the USAAF (U.S. Army Air Forces) as A-25A Shrike. Some Helldivers were delivered to the British Royal Navy, but they never saw combat. Over the years, further deliveries were made to Australia, France, Greece, Italy, Portugal and Thailand. A total of 7,140 Helldivers were built in various versions.

Considered a competitor to the new Helldiver was the Brewster SB2A Buccaneer, which entered service shortly before. The almost all-metal Helldiver was a low-wing monoplane with retractable landing gear and folding wings. Because the early variants still had shortcomings, additional attachments and modifications were necessary. This weight increase had a negative effect on flight characteristics and maneuverability. Therefore, in 1944, starting with the SB2C-3 version, the Helldiver received a more powerful radial piston engine of the type Wright R-2600-20 Cyclone with 1,900 hp instead of the previous 1,700 hp. With this, the aircraft reached a top speed of 256 knots (475 km/h) as well as a service ceiling of 29,100 feet (8,900 m). The range was about

A Curtiss SB2C-3 Helldiver in 1945. For protection against enemy fire, the aircraft had self-sealing fuel tanks and light armor. (U.S. Navy)

1,165 miles (1,012 nm; 1,875 km) with a 1,000 lb (450 kg) bomb-load, but could be increased by additional tanks. The armament included two fixed, forward-firing 20 mm guns in the wings and two movable 30 caliber (7.62 mm) machine guns in the rear cockpit. The Helldiver could carry either one aerial torpedo or up to two 900 lb (454 kg) bombs in its bomb bay. A 500 lb (227 kg) bomb could be mounted under each wing and, on the later SB2C-4 variant, unguided rockets against land and sea targets. The crew consisted of the pilot and the radio operator/gunner, who also operated the rear machine gun.

"Son of a Bitch, 2nd Class"

Many Helldiver pilots rated the Douglas SBD Dauntless, considered a predecessor, as a more capable aircraft type because, among other things, it was considered more durable. In addition, the Helldiver was not very popular with its crews because of its clumsiness and limited flight characteristics during takeoff and landing. Thus, it was also called "Son of a Bitch, 2nd Class" in reference to its official designation "SB2C."

When Helldivers from the carrier U.S.S. *Bunker Hill* flew their first combat missions in November 1943 near Papua New Guinea in the Pacific, it became apparent that the aircraft was underpowered, along with various other weaknesses. After increasing the engine's power and further improvements, Helldivers saw successful service in the battles for the Marianas, the Philippines, Iwo Jima, Okinawa, as well as in the attacks on the Japanese islands until the end of the war. Helldiver pilots also helped sink the Japanese battleships *Yamato* and *Musashi*—the largest ships of their kind. Today, several Helldiver SB2C bombers still exist in various museums.

A Helldiver taking off from U.S.S. *Lexington*'s (CV-16) deck, while other aircraft are getting ready for takeoff. (U.S. Navy)

Crewmen aboard U.S.S. *Bennington* (CV-20) maneuvering a SB2C-4 Helldiver of Bombing Squadron VB-82 into position on the flight deck. Note *Bennington*'s geometric air group identification symbol on the Helldiver. (U.S. Navy)

Aircraft handlers maneuver a SB2C-5 Helldiver of Bombing Squadron 95 (VB-95) into the hangar deck of U.S.S. *Bunker Hill* (CV-17) in the Pacific. Note the wing folding mechanism. (U.S. Navy)

A Helldiver smashed to pieces while landing on the U.S.S. *Shangri La* (CV-38). (U.S. Navy)

A SB2C-1 Helldiver banking before overflying the carrier U.S.S. *Yorktown* (CV-10). (U.S. Navy)

The Japanese battleship *Musashi* (foreground) and a destroyer under attack by carrier-based Helldivers and other U.S. aircraft in the Sibuyan Sea (battle of Leyte Gulf) on October 24, 1944. After being struck by an estimated total of 19 torpedoes and 17 bombs, *Musashi* went down. (U.S. Navy)

Curtiss SB2C-3 Helldiver General Characteristics

Length	36 ft 8 in (11.18 m)
Wingspan	49 ft 9 in (15.16 m)
Height	13 ft 2 in (4.01 m)
Powerplant	1× Wright R-2600-20 Cyclone radial piston engine (1,900 hp)
Maximum speed	256 knots (295 mph; 475 km/h)
Range	1,165 miles (1,012 nm; 1,875 km) with a 1,000 lb bomb
Crew	2
Service ceiling	29,100 feet (8,900 m)
Empty weight	10,547 lb (4,784 kg)
Gross weight	16,616 lb (7,537 kg)
Armament	2 × 20 mm cannons 2 × 30 caliber (7.62 mm) MGs 1 × torpedo 2 × 900 lb (454 kg) bombs or 2 × 450 lb (227 kg) bombs

In Profile:
Grumman TBF/TBM Avenger

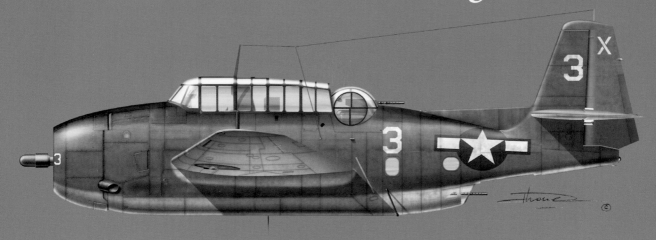

The TBM-1C (built by General Motors, BuNo. 46214) flown by future U.S. President George H. W. Bush. Assigned to VT-51 aboard the light carrier U.S.S. *San Jacinto* (CVL-30) as part of Task Force 58 in 1944.

Grumman TBF/TBM Avenger

(torpedo bomber and horizontal bomber)

In 1939 the development of the later Grumman TBF/TBM Avenger started because the U.S. Navy needed a new torpedo bomber to replace the obsolete Douglas TBD Devastator. After several manufacturers participated in the tender, Grumman was awarded the contract. The first flight of the prototype XBTF-1 took place in August 1941. After the attack on Pearl Harbor on December 7, 1941, the new aircraft was given the descriptive name "Avenger."

The three-seat torpedo bomber was an all-metal mid-wing monoplane with retractable landing gear and folding wings. Initially, the first TBF-1 version was powered by a Wright R-2600-8 Cyclone radial piston engine. Its power of 1,700 hp enabled the Avenger to reach a top speed of 242 knots (447 km/h) and a service ceiling of 22,600 feet (6,900 m). Its range was up to about 905 miles (786 nm; 1,456 km). Subsequent variants received more powerful engines. The most powerful was the TBF-3 with an output of 1,900 hp. The crew consisted of up to three men: the pilot, the bombardier, and the radio operator. The original armament included one forward-firing 30 caliber (7.62 mm) machine gun rigidly integrated into the fuselage and a dorsal turret mounting a 50 caliber (12.7 mm) machine gun in the rear of the cockpit. Later versions received two 50 caliber (12.7 mm) guns in the wings. In its bomb bay, the Avenger could carry either a 2,000 lb 53.3 cm torpedo or a total bomb load of 2,000 lb (907 kg). Unguided rockets could be mounted under the wings to engage ground or sea targets. Alternatively, it was possible to install an auxiliary fuel tank in the bomb bay and under each wing to increase range. The fuel tanks were self-sealing and the interior was lightly armored in places.

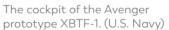
The cockpit of the Avenger prototype XBTF-1. (U.S. Navy)

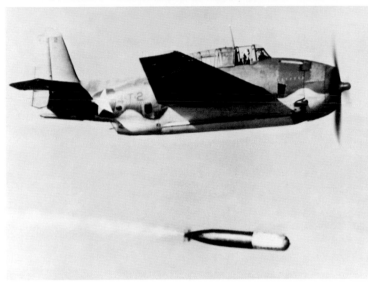

An Avenger after dropping his aerial torpedo. Alternatively, the aircraft could carry a total bomb load of 2,000 lb (907 kg). (U.S. Navy)

The first production aircraft did not arrive at Pearl Harbor until shortly before the battle of Midway (June 1942). However, this was too late to use them aboard the carriers. Thus, only six Avengers were able to participate in the battle without fighter protection. However, all but one of the aircraft were shot down. After Midway, the Avenger replaced the Devastator in all U.S. Navy torpedo squadrons. Shortly thereafter, the U.S. Marine Corps also converted its squadrons to the new Avenger. As more and more aircraft were needed during the war, additional Avengers were produced by General Motors starting in late 1942. These were given the designation "TBM," while the aircraft built by Grumman were named "TBF." Together, the two manufacturers built a total of about 9,836 Avengers. Until 1945, the successful design was only

slightly modified. Starting in 1943, a large number of these aircraft received radar equipment to detect enemy aircraft, surface ships and submarines. Some were equipped with cameras and searchlights for their use as reconnaissance planes.

During the war, the Avenger proved to be one of the most successful torpedo bombers ever built and made its contribution to Allied sinking successes in the Pacific and Atlantic. During the battles for Guadalcanal in 1943, Avengers were able to damage the Japanese battleship *Hiei* and sank the carrier *Hiyō* during the battle in the Philippine Sea the following year. Thanks to their

The Avenger: A durable design

After the war, Avengers continued to serve in numerous roles (e.g., as a reconnaissance, rescue and supply aircraft) in the United States and abroad. The U.S. armed forces retired the last Avengers by 1956. A variant used specifically for antisubmarine warfare was delivered to Great Britain, France, Japan, the Netherlands and Canada in the 1950s. Some Avengers are still in service, for example in Canada as observation and firefighting aircraft over the Canadian forests. In addition, numerous examples are still preserved in museums and collections today.

large payload capability, they were also able to provide airborne supplies to U.S. forces fighting in the Pacific Islands. Avenger pilots also played a major role in the sinking of the battleships *Yamato* and *Musashi*. In the Atlantic, Avengers operating from escort carriers helped protect vital supply convoys. In this role, they damaged or sank numerous German U-boats.

Some 1,000 aircraft were delivered to the Fleet Air Arm of the British Royal Navy under the designations Tarpon MK I and later Avenger MK I. The latter successfully operated the aircraft on its aircraft carriers in the Atlantic and Pacific. Some Avengers also served in the Royal New Zealand Air Force. The future American President George H. W. Bush was the youngest pilots in the U.S. Navy to fly an Avenger named "White 2" while stationed on the light carrier U.S.S. *San Jacinto* (CVL-30).

TBM-3E Avengers from the escort carrier U.S.S. *Vella Gulf* in formation flight. The service ceiling was about 22,600 feet (6,900 m). (U.S. Navy)

Grumman TBF-1 Avenger General Characteristics

Length	40 ft 1⁄8 in (12.195 m)
Wingspan	54 ft 2 in (16.51 m)
Height	16 ft 5 in (5.00 m)
Powerplant	1 × Wright R-2600-8 Cyclone radial piston engine (1,700 hp)
Maximum speed	242 knots (278 mph; 447 km/h)
Range	905 miles (786 nm; 1,456 km, depending on the source more)
Crew	3
Service ceiling	22,600 feet (6,900 m)
Empty weight	10,556 lb (4.788 kg)
Gross weight	15,536 lb (7,047 kg)
Armament	3 × 50 caliber (12.7 mm) MGs 1 × 30 caliber (7.62 mm) MG 1 × torpedo or 1 × 2,000 lb (907 kg) bomb or various smaller bombs or mines or 8 × rockets

An Avenger in Royal Navy service. It proved to be a successful submarine hunter on American and British escort carriers. (U.S. Navy)

Brewster F2A Buffalo

(fighter aircraft)

The Brewster F2A Buffalo was the result of a U.S. Navy request for proposals for a new carrier-based fighter. At that time, the aircraft manufacturer Grumman also submitted a design, which would later become the F4F Wildcat. After the maiden flight of the Brewster prototype XF2A-1 in 1937 and further comparative tests with the Grumman design, the U.S. Navy decided to order 54 Brewster F2A-1 aircraft.

The first Monoplane

The Brewster F2A-1, later designated the Buffalo, became the U.S. Navy's first monoplane fighter in 1939, replacing the aging Grumman F3F biplane. The single-seat, all-metal, mid-wing monoplane was equipped with folding wings and retractable landing gear. The first variant F2A-1 was not equipped with self-sealing tanks or any armor; these safety features were installed in later versions.

In Profile:
Brewster F2A Buffalo

Brewster Buffalo F2A-3 (BuNo. 01562), accepted into the U.S. Navy in September 1941. It first served with VF-2 aboard U.S.S. *Lexington* (CV-2), then with VF-6 aboard U.S.S. *Enterprise* (CV-6). After its deployment to Midway it was flown by USMC pilot Captain Kirk Armistead and badly damaged during the battle of Midway in early June of 1942. After being repaired, it was stationed in Pearl Harbor and then in San Diego before being scrapped in 1943.

Wind tunnel testing of the F2A Buffalo in 1938. (NACA/NASA)

Compared to other fighters of that era, the F2A Buffalo's design had a visually compact appearance. (U.S. Navy)

However, the associated increase in weight affected the flight performance. The power plant initially consisted of a Wright R-1820-34 Cyclone radial engine with about 950 hp, but was replaced by the more powerful R-1820-40 in 1941. With its approximately 1,200 hp, the agile Buffalo was capable of reaching a top speed of 279 knots (517 km/h) and a service ceiling of 33,200 feet (10,100 m). The maximum range was 965 miles (839 nm; 1,553 km). The armament consisted of two 50 caliber (12.7 mm) machine guns in the forward fuselage section and two more in the wings. Depending on the source, two 100 lb (45 kg) bombs could be carried under the wings. In 1939, Belgium ordered 40 Buffalos. However, only one aircraft could be delivered before Belgium was occupied by German troops in 1940. Another 44 aircraft were acquired by Finland. The British Royal Air Force did not want to use the Buffalo in Europe because of its inferiority to German fighters. However, Great Britain ordered about 170 aircraft, which served with mixed success in Asia as well as in the Pacific. The Buffalos acquired by the Dutch Air Force also scored some kills in the Dutch East Indies. The aircraft performed relatively well in air combat despite its design weaknesses.

In addition to the U.S. Navy, the U.S. Marine Corps also used the Buffalo. Stationed on Midway, the aircraft attempted to repel Japanese attacks on the archipelago in June 1942. However, the Buffalos were clearly outgunned by the Japanese Mitsubishi A6M Zero fighters, so that 13 of the 20 aircraft deployed were shot down.

An F2A Buffalo after crash landing on the escort carrier U.S.S. *Long Island* (CVE-1) in July 1942. (U.S. Navy)

Brewster F2A-3 Buffalos in service as training aircraft. (U.S. Navy)

Other factors in the high loss rate were the inexperience of the Buffalo pilots and flawed air combat tactics. By this time, it was also becoming apparent that this aircraft type had reached the end of its development capability. In addition, there had been repeated delays and problems in production. Therefore, from early 1942, the Buffalos stationed on U.S. aircraft carriers were replaced by proven and trusted Grumman F4F Wildcat fighters. Until the end of the war, the remaining aircraft were used to train new pilots. Of the total of approximately 509 Buffalos built, only one known example survives in the Aviation Museum of Central Finland in Tikkakoski. However, there are plans to recover the wreck of a Buffalo, which ditched off Midway in 1942 and sank there.

Brewster F2A-3 Buffalo General Characteristics

Length	26 ft 4 in (8.03 m)
Wingspan	35 ft 0 in (10.67 m)
Height	12 ft 0 in (3.66 m)
Powerplant	1 × Wright R-1820-40 Cyclone radial piston engine (1,200 PS)
Maximum speed	279 knots (321 mph; 517 km/h)
Range	965 miles (839 nm; 1,553 km)
Crew	1
Service ceiling	33,200 feet (10,100 m)
Empty weight	4,732 lb (2,146 kg)
Gross weight	7,159 lb (3,247 kg)
Armament	4 × 50 caliber (12.7 mm) MGs 2 × 100 lb (45 kg) bombs

Grumman F4F Wildcat

(fighter aircraft)

The Grumman F4F Wildcat was originally intended as a biplane to follow the successful F3F series. However, when the U.S. Navy needed a modern fighter and the competitor Brewster developed the later F2A Buffalo as a monoplane, Grumman decided in 1936 to redesign its XF4F-F1 into one as well. Although the prototype of the F2A Buffalo proved superior in comparative tests, Grumman improved its design several times until the XF4F-3 version. After overcoming the initial weaknesses, the XF4F-3 proved to be at least equal to the competing Brewster model. In 1938, the U.S. Navy decided to order 54 of each of the two competing aircraft types also as backup aircraft in case of possible problems with the Brewster.

The first series of the Grumman fighter, later known as the Wildcat, was designated the Grumman F4F-3. In 1940, France and Belgium also ordered the Grumman F4F. Due to the military defeat of both countries against Germany a few months later, however, these aircraft could no longer be delivered, so Great Britain took them over and commissioned them into the Royal Navy under the designation Martlet MK I.

The single-seat Wildcat was an all-metal, retractable-gear, mid-wing monoplane with a fuselage shape still reminiscent of a biplane. The second production model, designated F4F-4, went into production in November 1941. The Wildcat received folding wings, self-sealing fuel tanks, light armor and an initial armament of four 50 caliber (12.7 mm) machine guns. The Wildcat could either carry two 250 lb (113 kg) bombs, two 100 lb (45 kg)

In Profile:
Grumman F4F Wildcat

The F4F-4 Wildcat "White 23" (BuNo. 5093) flown by Lt. Cdr. John S. Thach, VF-3, U.S.S. *Yorktown* (CV-5) during the battle of Midway, in which he shot down at least three Japanese Mitsubishi A6M fighters.

The F4F Wildcat's appearance is similarly compact to that of the Brewster F2A Buffalo. (U.S. Navy)

Comparison of parking space needed for Wildcats with and without folded wings. (U.S. Navy)

The completed Wildcat fuselages before the wings were added. (U.S. Navy)

bombs or six unguided rockets for engagements against land or sea targets, depending on the version or mission profile.

The power plant consisted of one Pratt & Whitney R-1830-86 Twin Wasp radial piston engine. Its power of 1,200 hp enabled the Wildcat to reach a top speed of 288 knots (533 km/h) and a service ceiling of up to 39,500 ft (12,000 m, depending on the version and source). The maximum range of approximately 845 miles (734 nm; 1,360 km) could be increased using auxiliary drop tanks. In addition to the fighter variant, the Wildcat was also used as a seaplane and reconnaissance aircraft. The F4F-7 version, for example, was a long-range reconnaissance aircraft with a range of up to 3,100 nautical miles or 5,800 kilometers (or less, depending on the version and source). At the start of World War II, the maneuverable, rugged and powerful Wildcat was the U.S. Navy's standard fighter and bore the brunt of combat in the Pacific until 1943.

In the ultimately failed defense of Wake Island in December 1941, U.S. Marine Corps Wildcat pilots at least succeeded in sinking the Japanese destroyer *Kisaragi*. Land and carrier-based Wildcats were successfully deployed during the battle of Midway as well as in the battles for Guadalcanal and the Solomon Islands. Here, the technically inferior Wildcats were able to hold their own against the more maneuverable Mitsubishi A6M Zero fighters thanks to their skilled pilots and clever tactics. In addition to their role as fighters, Wildcats protected

Inspecting a Grumman Wildcat's Pratt & Whitney R-1830-86 engine on display at the U.S. Naval Training School, New York in 1945. (U.S. National Archives)

A Wildcat with its associated life raft. This became a lifesaver when the pilot had to ditch. (U.S. Navy)

Two Wildcats on a deck elevator aboard U.S.S. *Enterprise*. This photograph illustrates the practical value of folding wings. (U.S. Navy)

A Landing Signal Officer (LSO) on board the escort carrier *Marcus Island* (CVE-7) waves an FM-2 Wildcat aboard. (U.S. Navy)

convoys, attacked submarines and supported amphibious landing operations. When Grumman switched production to the new F6F Hellcat, the Wildcat was subsequently continued by General Motors (Eastern Aircraft Division). Unlike most carrier aircraft, it could take off from and land again on the short flight decks of escort carriers. This feature made the Wildcat so valuable, especially as a carrier-based fighter-bomber and submarine hunter, that Eastern Aircraft continued to produce this aircraft model until the end of the war. From 1943 on, however, its role on large fleet carriers was taken over by the F6F Hellcat.

The Royal Navy received more than 1,100 Wildcats under the Lend-Lease Act and gave them the designations Martlet (MK I–V) and later Wildcat MK VI. In Royal Navy service, they were successfully deployed in the Atlantic, Mediterranean, Pacific and Indian Oceans. The "Martlet/Wildcat" also proved itself on British escort carriers protecting supply convoys and as submarine hunters.

The First Cat

The Wildcat is considered to be the origin of the famous "cat family" of the Grumman Aerospace Corporation. Their tradition of naming aircraft after cat species continued until the F-14 Tomcat. Of the approximately 7,722 Wildcats built, a number of airworthy examples still exist today, plus others in various museums and collections around the world.

A Wildcat making an unsuccessful landing on an escort carrier. The propeller slices the wooden flight deck covering. The resulting wood splinters are whirled through the air. (U.S. Navy)

Pilots posing in front of F4F Wildcat for a photo aboard the escort carrier U.S.S. *Nassau* (CVE-16). (U.S. Navy)

Grumman F4F-4 Wildcat General Characteristics

Length	28 ft 9 in (8.76 m)
Wingspan	38 ft 0 in (11.58 m)
Height	11 ft 10 in (3.61 m)
Powerplant	1 × Pratt & Whitney R-1830-86 Twin Wasp radial piston engine (1,200 hp)
Maximum speed	288 knots (331 mph; 533 km/h)
Range	845 miles (734 nm; 1,360 km)
Crew	1
Service ceiling	39,500 ft (12,000 m)
Empty weight	4,907 lb (2,226 kg)
Gross weight	7,423 lb (3,367 kg)
Armament	6 × 50 caliber (12.7 mm) MGs 2 × 250 lb (113 kg) bombs or 2 × 100 lb (45 kg) bombs 6 × rockets

Vought F4U Corsair

(fighter aircraft)

In the late 1930s, the U.S. Navy required the development of a high-performance, high-speed fighter aircraft. The manufacturer Vought (United Aircraft Corporation) participated in the tender and built a prototype designated XF4U-1. The goal was to achieve the highest possible speed with minimal air resistance. To this end, the most powerful engine available was to be installed in the smallest possible fuselage. To be able to convert the power of the 1,800 hp Pratt & Whitney R-2800 radial engine into speed, a propeller with a diameter of 13 feet (four meters) was required. However, this made it difficult to use a conventional landing gear as the necessary safety distance between the propeller tips and the ground could not be achieved with such gear. The low-wing aircraft therefore received the famous "gull wing" giving the later Corsair its characteristic appearance. The downward bend increased the distance of the aircraft fuselage and thus of the propeller tips to the ground sufficiently.

In 1940, the prototype reached an impressive top speed of more than 380 knots (700 km/h) during a test flight. After some modifications and the installation of a more powerful engine, the first production aircraft, designated Vought F4U-1 Corsair, were delivered to the U.S. Navy starting in the summer of 1942. Compared to the prototype, these had a cockpit that was moved further to the rear. This made forward visibility more difficult, especially when landing on aircraft carriers. The first production model of the all-metal fighter was powered by a 2,000-hp Pratt & Whitney R-2800-8 radial engine. This gave the F4U-1 a top speed of app. 362 knots (671

In Profile:
Chance Vought F4U Corsair

Vought F4U-4 Corsair (BuNo. 96871) of Fighter Squadron 24 (VF-24), assigned to CVG-2 aboard the carrier U.S.S. *Philippine Sea* (CV-47) for a deployment to the Western Pacific and Korea from April 1 to June 9, 1951.

The successful Vought F4U Corsair, here pictured aboard the fleet carrier U.S.S. *Philippine Sea* (CV-47) in 1951, even saw action during the Korean War. (U.S. Navy)

km/h) and a service ceiling of 41,500 feet (12,600 m). The range was about 1,005 miles (873 nm; 1,617 km). By installing additional tanks under the fuselage and wings, the range of the F4U-1A variant could be increased to 1,506 miles (1,310 nm; 2,425 km). From 1944, the F4U-4 variant received, among other innovations, a more powerful engine in the form of a Pratt & Whitney R-2800-18W with 2,130 hp. This increased the maximum speed from 362 knots to 385 knots (671 to 714 km/h). The last series produced after the war, the F4U-7, received the most powerful engine with 2,350 hp, but this did not increase the speed significantly. The armament initially consisted of six fixed, forward-firing 50 caliber (12.7 mm) machine guns in the wings. Later models received increased armament as well as unguided rockets against sea and ground targets. The aircraft had self-sealing tanks as well as light armor protection for the pilot. Other Corsair variants were used as reconnaissance aircraft and night fighters.

A Corsair firing its unguided rockets at Japanese positions on Okinawa in 1945. (U.S. National Archives)

The F4U-4 Corsair's Pratt & Whitney R-2800-18W radial engine with 2,380 hp. (U.S. Air Force)

Pilots enjoy the image of a nude woman painted on a Corsair named "Skipper's Orchid." (U.S. Navy)

A Corsair XF4U-3 variant as a test aircraft for testing a new engine with a high-altitude turbo-supercharger. The objective of the proposed change to the turbo-supercharger system was to obtain greater speeds for the Corsair at higher altitudes. During evaluation tests in 1944, the supercharger system proved to be faulty and cumbersome and though there was a measurable increase in speed in the 30,000 feet region the project was cancelled. (U.S. Navy)

The deck of the escort carrier U.S.S. *Attu* (CVE-102) filled with Corsairs. The ship could carry 27 aircraft. (U.S. Navy)

A Corsair landing on the training carrier U.S.S. *Wolverine* on Lake Michigan. The "gull wings" are clearly visible. (U.S. Naval Aviation Museum)

A Corsair crash landing on the escort carrier U.S.S. *Charger* (CVE-30). (U.S. Navy)

A F4U-4-1A Corsair that had emergency-landed on Green Island (now Nissan Island, Papua New Guinea) during its repair in March 1944. (U.S. Naval Aviation Museum)

The new Corsair's first combat missions were flown in early 1943 by pilots of the U.S. Marine Corps during the battles for Guadalcanal in the Pacific. Here, the fighter's tremendous acceleration and high speed proved to be a great advantage. Because the relatively far aft cockpit limited forward visibility, the U.S. Navy was initially reluctant to use the Corsair on its carriers. However, the problem was largely solved by raising the pilot's seat and cockpit canopy. Nevertheless, the aircraft was difficult to control during takeoff and landing, especially for inexperienced pilots. For this reason, it was nicknamed the "Ensign-Killer."

The carrier-based Corsair was introduced to the U.S. Navy in the summer of 1944. By the end of the war, the Corsair had been successfully deployed in almost all major Pacific theaters, including Iwo Jima and Okinawa. Their mission profiles also included supporting amphibious landings and fending off Japanese kamikaze aircraft.

Starting in 1942/43, the Royal Navy urgently needed an agile long-range fighter. The British Skua and Roc models made by Blackburn had sufficient range, but were too cumbersome for direct air combat. The more maneuverable Hawker Sea Hurricane and Supermarine Seafire models, in turn, had too short a range for use over the open ocean. The Corsair, however, combined maneuverability with long range and was thus the first choice for the Royal Navy. For this reason, Great Britain received a total of 2,012 Corsairs under the Lend-Lease Act. Carrier-based British Corsairs were deployed in European and Pacific waters. These included attacks on the German battleship *Tirpitz* in Norway and participation in large-scale offensives against Japanese positions in the Pacific.

The New Zealand Air Force received 370 Corsairs. Produced until the early 1950s, the Corsair also saw service in various roles (fighter-bomber, reconnaissance, and "limited" fighter) during the Korean War. During that period, it also served in Argentina, France, El Salvador and Honduras. By 1970/71, the last aircraft had been decommissioned. A total of 12,571 Corsairs were produced by Vought and other manufacturers.

The Corsair proved itself in air combat against Japanese fighters such as the Mitsubishi A6M, Mitsubishi J2M, Kawanishi N1K-J and Nakajima Ki-84. (U.S. Navy)

Corsairs in service with the Royal Navy. (U.S. Navy)

A F4U-4 Corsair in 1950. Even today, a large number of these fighters still exist in airworthy condition. In addition, various examples can be found in museums around the world. (U.S. Navy)

Vought F4U-4 Corsair General Characteristics

Length	33 ft 8 in (10.26 m)
Wingspan	41 ft 0 in (12.50 m)
Height	14 ft 9 in (4.50 m)
Powerplant	1 × Pratt & Whitney R-2800-18W radial engine (2,380 hp)
Maximum speed	385 knots (445 mph; 717 km/h)
Range	1,005 miles (873 nm; 1,617 km)
Crew	1
Service ceiling	41,500 feet (12,600 m)
Empty weight	9,205 lb (4,238 kg)
Gross weight	14,670 lb (6,654 kg)
Armament	6 × 50 caliber (12.7 mm) MGs (later 4 × 20 mm cannons) 2 × 100 lb (45 kg) bombs 4 × rockets

In Profile:
Grumman F6F Hellcat

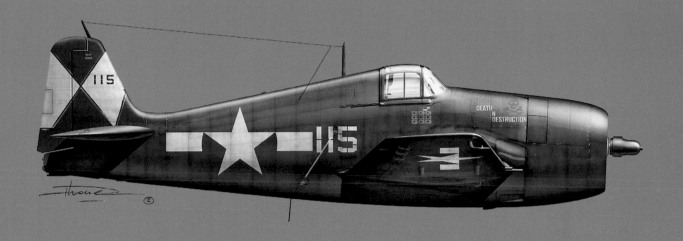

Grumman F6F-5 Hellcat "White 115" (BuNo. 72534) from VF-83, U.S.S. *Essex* (CV-9), May 1945.

Grumman F6F Hellcat

(fighter)

When the Grumman F4F Wildcat formed the backbone of the carrier-based fighter aircraft force in 1941, the U.S. Navy had already ordered a potential successor in the form of the prototype XF6F-1. Its development was to benefit from the experience gained in air combat with the Japanese Mitsubishi A6M Zero in order to have an equal or even superior fighter aircraft available in the near future. During the testing of the XF6F-1 it turned out that extensive modifications were still necessary. After successful testing of another improved prototype in the summer of 1942, series production soon began. The first aircraft, designated Grumman F6F-3 Hellcat, were delivered to the U.S. Navy that same year.

The single-seat Hellcat was an all-metal low-wing monoplane with folding wings. Unlike the mid-wing Wildcat, the landing gear was relocated from the fuselage to the wings. This increased directional stability during takeoff and landing. The F6F-3 was powered by a Pratt & Whitney R-2800-10 radial engine with about 2,000 hp. With this, the aircraft reached a top speed of 330 knots (612 km/h) and a service ceiling of 38,500 feet (11,745 m). The range was about 1,085 miles (942 nm; 1,745 km). The armament initially consisted of six 50 caliber (12.7 mm) machine guns in the wings but was slightly modified in later versions. The Hellcat could carry a bomb load of about 2,000 lb or 900 kilograms (depending on the version). Designed to be very robust, the aircraft was fitted with self-sealing tanks and extensive armor protection. The Hellcat could carry up to six unguided rockets to engage ground and sea targets and was also used for reconnaissance and as a night fighter. The range could be extended by additional drop tanks. Engine power was increased by about 200 hp in the F6F-5 variant. This led to a slight improvement in flight performance.

A Hellcat F6F-5 with streamlined cowl and canopy in 1945. (U.S. Navy)

Although they participated in numerous operations, Hellcat pilots achieved their greatest success during the 1944 air and naval battle in the Philippine Sea. During the fighting, some 480 Hellcats and 420 bombers from 15 U.S. carriers succeeded in destroying more than 400 Japanese aircraft as well as three carriers. The Japanese Navy was not able to recover from this defeat. Even in direct air combat against the famous (but by then obsolete) Mitsubishi A6M Zero, the Nakajima Ki-84 and the Mitsubishi J2M, the kill figures were clearly in favor of the Hellcat. In addition to the material and numerical superiority of the Hellcat, the success was also due to the increasingly poor level of training of Japanese pilots from 1944 onward. Alongside the Vought F4U Corsair, the Hellcat became the best and most successful Allied carrier-based fighter in the Pacific War.

A Hellcat caught fire after crash landing on the carrier U.S.S. *Enterprise* (CV-6) on November 1, 1943. However, pilot Byron M. Johnson was rescued from the burning aircraft without major injury. (U.S. Navy)

A Hellcat F6F-5 with wings folded aboard U.S.S. *Lexington* (CV-16). (U.S. Navy)

View through U.S.S. *Yorktown*'s (CV-10) hangar deck. A Hellcat on the flight deck is about to take off. (U.S. Navy)

A successful Successor

Although larger and significantly heavier than the previous Wildcat, the Hellcat performed substantially better in U.S. Navy and Marine Corps service. This new fighter made an enormous contribution in achieving American air supremacy in the Pacific by the end of the war. Of the approximately 6,477 confirmed U.S. Navy aerial victories, the Hellcat accounted for a total of 4,947, or 75 percent of all aerial victories.

The British Royal Navy received some 1,200 Hellcats under the "Lend-Lease Act." Under the designation Gannet the aircraft served successfully in antisubmarine warfare in the transatlantic convoy service. Further missions followed in the Mediterranean, the Pacific and the Indian Ocean. British Hellcat pilots were able to achieve 52 aerial victories.

Hellcat production at Grumman ended after 12,272 aircraft were built in November 1945. The following year, the Hellcat served for a few weeks as the first aircraft of the Navy's "Blue Angels" aerobatic squadron. Beginning in the late 1940s, Hellcats were delivered to Argentina, Paraguay and France. During the Korean War, the United States used converted Hellcats as guided missiles (drones) against targets in North Korea. French aircraft were used in the Indochina War. By the early 1960s, the last Hellcats had finally been decommissioned. Today, numerous examples of this type still exist in museums and collections, with some of them in airworthy condition.

A Hellcat pilot on his aircraft's wing posing for the camera. Note the wing's folding mechanism. (U.S. Navy)

An F6F Hellcat overflying an island in the Pacific. Its appearance shows similarities to its predecessor the F4F Wildcat. (U.S. Navy)

A F6F-3 Hellcat aircraft being raised from the ocean floor southwest of San Diego, California, by the salvage team of the U.S.S. *White Sands* in October of 1970. (U.S. Navy)

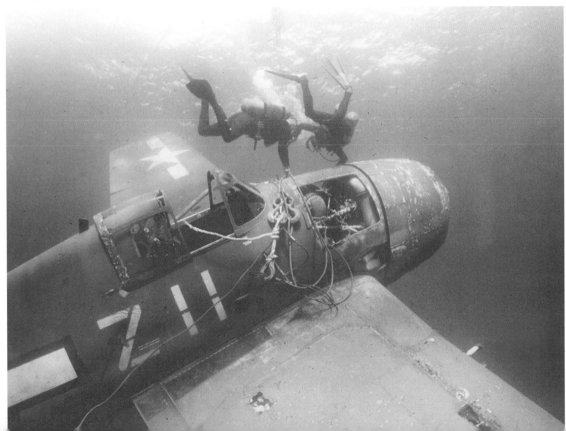

In 1952, Guided Missile Unit 90 used F6F-5K Hellcat drones, each armed with a 2,000 lb (900 kg) bomb, to attack bridges in Korea; flying from U.S.S. *Boxer* (CV-21), radio controlled from an escorting AD Skyraider. (U.S. Navy)

A Sidewinder 1-A missile fired from an F9F Cougar strikes an F6F-5K Hellcat target drone over Naval Ordnance Test Station (NOTS) China Lake, California on May 2, 1958. (U.S. Navy)

Grumman F6F-5 Hellcat General Characteristics

Length	33 ft 7 in (10.24 m)
Wingspan	42 ft 10 in (13.06 m)
Height	13 ft 1 in (3.99 m)
Powerplant	1 × Pratt & Whitney R-2800-10W Double Wasp radial piston engine (2,200 hp)
Maximum speed	340 knots (391 mph; 629 km/h)
Range	945 miles (821 nm; 1,521 km)
Crew	1
Service ceiling	37,300 feet (11,400 m)
Empty weight	9,238 lb (4,190 kg)
Gross weight	12,598 lb (5,714 kg)
Armament	6 × 50 caliber (12.7 mm) MGs Bombload: 2,000 lb (900 kg) 6 × rockets

Glossary

Carrier-based Aircraft

Carrier-based aircraft had special features. They had reinforced landing gear to absorb the hard impacts of landing, and a tailhook that hooked into the landing cable, which was stretched across the deck. In addition, there was a structurally reinforced fuselage and folding wings to save space. Enlarged fuel tanks and additional drop tanks provided sufficient reserves for the return flight to the carrier during long missions over the sea. Before the introduction of radio and direction-finding equipment, some carrier aircraft also had a navigator as a second crew member.

Fighters

Their mission was essentially directed against enemy fighter aircraft. As fast, maneuverable, and powerful fighters, they were intended to achieve air superiority in friendly or enemy territory. In this role, they were also used as interceptors against bombers or to protect their own bombers. Examples of this type were the Grumman F6F Hellcat (U.S.) Supermarine Seafire (Great Britain), and the Mitsubishi A6M Zero (Japan).

Escort Fighters

Escort fighters protect bombers during their missions from attacks by enemy fighters. The escort fighter had to have the same range to protect the vulnerable bombers during the entire mission, including the return flight to the carrier. Examples of this type were the Grumman F6F Hellcat (U.S.), Supermarine Seafire (Great Britain) and the Mitsubishi A6M Zero (Japan).

Interceptors

Fast fighters with a high rate of climb were suitable as interceptors. Their task was to intercept approaching enemy bombers with their escort fighters as well as reconnaissance aircraft. Examples of this type were the Grumman F6F Hellcat (U.S.), Supermarine Seafire (Great Britain) and the Mitsubishi A6M Zero (Japan).

Fighter-bombers

Most fighters could be converted to fighter-bombers by attaching bomb racks. Aircraft that were no longer capable of the required performance as fighters were often used in this role. Many fighters were also designed as fighter-bombers so that carriers, with their limited space, could carry as few different types of aircraft as possible. Fighter-bombers could attack sea and land targets by bombs or (unguided) rockets. Examples of this type included the Grumman F4F Wildcat and the Vought F4U Corsair (both U.S.).

Night Fighters

Since darkness and the resulting lack of visibility made night operations of carrier aircraft ineffective and even dangerous, they were given radar. However, the size of the first units meant that an additional crew member was needed to operate them, so two-seat aircraft in particular were used as night fighters. Further development of radar after 1945 blurred the line between "conventional" fighters and night fighters, as soon many fighters were capable of operating at night or in bad weather. Examples of this type were the Vought F4U Corsair (U.S.) and the Fairey Firefly (Great Britain).

Dive Bombers

Dive bombers were relatively light bombers. Compared to the heavier horizontal bombers, they were equipped with lighter bomb loads (usually 500–1,000 lb.) so that they could attack point targets in a dive. Primary targets included primarily ships and bunkers, but also industrial plants, military columns, and troop concentrations. Guided missiles and improved air defense systems made dive bombers obsolete after 1945. Examples of this type were the SBD Dauntless (U.S.), the Fairey Barracuda (Great Britain) and the Aichi D3A (Japan).

Horizontal Bombers

Horizontal bombers could destroy targets such as ships or bunkers from high altitudes (up to 9,000 feet). Despite the heavier bomb load, the targeting capability was less accurate than that of a dive bomber. Examples of this type were the Douglas TBD Devastator (U.S.) and the Nakajima B5N (Japan).

Torpedo Bombers

A torpedo bomber could attack ships in the open sea or in harbors by means of a torpedo carried under the fuselage. This then struck like a submarine torpedo usually below the waterline of the enemy ship. Guided missiles and improved air defense systems made torpedo bombers obsolete after 1945, with the exception of antisubmarine warfare. Examples of this type were the Grumman TBF/TBM Avenger (U.S.), the Fairey Swordfish (Great Britain) and the Nakajima B5N (Japan).

Reconnaissance Aircraft

Carrier-based reconnaissance aircraft were mostly converted fighters or, in some cases, bombers, equipped with a larger tank to increase range and cameras. An exception was the Japanese Nakajima C6N, which was designed primarily as a reconnaissance aircraft. The task of reconnaissance aircraft was to obtain information about the enemy by means of reconnaissance flights in order to provide a basis for operational or tactical decisions. This included fleet and troop movements and the condition and strength of enemy forces. Examples of this type were the F4F Wildcat (U.S.), the Fairey Fulmar (Great Britain) and the Nakajima C6N (Japan).

5

U.S.S. *Saratoga*: A Dive into History

If U.S. military commanders had their way, a new era was to begin for warfare in 1946. The year before, the dropping of two atomic bombs on the Japanese cities of Hiroshima and Nagasaki had already demonstrated the devastating destructive power of this weapon. Experts now wanted to research the effects of nuclear weapon explosions on warships and other weapons systems. The United States had chosen Bikini Atoll in the Pacific for this purpose. This largest field test in history was named Operation *Crossroads* because the term "Crossroads" literally represented a crossroad between conventional and nuclear warfare. Some 90 ships, among them battleships, cruisers and two aircraft carriers, were to be expended. U.S.S. *Saratoga*, considered obsolete, was one of the target vessels.

One July 1, 1946, the first 23-kiloton atomic bomb named "Test Able" was dropped from a B-29 Superfortress bomber detonating 518 feet (158 m) above sea level sinking five ships. U.S.S. *Saratoga*, anchored 2,265 yards (2,070 m) away, survived the explosion with only minor damage, including the ignition of her flight deck's teak wood. The following day a skeleton crew boarded the carrier preparing her for the next test: On July 25, 1946, the 23-kiloton underwater blast named "Test Baker" detonated under the landing ship *LSM-60* some 400 yards

Frontal view of "Test Able's" mushroom cloud. The burning U.S.S. *Saratoga* is visible on the far left. (U.S. Navy)

Mushroom-shaped cloud and water column from the underwater nuclear explosion "Baker" of July 25, 1946. Photo taken from a tower on Bikini Island. Since U.S.S. *Saratoga* was anchored on the opposite side, she is not in the picture. (U.S. Dept. of Defense)

Undefeated in World War II, U.S.S. *Saratoga* finally sinks on July 25, 1946, after "Test Baker" had caused severe leaks to her hull, making it impossible to save the contaminated carrier. (U.S. Navy)

(370 m) from the carrier. The explosion's force lifted the carrier out of the water, knocked everything off her flight deck and knocked most of her funnel onto the flight deck. U.S.S. *Saratoga* sank shortly thereafter with her stern first. Less than 10 of the 90 target vessels expended in Operation *Crossroads* survived this unique experiment which had proven that atomic bombs could destroy entire fleets and contaminate those ships that remained afloat after the blast.

Daniel J. Lenihan served as Chief of the "Submerged Cultural Resources Unit" (SCRU) based in Santa Fe, New Mexico (later renamed the NPS Submerged Resources Center) from 1975–2000. This mobile team of underwater archaeologists was fielded by the U.S. National Park Service, the lead federal agency in historic preservation in America. Daniel was accompanied by Larry Murphy (deputy project director), Larry Nordby and Jerry Livingston (illustrators), all from Santa Fe, and James Delgado, a maritime historian from the NPS Washington office. Daniel describes how he and his team took archaeology to the aircraft carrier U.S.S. *Saratoga* and the other ships expended during Operation *Crossroads*:

> Our specialized team were early practitioners of no-to-low impact underwater archaeology. This meant doing as much research as possible with the least disturbance to fragile sites. That principle is still a hallmark of American archaeology on land or underwater. But it was a bit ironic in the context of Bikini Atoll. It is hard to imagine disturbing a site more than detonating an atomic bomb near it. And that was the case with U.S.S. *Saratoga*, the largest of the 10 ships sunk at Bikini. The bombs were birthed in Los Alamos, New Mexico, a 45-minute drive to the north of SCRU headquarters in Santa Fe. The 'device,' as referred to in hushed correspondence, was first tested at the 'Trinity Site,' a few hours to our south. It seemed we had some strange connection to these… devices. Now we would follow them out to the Marshall Islands in the Pacific Ocean. In Japan, they were used to end a hot war and in Bikini—maybe a test or perhaps as an early warning growl in a cold war with the Soviet Union.
>
> The world's fourth and fifth atomic explosions were conducted on a test fleet, anchored in clear water in July of 1946. World War II had ended a year earlier, leaving a legacy of destruction and death. The shipwrecks at Bikini reminded me of our research on the battleship U.S.S. *Arizona* in Pearl Harbor where we documented a traumatic loss of life in our nation's history. There, 1,177 men died before World War II was even 10 minutes old for Americans.
>
> At Bikini, we hadn't the same emotional impact as working on U.S.S. *Arizona* where so many died and were never recovered. But in the wreckage around us was something perhaps more ominous—10 warships destroyed by only two bombs. This was a target fleet of 20th century warships mangled by the same class of weapons the U.S. had used on the Japanese at Hiroshima and Nagasaki.
>
> Battleships like the *Arizona* in Pearl Harbor and the Japanese *Nagato* (the latter had been captured by the war's end) at Bikini were traditionally the sluggers. But by the end of World War II, aircraft carriers had taken prominence. One of them was U.S.S. *Saratoga*, now at the bottom of the Bikini lagoon. She in particular, made a connection with us. Her sheer size is difficult to comprehend under-water but she would become the main focus of our attention at Bikini. We began mapping the

Perspective drawing of *Saratoga* made in 1990. She lies in 180 feet (55 m) of water on the port bilge at a -10 to -15 degree angle rising to within 40 feet (12 m) of the surface, with the island and mast (which has collapsed in the meantime) visible from the surface. The U.S. Navy determined from oil leaks that the bottom shell plating had ruptured. This, they concluded, along with a tear in the hull near the starboard quarter, and the failure of sea chests and valves, had sunk *Saratoga*. (Drawing: Jerry Livingston and Larry Nordby, U.S. National Park Service)

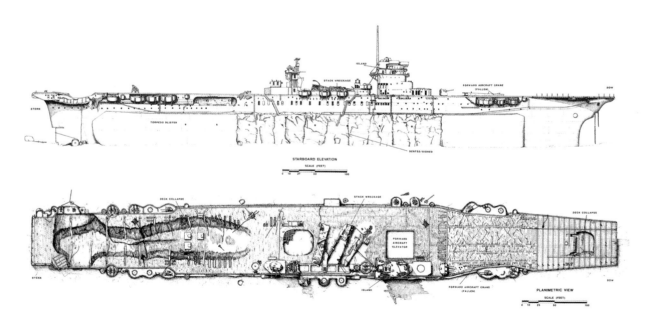

Profile views of *Saratoga*, 1990. U.S.S. *Saratoga* readily evidences the effects of the "Baker" bomb's detonation. More precisely, the ship shows the aftermath of a nearby atomic detonation's pressure wave, the effects of being lifted 29 to 43 feet, being hit by enormous waves, and the results of tons of water thrown up by the blast falling on the decks. Below the flight deck level, damage primarily consists of dishing along the starboard hull shell plating, most noticeably on the torpedo blister, which is pushed inward between frames to a depth of six feet in some areas. (Drawing: Larry Nordby and Jerry Livingston, U.S. National Park Service)

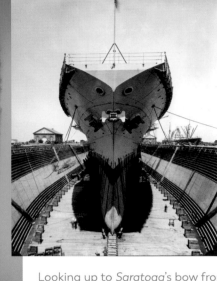

Looking up to *Saratoga*'s bow from the seafloor. This was the perspective shipyard workers had when she was in dry dock (as seen in the inset photo). A few years ago, however, the stern quarter—already weakened by the atomic blasts and the sinking—has largely collapsed. (Pete Mesley; inset U.S. Navy)

Face to face with *Sara*'s bow. Unlike her successors, she and her sister ship *Lexington* were built with enclosed "hurricane bows." (Pete Mesley)

Saratoga's mighty bow as seen from the side. (Pete Mesley)

This 1990 photo shows an area near the bow, where the flight deck is partially collapsed. This collapse generally conforms to an area damaged by kamikaze attack off Iwo Jima on February 21, 1945, and subsequently repaired for quick return to service. The deck collapse in this area may also be post-depositional and attributable to a twice damaged area weakening with corrosion and finally collapsing after the sinking. The inset photo shows the intact deck in 1936. (Larry Murphy, U.S. National Park Service / Submerged Resources Center; inset U.S. Navy)

A more recent photo of this area near the bow shows that it had further collapsed. (Pete Mesley)

sunken ships in 1989, the same year the 'Berlin Wall' came down, a rare good omen in a cold war still quietly raging as thermonuclear warfare wasn't a vague possibility in those days.

Before accepting this mission, I had to feel assured I wasn't taking the team someplace that could hurt them. Besides consulting with Dr. Robison, a respected scientist involved in research at Bikini, I wanted more. I drove 'up the hill' to Los Alamos to discuss it all with Jim Sprinkle, a family friend

Antiaircraft emplacements on the starboard side just below the flight deck. Inset photo: *Saratoga's* antiaircraft guns firing during World War II. (Pete Mesley; inset U.S. Navy)

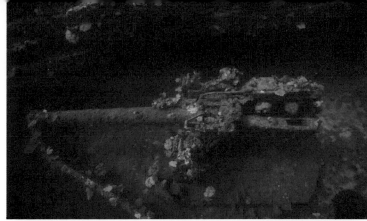

One of the 12 5-inch (12.7 cm) single antiaircraft guns photographed in 1989–1990. (Larry Murphy, U.S. NPS / SRC)

One of the remaining 5-inch (12.7 cm) antiaircraft guns, photographed in 1989–1990. (Larry Murphy, U.S. NPS / SRC)

who often flew off to Soviet sites to consult on such problems. I explained what we would be doing. He responded, "should be alright." I then asked, "would you let your kids dive there?" He smiled. "Okay, let me talk to some people." Later that evening he called me at home and said "yes, I would." Understandably, two of the six I asked to go, still declined.

The front of *Saratoga*'s island superstructure. The 8-inch (20.3 cm) twin gun, which is missing, was removed before the carrier sailed to Bikini Atoll. The large opening in the deck is the open deck elevator shaft. (Pete Mesley). The inset photo shows *Saratoga*'s island from a similar perspective in 1933. Note the funnel behind the island which was destroyed during Operation *Crossroads*. (U.S. Navy)

Remains of the funnel on the flight deck. The atomic blast wave or the water column's falling mass caused the collapse before the ship sank. (Larry Murphy, U.S. NPS / SRC)

At Bikini, our underwater video systems were critical for gaining detail that permitted mapping coherent images of such large ships. Excellent visibility made that possible. We have to consider that U.S.S. *Saratoga* was almost as long as skyscrapers are tall. It was the most impressive shipwreck I have seen underwater; not just a 'site' in the archaeological sense but an extraordinary 'sight' to ponder. Unlike the clumsy black and white videotape cameras we used in the 1970s and early 1980s, these were color. Ironically the popular cameras were made in Japan. They were useful for our earlier work in Pearl Harbor where visibility was only 5 to 7 feet. Even more so in Bikini where the sites were so large and our team, so small. We could often see 100 feet in front of us, important when mapping a 888 feet (270.7 m) long aircraft carrier. The illustrators could make scans of large reaches of the flight deck, *Saratoga* was upright with the deck varying from 100 to 120 feet deep. The hull stretched below to 180,' where it dug deep into the silty bottom. The problem was, seeing 100 to 120 feet' on *Saratoga* is not as useful as seeing that far on most sites that underwater archaeologists map. That's about 1/8th of the flight deck. Cruising down the length of that deck at 120 feet deep is tiring, particularly if you are pushing a video camera in front of you.

Rear view of the remains of the island. (Pete Mesley)

Front view of the bridge with pilot house inside in 1989–1990. (Larry Murphy, U.S. NPS / SRC)

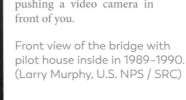

Interior of the pilot house. Most of the equipment remains inside. A chart table is first encountered on entering through the starboard bulkhead. The helm (with the wheel missing) and binnacle (missing the compass and cover) are easily identifiable. Mounts for the signal telegraph and a navigational radar set can be seen too. (Pete Mesley); The inset image shows the pilot house of an *Essex*-class carrier resembling the one aboard *Saratoga*. (U.S. Navy)

Daniel Lenihan examining a ceiling lamp in 1989–1990. As objects like this, as well as the supporting structures, have become increasingly unstable over the years, the interiors of shipwrecks can quickly become deadly traps for divers. (Larry Murphy, U.S. NPS / SRC)

Live 5-inch (12.7 cm) caliber cartridges, without warheads, in aluminum cartridge cases in Saratoga's handling room, photographed in 1989–1990. (Larry Murphy, U.S. NPS / SRC)

Five general purpose 500 lb (227 kg) bombs on their bomb carts, on *Saratoga*'s hangar deck. Lying in front of the bombs is a single 350 lb (160 kg) depth bomb. Photographed in 1989–1990. (Larry Murphy, U.S. NPS / SRC)

Fantastically illuminated by diver Pete Mesley, this photo allows an in-depth view into *Saratoga*'s dentist's office. Some of the equipment and the furniture is still intact. (Pete Mesley) The inset photo shows the dentist's office aboard the carrier during the 1930s. (U.S. Navy)

The toilets "heads" slowly filling with sediment. Note the bulkhead still has its white paint. (Pete Mesley)

Two diver helmets that once belonged to *Saratoga*'s divers who were in charge of hull inspection, mine clearance, propeller inspection, maintenance and debris removal. (Pete Mesley)

One of the three Curtiss SB2C Helldiver dive bombers that were observed on the hangar deck during the dives in 1989–1990, stowed with their wings folded. (Larry Murphy, U.S. NPS / SRC)
The inset photo shows a Helldiver with folded wings during World War II. (U.S. Navy)

Close-up of the Helldiver's cockpit. (Larry Murphy, U.S. NPS / SRC)

The same Helldiver which had been examined in 1989–1990, photographed more recently with the ceiling still being relatively intact. (Pete Mesley)

Operations at Bikini were unusually smooth and free of weather problems. The lagoon was 180 feet deep and we used air with its well-known narcotic effects at depth a constant issue. We traveled to the sites in small boats operated by natives of Bikini—their grandparents and older family members had been displaced by our military for these same tests. The U.S. Navy had done a great job fixing buoys, fore and aft, to all wrecks, which was critical. Our task would have been impossible without the help of Commander Dave McCampbell and his MDSU-1 team from Pearl Harbor. These ships had been hardly explored or imaged in the past due the residual radioactivity. We would deploy a team to a wreck to reconnoiter for general sketching, while another gathered underwater video. Sometimes we used measured baselines on heavily damaged areas. Larry Nordby, who created the masterpiece line-drawings of U.S.S. *Saratoga*, videotaped portions of the complicated superstructure for later inclusion in the master.

The Helldiver photographed not too long after the previous image was taken. The ceiling had come down at an angle on the port side so that it was almost touching the aircraft's left side. (Pete Mesley)

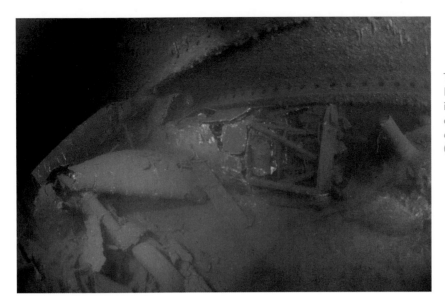

This latest image of the Helldiver photographed in 2015 shows that the ceiling has collapsed onto the fuselage. (Pete Mesley)

We returned in 1990 and again emphasized *Saratoga*, with many penetrations to the hangar deck and deeper into the vessel which were particularly costly in overall hours spent decompressing—releasing in stages the high-pressure air we had breathed. Our illustrated report, *The Archaeology of the Atomic Bomb* was printed in 1991 including a series of detailed drawings of U.S.S. *Saratoga* visualizing the effort by the illustrators Larry Nordby and Jerry Livingston to obtain and convey this information more than three decades ago before the smartphone was even a dream in the haunts of some budding genius mind.

Pete Mesley, one of the Southern Hemispheres most experienced technical diving instructors and explorers, started specializing in rebreather and technical diving trips in 1998, and dedicated himself to researching, finding, diving, photographing and leading expeditions to wreck diving meccas including the wrecks at Bikini Atoll. Because U.S.S. *Saratoga* has always held a special fascination for him and he is very familiar with wreckage, Pete has been able to see the wreck's deterioration in recent years since the National Park Service survey in 1989–1990:

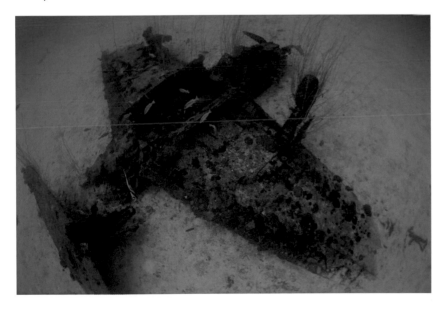

A Helldiver dive bomber wreck lying upside down off the starboard side of *Saratoga*. This aircraft was blown or washed off the ship's flight deck during Operation *Crossroads*. (Pete Mesley)

I did my first trip to Bikini Atoll in November 2010. For decades, I have wanted to dive what was deemed the ultimate wreck diver's paradise, which hosted the world's largest concentration of battleships, destroyers, submarines and an aircraft carrier. So, over the next 10 years and frequenting the atoll over 18 times I have had a unique opportunity to watch the wrecks change over time. The ship that showed the largest change over time was U.S.S. *Saratoga*, which had borne the brunt of two atomic explosions and this was beginning to show. On my first trip in 2010 the flight deck was already well on its way and had collapsed in many places aft of the forward elevator shaft. There was a row of aircraft on the port side of the hangar deck. The most recognizable aircraft, a Curtiss SB2C-5 Helldiver, was the one most forward with its wings folded up for storage in the hangar deck.

In order to gain access to the aircraft you would have to be extremely careful—wide flat sheets of steel would hang precariously from the ceiling. This is why utilizing the latest in technology in diving equipment really assisted in our safety in accessing these fragile wrecks. Closed circuit rebreathers (CCRs) are common in today's diving practices especially in the technical diving world. Rebreathers recirculate the exhaled gas back into a loop where carbon dioxide is removed and oxygen is replenished. An ingenious invention which has enabled divers to carefully explore delicate areas deep inside wrecks and caves.

It is the bubbles exhaled by open circuit divers that cause the most damage, dislodging and agitating debris above one's head, which can collapse at any one given moment or cause "percolation" which is where the bubbles dislodge silt causing the visibility to reduce to zero in seconds making it extremely dangerous for divers to exit a wreck or cave. It is the use of these CCR's that have enabled us to extensively explore, deep inside these wrecks for extended periods of time, giving us a lot of opportunity to capture and document key areas of the ship.

The ceiling had come down at an angle on the port side so that it was almost touching the left side of the aircraft. This ceiling had been firmly in place for a number of years until 2015. The Helldiver had become a major landmark for divers to go and see, so when I went to the site it was a sad sight to see that the ceiling had now collapsed further. Its weight had pushed hard on the fuselage crushing most of it into the wreckage.

There are many areas on the mighty *Saratoga* that are showing their signs of wear and it is becoming increasingly dangerous to dive inside many of the areas. The bridge on the island has been deemed unsafe to dive since 2005 because of its precarious looking base structure. But she still stands tall today. The stern quarter, on the other hand, has largely collapsed.

Another Helldiver that came to rest about 160 feet (50 m) away from *Saratoga*. (Pete Mesley)

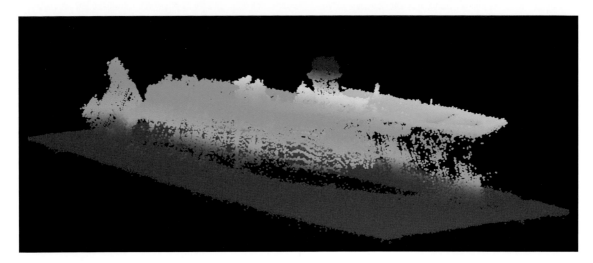

Multi-beam sonar point cloud image of *Saratoga* as viewed from the starboard bow looking aft. Created by the University of Delaware's Coastal Sediments Hydrodynamics and Engineering Laboratory (College of Earth, Ocean, and Environment) with a PingDSP sonar during a Bikini Atoll survey in 2019. The rear of the carrier is in the stages of collapse. (CSHEL University of Delaware)

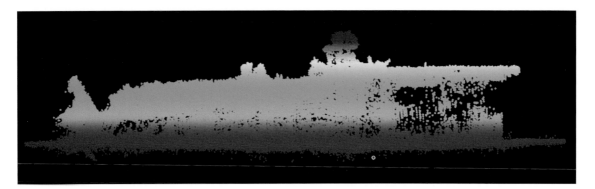

Saratoga as viewed from the starboard side (2019). This image clearly shows the collapsed stern section. (CSHEL University of Delaware)

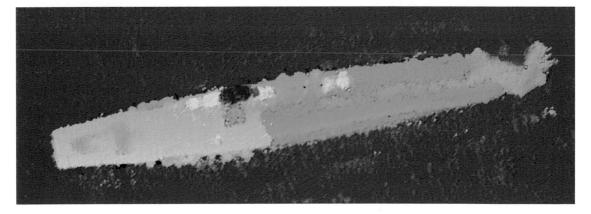

Saratoga as viewed from the top looking down (2019). This image reveals that not only the stern but also parts of the flight deck have collapsed. (CSHEL University of Delaware)

6

U.S.S. *Hornet*: A Guided Tour

U.S.S. *Hornet* (CV-12) is one of four surviving U.S. Navy aircraft carriers that saw action in World War II. Along with her three sister ships of the *Essex*-class, U.S.S. *Yorktown* (CV-10), U.S.S. *Intrepid* (CV-11) and U.S.S. *Lexington* (CV-16), she serves as a world-class floating museum, offering visitors from around the world the opportunity to relive World War II (and the Cold War) at sea as well as life and work aboard such a mighty ship.

Chuck Myers, one of the *Hornet*'s senior docents, takes us aboard on a tour of the famous aircraft carrier:

U.S.S. *Hornet* had an extraordinary combat record in World War II, engaging the enemy in the Pacific in March 1944, just 21 months after the laying of her keel and the shortest shakedown cruise in Navy history (two weeks). For 18 months, she never touched land. She was constantly in the most forward areas of the Pacific

U.S.S. *Hornet* (CV-12) preserved as a floating museum in Alameda, California. (U.S.S. *Hornet* Sea, Air and Space Museum)

war—sometimes within 40 miles of the Japanese home islands. Her pilots destroyed 1,410 enemy aircraft and over one million tons of enemy shipping. Her aircraft stopped the Japanese super-battleship *Yamato* and played the major part in sinking her. She launched the first strikes in the liberation of the Philippines, and in February 1945, the first strikes on Japan since the Doolittle Raid in 1942. The "Grey Ghost" participated in virtually all of the assault landings in the Pacific from March 1944 until the end of World War II, earning nine battle stars and the Presidential Unit citation. After two modernizations, she played a role in the Vietnam War during the 1960s and in the Apollo program, recovering the Apollo 11 and Apollo 12 astronauts as they returned from the Moon. In June 1970, U.S.S. *Hornet* was retired from active service and assigned to the reserve fleet in Bremerton, Washington, where she was designated as a National Historic Landmark in 1991.

The following year, the ship was ironically sold for scrap and moved back to the Bay Area for that purpose. Fortunately, the environmental laws in California were such that scrapping was delayed and ultimately determined to be impossible and *Hornet* was acquired by the Aircraft Carrier *Hornet* Foundation in 1995 and opened as a floating museum in October 1998. Today, *Hornet* resides at Pier 3 in Alameda, California at what was Naval Air Station Alameda, once her home port, and she has a new persona as the U.S.S. *Hornet* Sea, Air and Space Museum. Much of the ship has been restored and restoration is an on-going proposition, with new spaces opened periodically. The crew's objective is to maintain the ship as it was on retirement in 1970.

U.S.S. *Hornet*'s flight deck with aircraft from various eras on board. (Michael Layefsky)

Flight Deck and 01 Level

An aircraft carrier's flight deck is one of the busiest places on the ship. With an average of 300 men working among dozens of aircraft, flight decks are among the most dangerous workplace in the world. Add to that jet engine blasts or propellers, ordinance being loaded, and the challenges of landing with just about 200 feet (65m) of airstrip, and it was always an exciting place to be! As designed, U.S.S. *Hornet* was a "straight deck carrier," meaning that aircraft landed and launched parallel to the keel. In 1953, she (and most of her sister ships in the same period) were modified to handle jet aircraft, which were heavier and landed at faster speeds, requiring modifications for both launch and recovery, including stronger catapults, heavier arresting gear, and a strengthened flight deck. And in her last major overhaul she was, in 1956, converted to an "angled deck carrier" and soon designated as a CVS and tasked for antisubmarine duties.

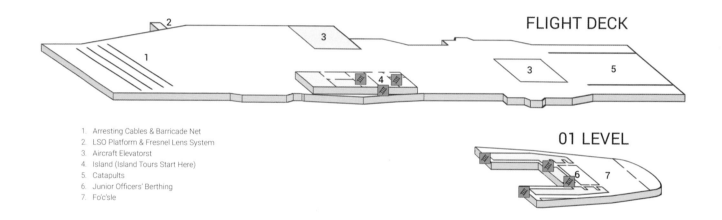

FLIGHT DECK

01 LEVEL

1. Arresting Cables & Barricade Net
2. LSO Platform & Fresnel Lens System
3. Aircraft Elevatorst
4. Island (Island Tours Start Here)
5. Catapults
6. Junior Officers' Berthing
7. Fo'c'sle

Map of the flight deck and 01 level. (U.S.S. *Hornet* Museum)

The newly commissioned carrier with its straight deck in 1943. (U.S.S. *Hornet* Museum)

After her 1953 modernization, U.S.S. *Hornet* was able operate jet aircraft, which were heavier than the World War II-era propeller aircraft. (U.S. Navy)

U.S.S. *Hornet* after her 1956 conversion to an "angled deck carrier." This meant that aircraft landed eleven degrees to port from the centerline and permitted the ship to launch and recover aircraft simultaneously and made flight deck operations safer in the process. The flight deck is 846 × 108 feet or 258 × 33 meters (about 2.1 acres or 0,84 hectares) and is made out of 3 1/2-inch teak and pine wood over a thin steel base. Part of it was replaced with aluminum plate during the jet era to prevent setting the wooden deck on fire. (U.S. Navy)

1. and 2. Landing Area

Landing an aircraft on an aircraft carrier's flight deck at sea is a dangerous task reserved only for highly trained pilots. All aircraft built for carrier use were equipped with "tailhooks," hooks that lower from the back end of the aircraft designed to catch an arresting cable. Once the angled deck was in place, *Hornet*'s flight deck had four arresting cables stretching across the landing area of her deck, each one able to trap and stop an aircraft.

A successful landing often came down to watching and obeying the Landing Signal Officer (LSO), who guided pilots into their landing from the small, framed platform on the port side of the flight deck off the landing area. In World war II, propeller aircraft were slower, and the LSO could use brightly colored paddles to direct approaching aircraft. Jet aircraft became too fast for this manual system and so the digital Optical Landing System (OLS) was installed about two-thirds of the way down the port side of the landing area. The OLS is a light device utilizing a fresnel lenses and reference lights in such a way that, if a pilot is correctly approaching, he will see the correct fresnel lens lit and know that he is level with the deck and can expect a successful landing. If the approaching aircraft had a damaged tailhook or some other trouble that prevented use of the arresting cables, the flight deck crew could erect a barricade net stretching across the deck between two stanchions. The pilot would fly into the net which would then wrap around the aircraft and drag it to a stop.

A TBM-1C Avenger catching a wire upon returning to U.S.S. *Hornet* in World War II. (U.S.S. *Hornet* Museum)

A Lockheed S-3 Viking with a damaged tailhook flying into the barricade net dragging it to safely stop. (U.S. Navy)

3. Aircraft Elevators

U.S.S. *Hornet* and her sister ships have three aircraft elevators (smaller carriers had two). The first is forward centerline and connects hangar bay 1 to the flight deck near the catapults. The elevator is usually kept in the up position, flush with the flight deck. The other two were built on the port and starboard sides of the ship, with one in hangar bay 2 and the other in hangar bay 3. These elevators were used to quickly move aircraft between the hangar deck and flight deck, and each could move 20 tons, the weight of a fully fueled and loaded aircraft, between decks in under 10 seconds. Elevators are suspended on twelve cables controlled by a hydraulic piston. When the elevators weren't in use, they could be used as recreation spaces for playing volleyball or basketball.

The aft centerline elevator, which was present before the angled deck conversion. In World War II and until 1956–7, there were two centerline elevators and one on the port side. (U.S.S. *Hornet* Museum)

The midships elevator aboard U.S.S. *Enterprise* (CV-6) with a F6F Hellcat fighter on it in 1944. (U.S. Navy)

4. Island Superstructure

The "Island" is the superstructure rising from the flight deck. It served as the command center and held the captain's bridge, pilot house, navigation, primary flight control, and, at its base, combat information center. The captain's bridge and pilot house are where the captain was expected to be when the ship was at sea. From his bridge, the captain could see 25 miles (40 km) in all directions and would give orders to steer the ship back into the pilot house where the helmsman would control the ship's wheel while the lee helmsman controlled the ship's speed.

On *Hornet*, there are eight levels of restored spaces in the island and visitors can explore many of them. (U.S.S. *Hornet* Museum)

The lower bridge is the flag bridge, whereas the one above is the captain's bridge. Above the island are an array of antennas for various types of radar and some radio equipment as well. On special days, you will see the biggest antenna, sailors call it the "bed spring antenna" rotating as it did at sea. (U.S.S. *Hornet* Museum)

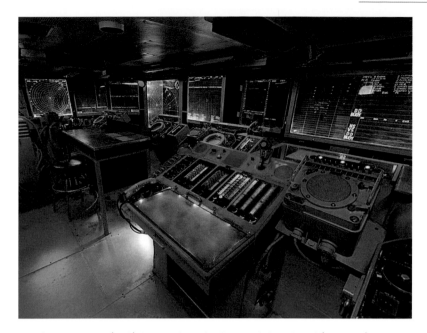

The combat information center (CIC), located at the base of the island (02 level), was the space where the ship gathered information about the vessels and aircraft around it. Equipment in CIC was used to track and identify movement under the water, along the surface of the water, and up in the air. Ships and aircraft would be identified as friend or foe based on the radio signals they emitted and other identifiers and their movements would be tracked on large plotting maps. (U.S.S. *Hornet* Museum)

The plotting room, the predecessor to the more complex CIC, aboard an *Essex*-class carrier during World War II. (U.S. Navy)

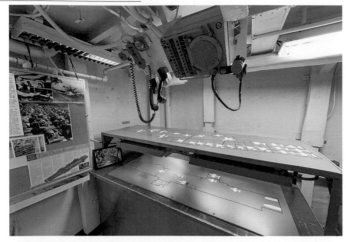

Inside the island, on flight deck level (03 level), is the flight deck control. There, the Ouija "wee-gee" board is used to keep track of the placement and status of each aircraft on the flight deck and hangar deck. The aircraft silhouettes represent each type of aircraft on board and are moved as the aircraft moves. (U.S.S. *Hornet* Museum)

The flag bridge on the 05 level with its bow view for use by an admiral (when on board) and his staff while the captain commands the ship from the main bridge above (06 level). (U.S.S. *Hornet* Museum)

The captain's bridge is three levels above the flight deck (06 level) just forward of the pilot house and is his "office" and command center while the carrier is at sea. He has company on the bridge, typically four officers on watch at all times. The picture shows the captain's chair on the port side, surrounded by devices conveying various types of status. Above on the right side are wind speed and direction indicators—vital for launching or recovering aircraft. Below that are three devices showing the status of the port and starboard engines and the rudder angle indicator. The windows in front—facing the bow—and to the side permit a view of most of the flight deck, making it easy to watch all launches and landings from this position. (U.S.S. *Hornet* Museum)

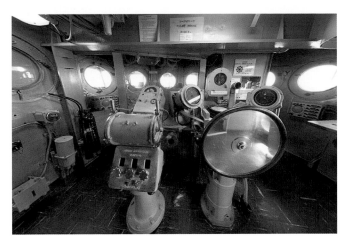

The pilot house is behind the captain's bridge. Pictured below are some of the main attributes of this space, namely the engine order telegraph, the RPM annunciator on the left and the helm on the right. Above the helm are two gyro-compass repeaters, one operated by the forward gyro and one by the aft so that if one goes bad there is a redundant capability already in place. Above and between the two is the rudder angle indicator, showing the helmsman exactly where the rudder is at any time.

The lee-helm position to the left communicates to the engineering spaces, including engine rooms and fire rooms, just exactly how fast the ship should be traveling. The big handles on top communicate speeds in standards, both forward and aft and moving those handles causes bells to ring to alert the watch that a change is being made. The three crank handles on the device below communicate exact RPMs to the throttle men in the engine rooms. (U.S.S. *Hornet* Museum)

The pilot house of an *Essex*-class carrier during World War II. (U.S. Navy)

The captain's sea cabin right next to the pilot house. In case of an emergency he would be able to immediately enter the pilot house and the nearby bridge. The captain had his own steward serving him his meals. Located on the 02 level (below the flight deck) are in-port cabins for the captain and the admiral. (U.S.S. *Hornet* Museum)

Navigation is on the same level (level 06) as the captain's bridge and pilot house. The navigation crew had several ways to determine the ship's position including piloting, celestial navigation, LORAN, and the dead reckoning tracer. The LORAN (Long Range Navigation) system worked using a receiver on the ship that could sense low-frequency radio signals transmitted by fixed land-based beacons that then triangulate the ship's position based on the signals it received. The dead reckoning tracer (seen here on the table), was an analog computer that required the ship's longitude and latitude but could then follow a changing position through speed and direction. Both methods have been superseded by modern GPS. (U.S.S. *Hornet* Museum)

Primary flight control (PriFly) is the uppermost glass room on the island (level 08) two levels above the bridge. PriFly controls all launches and recoveries and is responsible for the launched aircraft during the initial ascent and for aircraft on final approach to the carrier. This is the domain of the Air Boss, who kept track of the aircraft and crew movement down on the flight deck below. His job was made slightly easier since the flight deck crew wore color-coded uniforms which indicated their duties so he could be sure that they were all where they were supposed to be. (U.S.S. *Hornet* Museum)

5. Aircraft Catapults

The ship's two hydraulic catapults made it possible to launch aircraft with a limited runway. Powered with compressed air and a hydraulic ram, they could take the aircraft from 0 to 120 mph (190 km/h) in about 3 seconds. The machinery to power the catapults is over six decks below with more than 1,000 feet (300 m) of cable connecting the machinery to the flight deck track. Aircraft were launched basically being pulled off the deck at high speed. They were attached to the catapult with a "bridle" affixed under its wings that then wrapped around a shuttle on the catapult. They were also then attached to the flight deck by a "holdback bar" allowing the aircraft to bring their engines to full power. When the pilot was ready, he would signal to the deck crew and the catapult was launched. The combined power of the catapult stroke and the aircraft's engines would snap the holdback bar at its thinnest point and the aircraft would go flying forward and off the deck.

An aircraft taking off from U.S.S. *Hancock* (CVA-19) with the combined power of the catapult stroke and the aircraft's engines. (U.S. Navy)

6. Junior Officers' Berthing

An aircraft carrier is, at its heart, an airport that can cross oceans. An *Essex*-class carrier would typically deploy with a carrier air group made of three to six squadrons. During World War II, air groups would usually include a fighter squadron, bombing squadron, scouting squadron, and torpedo squadron and consisted of over 100 aircraft. Later, different squadron types, such as antisubmarine and helicopter squadrons, would be added to the mix. Each squadron had 12–24 aircraft and pilots.

Junior officers' berthing. Air conditioning was installed after World World II. During the 1940s, the only areas that were air conditioned were Sickbay and spaces with sensitive machinery. (U.S.S. *Hornet* Museum)

All pilots are officers, most are junior officers, and they generally stayed in the forward section of the ship along with the officers of the ship's company. Junior officers' berthing or "J.O.B." was the "worst" accommodations an officer could expect aboard the carrier, still far better than most enlisted compartments, and was home to some of the ship's newest pilots. In this room, you can see safes where the pilots would store their sidearms when they weren't flying—aboard the ship, only Marines could carry firearms.

7. "Foc's'le"

The name "Foc's'le" is shorthand from "forecastle" referring to the castle-like structure which rose above the front of old wooden sailing ships. Its primary function aboard a carrier is to hold the two anchors. Each anchor chain is raised with the aid of a winch called a "wildcat," which are the brass domes that the chains wrap around. Each wildcat sits atop an anchor windlass, which uses a hydraulic motor to raise the anchor. When the anchor is fully raised, the chain is secured to the deck by clamps called pelican hooks, so-called because they look like large bird beaks.

U.S.S. *Hornet*'s "Foc's'le" with the massive anchor chains visible. (U.S.S. *Hornet* Museum)

Hangar Deck

The hangar deck is the carrier's main deck. Think of its main function as the parking garage and maintenance space for the ship's aircraft. As the largest open space, it was also a popular place for ship-wide events for all of the ship's sailors such as sport tournaments, movies, shows, church services, and other large assemblies. Today, the hangar deck features most of the *Hornet* Museum's historic aircraft, the flight simulator, ship's store, and an exhibit on the space race and Apollo 11 and 12 programs.

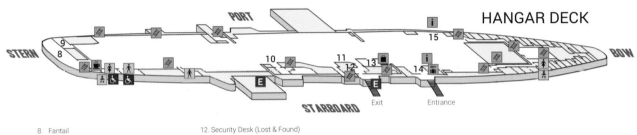

HANGAR DECK

8. Fantail
9. Friends of Nisei Exhibit *(up one ladder from Hangar Bay)*
10. Apollo Splashdown Exhibit
11. Special Exhibition
12. Security Desk (Lost & Found)
13. Ship's Store
14. Admissions & Information
15. Orientation

Map of hangar deck (00 level). (U.S.S. *Hornet* Museum)

8. Fantail

The fantail is the rear or aft deck of a ship. Below the fantail are the four propellers that propel the ship, each 15 ft (4.5 m) in diameter. It was one of the open areas on the ship and served as a crew lounge for men who were not standing watch, a classroom for learning skills such as rope tying, a platform for fishing, and a location for occasional ceremonies and services. When the ship was at sea, a lookout was also posted here, alert for men overboard.

The U.S.S. *Hornet's* fantail. The landing area of the flight deck is directly overhead making this an exciting, if not potentially dangerous, place to stand while aircraft were landing. (U.S.S. *Hornet* Museum)

9. Friends of the Nisei

This exhibit was installed by the Friends of the Nisei, a non-profit who worked with the *Hornet* Museum for this project. It deals primarily with the internment of Americans of Japanese descent and their dedicated combat and military intelligence service in the Pacific and especially in Europe during World War II.

10. Apollo Splashdown

On July 20, 1969, Apollo 11 astronauts Neil Armstrong and Buzz Aldrin became the first men on the Moon while Michael Collins orbited it in the CSM *Columbia*. On November 19, 1969, Apollo 12 astronauts Pete Conrad and Alan Bean became the second Moon walkers, while Dick Gordon piloted the CSM *Yankee Clipper*. On the return to Earth, both Apollo 11 and 12 were recovered in the South Pacific by U.S.S. *Hornet*. (11.15. on map: Special Exhibitions, Ship's Store, Admissions and Orientation)

Recovery of the Apollo 11 capsule after splashing down in the Pacific. (U.S.S. *Hornet* Museum)

The hangar deck (00 level) with various helicopters on display. The Apollo exhibit is visible at left. (U.S.S. *Hornet* Museum)

Saving and Restoring Historic Aircraft

The U.S.S. *Hornet*'s displayed aircraft include two World War II-era planes, a FM-2 Wildcat fighter and a TBM Avenger torpedo bomber.

FM-2 Wildcat

This fighter was accepted into the Navy on April 27, 1944 and was last operational with Carrier Qualification Training Unit at Naval Air Station Glenview in Illinois. On June 14, 1945, it was flown by Ensign E. J. Robinson off of U.S.S. *Wolverine* (IX-64) in Lake Michigan. The engine gave out while he was qualifying for carrier landings and he had to ditch in the lake. The cold, fresh water preserved the aircraft until it was recovered in 1995 by A & T Recovery. In 2006, it was transferred to the U.S.S. *Hornet* Museum for a seven-year-restoration project and is on loan from the National Museum of Naval Aviation in Pensacola, Florida.

The Wildcat on display on *Hornet*'s hangar deck (all four images: U.S.S. *Hornet* Museum)

The Wildcat after its recovery from Lake Michigan.

The Wildcat's folding wings today...

...and before its restoration.

The Wildcat's tail...

and its cockpit...

Avenger TBM-3

The torpedo bomber was purchased by the Aircraft Carrier *Hornet* Foundation in 1998 (after it had been used as a fire-fighting aircraft), and it was restored by volunteers with funds provided through donations. This Avenger has been painted in the squadron markings of VT-17, a squadron that flew from the deck of U.S.S. *Hornet* (CV-12) during World War II.

...have been restored by volunteers with funds provided through donations. (all three images: U.S.S. *Hornet* Museum)

From 1943 until the end of World War II, U.S.S. *Wolverine* (IX-64), along with her sister ship U.S.S. *Sable* (IX-81), were used for the training of 17,000 pilots, landing signal officers and other navy personnel on the Great Lakes. Converted from side-wheel steamers, these "fresh water carriers" were not equipped with armor, hangar deck, or elevators. Both ships were scrapped after the war. (U.S. Navy)

With a length of about 535 feet (163 m), U.S.S. *Sable* (IX-81) and U.S.S. *Wolverine* (IX-64) were shorter and lower to the water than many of the aircraft carriers of the day, but they were instrumental in the pilot training mission. (U.S. Navy)

The Avenger during restoration before being painted. (U.S.S. *Hornet* Museum)

The restored Avenger torpedo bomber on display in the hangar bay. (U.S.S. *Hornet* Museum)

Second Deck

A ship's second deck was a mix of living and working spaces but has the largest number of individual spaces available for self-touring.

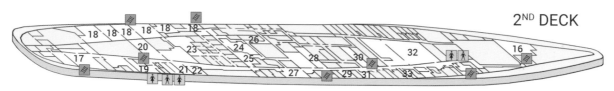

2ND DECK

16. Forward Auxiliary Emergency Generator
17. Chief Petty Officers' Mess & Lounge
18. Sister Ship Row
19. Chapel & Ship's Library
20. Torpedo Workshop

21. Task Force Exhibit
22. Women in the Military Exhibit
23. Sickbay
24. Hornet Legacy Exhibit
25. Bluejacket Family Activity Room

26. Post Office
27. Marine Detachment
28. Ready Room 4
29. Anti-Submarine Warfare Exhibit
30. Special Exhibition

31. Ray Vyeda Memorial Exhibit
32. Officers' Wardroom
33. Air Group 11 Exhibit

Map of second deck (below hangar deck). (U.S.S. *Hornet* Museum)

16. Forward Emergency Generator

The carrier has two emergency diesel generators (one forward, one aft), which could supply all critical electrical power needs in case the main generators failed or shut down. Crewmen would monitor the generator when it was not in use and tested it periodically to make sure it was in working order. Each generator had an engine that started using 250 psi compressed air and was rated at 1,416 hp and generated 1,000 kilowatts (1,600 amps).

17. Chief Petty Officers' Mess and Lounge

The rate, chief petty officer (CPO), is the seventh enlisted rate in the U.S. Navy, just above petty officer first class and below senior chief petty officer. Advancement into the chief petty officer grades is the most significant promotion within the enlisted naval grades. At the grade of chief petty officer, the sailor takes on more administrative duties. In the U.S. Navy, their uniform alters to reflect this change of duty, becoming nearly identical to that of an officer's uniform except with different insignia. Personnel in the three chief petty officer rates (E-7 through E-9) also had conspicuous privileges such as separate dining and living areas. Their mess was off-limits to anyone who was not a chief, including the captain himself, except by specific invitation.

The Chief Petty Officer (CPO) mess is where the CPOs (senior enlisted men) ate their meals. Adjacent to this space is the CPO lounge where the rudder centering device is located. This device was used to center the rudder and lock it into position if the steering mechanism was out of order. (U.S.S. *Hornet* Museum)

18. Sister Ship Row

The portside of the 2nd deck is dedicated to *Hornet*'s sister ships, so called because all 24 *Essex*-class aircraft carriers were built from the same basic blueprint. Out of all 24 sister ships, only four remain today: U.S.S. *Hornet*, U.S.S. *Intrepid*, U.S.S. *Lexington*, and U.S.S. *Yorktown*, all of which are museums you can visit.

19. Chapel and Library

As with most of the U.S. Navy's larger ships, a carrier crew included one or two chaplains. They have a specific faith group they follow and represent, but they also facilitated religious support for sailors of all faiths while they were aboard. If any faith group didn't have a chaplain aboard who represented them, a sailor of that faith volunteered as a certified lay leader. This compartment also contained the ship's library resembling a public library.

Navy Chaplain Allen A. Zaun standing at an altar set up for Christmas services aboard U.S.S. *Hornet*. (U.S.S. *Hornet* Museum)

20. Torpedo Workshop

Although an aircraft carrier could not launch torpedoes like a submarine can, but did, at times, carry bomber aircraft that could carry one torpedo and so needed to keep torpedoes on board during those times. The bulkhead (wall) opposite the torpedo workshop also contains one of the locations from where the ship can be steered if she were damaged in battle. It was made to be used only if the island and "Sec Conn" in the "Foc's'le" were not operational, which would mean that the ship would be in dire straits. The steering console includes a rudder angle indicator, a compass, a toggle switch to direct the rudder, and sound-powered headphones to listen to directions on how to steer the ship out of danger.

The U.S.S. *Hornet*'s torpedo workshop with various types of torpedoes. (U.S.S. *Hornet* Museum)

21. Task Force Exhibit

A task force is a group of ships assembled for a specific assignment, bringing together different divisions and squadrons without the need for a formal fleet reorganization. Task forces work well for the changing needs of war, and, by the end of World War II, about 100 task forces had been created by the U.S. Navy. Task forces could comprise many different types of ships including aircraft carriers, submarines, destroyers, light cruisers, and more. The task force would also be given a designated number (even numbers for the Atlantic and odd numbers to the Pacific) and could also be broken down into various subgroups: battle groups, task units, and task elements. Whenever a U.S. Navy aircraft carrier is called out to sea it is part of a battle group. A carrier battle group is a battle group specifically centered around one or more aircraft carriers with escorts. These other ships can include destroyers, smaller escort carriers, and more.

22. Women in the Military

This exhibit honors the service of women in the American military from its beginnings during the Revolutionary War as nurses to their combat service in the present.

23. Sickbay

Major warships such as aircraft carriers had a fully functional hospital, called "sickbay," to take care of an average 3,500 men. Staff included four doctors and about 24 corpsmen. Sickbay was equipped with a general examination room, x-ray room, bacteriological lab, vision and sound testing rooms, a laboratory, pharmacy, offices, and two surgical rooms. It also hosts a ward that can sleep some fifty sailors who were too ill or injured to return to their regularly assigned bunks.

The sickbay's ward during World War II and today. (U.S. Navy / U.S.S. *Hornet* Museum)

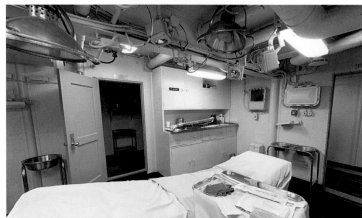

Sickbay for examinations and surgical operations. (U.S.S. *Hornet* Museum)

24. U.S.S. *Hornet* Legacy Room

This room honors all the ships named U.S.S. *Hornet* as this name dates back to the earliest days of the United States and has been carried through eight ships, the last being the aircraft carrier CV-12. This ship performed so admirably during its service that the name *Hornet* was carried on to the F/A-18 Hornet and Super Hornet jets even though the ship still floats.

26. Post Office

Mail is very important to sailors deployed at sea. Mail from home delivers emotions, connections, love, and a touch of family. Reading and writing letters are an easy escape from the harrowing experience of war. It brings sailors a reminder of people and places that they love and provides moments of normalcy and reassurance. Sending and delivering mail is made possible by exchanging mail at port of call, or at sea through "underway replenishment (UNREP)." UNREP is the process by which two ships moving parallel to each other exchange information, mail, or supplies from one to another while at sea. Mail was also transferred both ways by aircraft, often call the "COD."

The post office aboard an *Essex*-class carrier during World War II. (U.S. Navy)

27. Marine Detachment

A Marine detachment was a separate division on board a U.S. Navy ship. Aboard an *Essex*-class carrier, it consisted of about two officers and 46–55 Marines. They were the only ones aboard the ship allowed to carry firearms. The Marine detachment performed several functions. They acted as part of the ship's landing force if needed, provided the captain with guards dating back to older sailing days where mutiny was more likely. They also operated the ship's brig and manned several of the antiaircraft guns. Over time, the role of Marine detachments diminished until they were disestablished in 1998. Marines are still aboard U.S. Navy amphibious ships, however, to continue serving as the navy's landing force.

28. Ready Room

Ready rooms were used by pilots aboard aircraft carriers before, during, and after missions and, outside of combat, as a training room. When a carrier air wing was assigned to a carrier, each of its squadrons were given their own ready room. To the pilots, this area was like a clubroom as well as a place to store their flying gear which would have included parachutes, harnesses, and helmets.

Pilots were an essential part of the ship. To become a carrier pilot, men and women must pass strict requirements and go through intense training programs. Between January 1941 and August 1945, nearly 325,000 young men entered the cadet training program to fly in World War II. About 191,000 of them, or 59 percent, graduated. Most of the remaining dropped out while some perished in accidents during training.

Pilots being briefed in the ready room aboard U.S.S. *Hornet* during World War II. One pilot holds a dog, probably the air group's mascot. (U.S.S. *Hornet* Museum)

One of U.S.S. *Hornet*'s ready rooms today. (U.S.S. *Hornet* Museum)

29. Antisubmarine Warfare Exhibit

Antisubmarine Warfare (ASW) is the tactic of denying the enemy the effective use of their submarines. In World War II, German U-boats in the Atlantic caused heavy losses to merchant convoys transporting war materials to Europe and Africa. The U.S. Navy developed new combat techniques with aircraft such as the Grumman Avenger torpedo bombers and Wildcat fighter aircraft. Their aircraft carriers and the ships that protected them became known as Hunter Killer Groups (HUK) and helped stem heavy shipping losses. After the war, nuclear-powered submarines were built that could launch ballistic missiles, and ASW tactics quickly evolved during the post-WWII era and through the Korean War, becoming essential to the Cold War between NATO and the Warsaw Pact nations. New inventions such as sonobuoys, SONAR systems, and antisubmarine rockets helped carriers and other ships find, identify, and destroy enemy submarines.

30. Special Exhibit Room

This area is used to display some of the more interesting artifacts in the Museum's collection. These artifacts are changed out on a regular basis. There is also information on how artifacts are maintained in good condition.

31. Ray Vyeda Memorial Exhibit—From Mothballs to Museum

This exhibit honors the group called "The U.S.S. *Hornet* Historical Museum Association Inc.," which was formed to save the carrier and turn it into a museum. Thanks to the great efforts that these dedicated volunteers started, *Hornet* was rescued from being scrapped.

The officers' wardroom. Officers made up only about 10 percent of the crew, or around 300 to 350 men. (U.S.S. *Hornet* Museum)

32. Officers' Wardroom

Officers and enlisted sailors might have all been aboard aircraft carriers together, but their experiences were very different. The forward third section of the ship is mostly dedicated to officers. They had staterooms similar to college dorm rooms that they shared with a few roommates and usually ate in the wardroom. This was the main mess area for the officers of the ship. Unlike the cafeteria-style chow line that the enlisted crew had down on the third deck, food here was served as in a restaurant, with stewards acting as cooks, waiters, and bussers. Also unlike the enlisted men, officers had to pay for their meals whereas food from the enlisted mess was given for free. The tables in the wardroom were set with tablecloths, silverware, and china and officers were expected to dress in the uniform of the day. The flight suit mess, wardroom galley, and wardroom pantry were operational 24-hours-a-day to accommodate erratic mission schedules, though officers would have access to more limited menu options off-hours from breakfast, lunch, and dinner.

Stateroom for two officers, who had more privacy than the enlisted men who had to sleep in larger quarters. (U.S.S. *Hornet* Museum)

An officer enjoying a certain privacy in his stateroom aboard an *Essex*-class carrier in World War II. (U.S. Navy)

Berthing for the enlisted men aboard U.S.S. *Hornet*, who made up 2/3 of the crew. In some of these quarters, forty or even more men would sleep in one room. (U.S.S. *Hornet* Museum)

Enlisted crew members relaxing in their quarters aboard an *Essex*-class carrier during World War II. The only "privacy" was provided by closing a curtain in front of their bunk. (U.S. Navy)

33. Air Group 11 Exhibit

This exhibit is dedicated to Air Group 11, which flew off U.S.S. *Hornet* from 1944–1945 attacking targets on Okinawa, Formosa, the Philippines, French Indochina, and Hong Kong. The air group faced the threat of kamikaze attacks, foul weather, and antiaircraft fire over intended targets. By the end of January 1945, it claimed 105 enemy aircraft shot down and 272 aircraft destroyed on the ground, over 100,000 tons of enemy shipping sunk and more than 100 Japanese ships damaged. These great accomplishments did not come without a price. In four months of flying, the air group lost over fifty aircraft and had more than 60 men killed, missing-in-action, or wounded.

Exhibit honoring Air Group 11. Over the years, numerous former crew member have been donating or loaning their former uniforms or equipment to the museum in order to make them available to the public, thus helping to tell the personal stories of veterans who have served aboard the ship. (U.S.S. *Hornet* Museum)

Third Deck and Below

The 3rd Deck was perhaps more utilitarian but also features wider passageways than the 2nd Deck above. This was, in part, because it was mostly dedicated to the enlisted sailors aboard the ship who made up approximate 2/3 of the ship's crew! It also leads down into the ship's engineering spaces like the engine and fire rooms.

3RD DECK

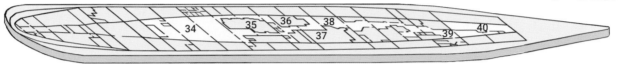

34. Enlisted Mess
35. Enlisted Galley
36. Engine Room Ladder (Engine Room is Two Decks Down)
37. Fire Room Ladder (Fire Room is Two Decks Down)
38. Ge-Dunk
39. Brig
40. Catapult Machinery Room

Map of third deck (below second deck). (U.S.S. *Hornet* Museum)

34. and 35. Enlisted Mess and Galley

The enlisted mess served four meals a day: breakfast, lunch, dinner, and midnight rations. This was built-in to feed the enlisted crew no matter what shift they were assigned. With so many mouths to feed, the mess crew were producing approximately 10,000 servings of food a day! They used oversized kitchen equipment to get the job done–massive soup pots, ladles the size of whole bowls, and stand mixers as large as most people's oven! The galley had a bakery nearby that produced bread for not only the aircraft carrier but also all the other ships that sailed with her in her battle group (smaller ships usually did not have bakeries of their own).

U.S.S. *Hornet*'s bakery could not only produce bread, but also doughnuts, pastries, pies and more. (U.S.S. *Hornet* Museum)

Work in a bakery aboard an *Essex*-class carrier during World war II. (U.S. Navy)

The machine ship aboard U.S.S. *Hornet*. Since repairs were frequently needed on a large ship or machine parts were damaged by battle effects, a machine shop was an important asset. (U.S.S. *Hornet* Museum)

Skilled crew men of an *Essex*-class carrier working in the machine shop during World War II. (U.S. Navy)

36. Engine Room

Essex-class carriers were built with two engine rooms, each of them having two main engines and associated machinery, for a total of four. Each main engine has two completely separate turbines working in unison, and jointly connected, through a single set of reduction gears, to a single propeller shaft. There are four propellers that drive the ship. Each engine can produce 37,500 shaft horsepower. Starboard engines (1 and 3) turn clockwise, and port engines (2 and 4) turn counterclockwise. The four engines produce 150,000 hp in total, and the turbines turn at approximately 5,000 rpm at full power. The ship often ran two of its engines at any one time while the others were serviced but it could run all four engines if it were trying for top speed, which was 33 knots (38 mph or 61 km/h).

One of the four turbines aboard U.S.S. *Hornet* producing 37,500 shaft horsepower. (U.S.S. *Hornet* Museum)

One of the four reduction gear boxes located between the turbines and one of the shafts connected to the ship's propeller. The gear box is used to reduce the speed of the input, from the turbine, while also multiplying the torque the input creates. (U.S.S. *Hornet* Museum)

The panel used by an enlisted sailor to control each of the four engines. This view shows the forward steam throttle as the wheel on the left, below the RPM dial and to the right of the devices that relay orders from the bridge in both speed and RPM. (U.S.S. *Hornet* Museum)

This view shows the main panel of the generator and a portion of the reduction gear box, the gray device in the lower center background. (U.S.S. *Hornet* Museum)

37. Fire Room

There are eight Babock & Wilcox separately fired superheated boilers situated in four fire rooms, two per fire room. They produce saturated and superheated steam; saturated (auxiliary) steam for auxiliary machinery, heating, etc., and superheated (main) steam that traveled into the engine rooms at 600 psi and 850 degrees Fahrenheit for use in the main engines and main generators. It was hot working down there, about 30 degrees hotter than the temperature outside.

Fire rooms 1 and 2 supplied the forward engine room for engines 1 and 4, while fire rooms 3 and 4 supplied the after engine room for engines 2 and 3. Each fire room and engine room is an isolated, self-contained, watertight compartment. Each of these rooms has two levels—upper and lower. All boilers and engines can be inter-connected in case of damage to any one or combination thereof.

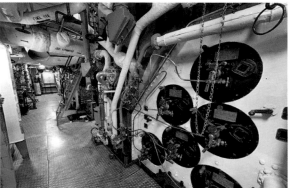

This shows the lower half of one of the two boilers. The two sets of burner panels can be seen to the right of the picture. The grey periscope in the upper right center gives the fireroom crew access to the smoke going out of the stack many levels above. (U.S.S. *Hornet* Museum)

This view shows some of the burners—each of the round black circles is a single burner with the capability to handle burner nozzles of various sizes, depending on how much steam is needed. The nozzles can be changed quickly, one by one, while the boiler is in use. (U.S.S. *Hornet* Museum)

38. "Ge-Dunk"

The third Deck was almost entirely devoted to living spaces and spaces for personal services of the enlisted crew including access to the Barber shop on the fourth deck, one of the ship's stores for the enlisted crew, and a snack bar called the "Ge-Dunk." While sailors ate for free at the enlisted mess, they had to pay for their food at the "Ge-Dunk" but it was open all day and offered different options such as hot sandwiches, hot dogs, ice cream, candy bars, and other types of easy food. There are a few legends for the origin of the name "Ge-Dunk," but one favorite is that it was introduced in ships originally as an early vending machine and the food or candy hitting the tray at the bottom of the vending machine made a "Ge-Dunk" sound.

39. Brig

The ship's brig, or its jail, was managed by the Marine detachment. Only the captain could assign brig time and the reasons for it were a.) if a sailor put the crew in danger or b.) if a sailor put the ship in danger. Worse offenders would have been taken off to be tried and jailed on shore, but sailors could be assigned to the brig just overnight or up to 30 days. The captain could also assign them to just bread and water for the first three days of their stay.

Prisoners in the brig were expected to wake up at 4:30 a.m. and do hard labor during the day. When out of their cells, they were marched together and led through the passageways by Marines. Others in the area would have to "make way" to socially isolate them as part of the punishment. The point of the brig was to make it a terrible time. With approximately 3,500 men, and an average age of nineteen, a quick but tough punishment for offenses was used to keep order.

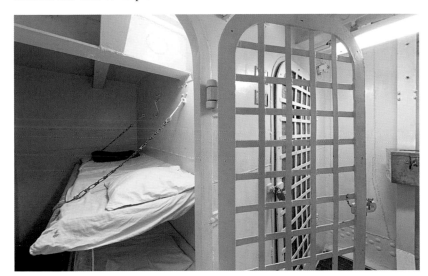

The ship's brig was small with only 13 beds available, but it was meant to send a message quickly. (U.S.S. *Hornet*)

40. Catapult Machinery Room

Essex-class carriers used two hydraulic catapults on their flight deck to launch aircraft. The machinery that powered those catapults was located far below in two machinery rooms. Both are on the third deck and about a mile of cable run between them and the flight deck. Each catapult room has four high-pressure air tanks and one hydraulic fluid tank which connects to a large piston. When an aircraft is ready to fire, high-pressure air is piped into the hydraulic fluid tank. A switch is flipped, and that hydraulic fluid threw the piston forward. The piston worked on a 1:10 ratio with the catapult on the flight deck; for every foot that the piston moved forward, the aircraft attached to the catapult on the flight deck moved 10 feet forward.

The port side catapult affectionately named the "Port Cat." Some *Essex*-class carriers were converted to steam catapults required for launching jet fighter and attack aircraft—like *Oriskany*, *Hancock* and *Ticonderoga*. (U.S.S. *Hornet*)

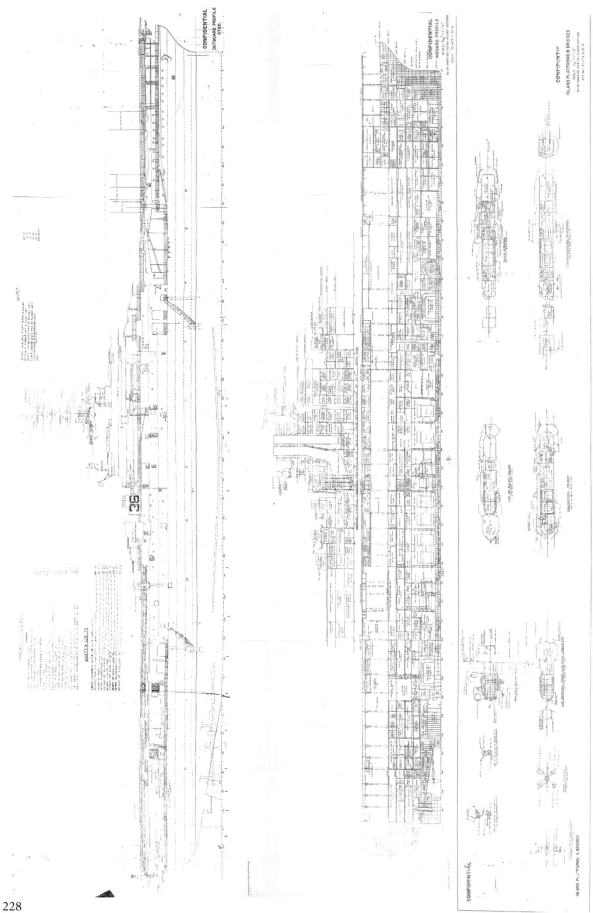

A set of plans of an *Essex*-class carrier (U.S.S. *Antietam*, CV-36) (Drawings: U.S. Navy)

7

The *Essex*-class beyond World War II

When World War II ended, the U.S. Navy was unchallenged on the world's oceans. With a fleet of almost 2,500 major combatant vessels (aircraft carriers, battleships, cruisers, destroyers, destroyer escorts, and submarines) and various amphibious transports, it had nearly twice the size of the British and Dominion navies combined. Its naval aviation component numbered more than 90 aircraft carriers and more than 41,000 aircraft.

This epic conflict firmly established the decisive role of aviation within naval and amphibious operations and carriers replaced battleships as the primary surface warship. Moreover, by the late 1940s, carrier-based aircraft, which had transitioned from propeller to jet propulsion, initially became the preferred U.S. Navy's means to carry out nuclear strikes in case of war (alternatively, these weapons could be launched in the form of guided missiles from submarines or various surface ships).

To meet this objective, the fleet was centered on the carrier attack force. Due to restricted defense budgets in the early postwar years, the Navy was not authorized to construct new carrier classes. However, it was possible to convert existing ships and complete vessels begun during the war (*Midway*-class carriers). As such, the 24 *Essex*-class carriers available after 1945 provided the Navy with its initial fleet of postwar attack carriers. Most of these capable ships were modernized under various conversion programs beginning in 1948 and continuing into the 1960s, in which they received angled decks, steam catapults, and upgrades in weapon and fire control systems, thus resembling the postwar designed *Forrestal*-class, the first "super carriers." These various modifications enabled the *Essex*-class to meet the postwar naval mission until replaced by new carriers and re-designated to serve in antisubmarine, training, or other carrier support roles.

1960s concept artwork of a "Satellite Launching Ship" depicting an *Essex*-class carrier converted for launching space satellites into orbits not readily accessible from launch sites in the United States. The rocket shown is an "Atlas" type. This concept was never implemented. (U.S. Naval Photographic Center)

U.S.S. *Bennington* (CVA-20) passes the wreck of the battleship U.S.S. *Arizona* (BB-39) in Pearl Harbor, Hawaii, on Memorial Day, May 31, 1958. *Bennington's* crew is in formation on the flight deck, spelling out a tribute to the *Arizona's* crewmen who were lost in Japanese attack on Pearl Harbor on December 7, 1941. Note the outline of *Arizona's* hull and the flow of oil from her fuel tanks. (U.S. Navy)

Aerial photograph showing the U.S.S. *Oriskany* (CV-34) on the day of her last return from a deployment on March 3, 1976. The carrier was decommissioned as the last active *Essex*-class carrier in September 1976. (U.S. Navy)

After 25 years of service on operations in Korea, Vietnam and the Mediterranean, U.S.S. *Oriskany* (CV-34) awaiting her fate to be sunk as an artificial reef off the coast of Florida in 2006. Although she was completed after World War II and did not enter service until the 1950s, she was one of the longest-lasting ships of the *Essex*-class. (U.S. Navy)

Detonations aboard U.S.S. *Oriskany* causing flooding the ship's compartments. (U.S. Navy)

The 911-feet (278 m) long carrier slowly sinking by the stern first. (U.S. Navy)

Besides serving during the Korean and Vietnam wars, several of the carriers played a part in the U. S. spaceflight program, as recovery ships for unmanned and manned spaceflights, between 1960 and 1973. U.S.S. *Hornet* recovered the astronauts from the first two moon landing missions, Apollo 11 (July 1969) and Apollo 12 (November 1969).

The last active ship of the class, U.S.S. *Lexington* (CV-16, later AVT-16), which was used as a training carrier, retired from the fleet in 1991 after 48 years of service and found a new use as a museum ship. Three of her sister ships, *Yorktown* (CV-10), *Intrepid* (CV-11), and *Hornet* (CV-12), also have been preserved as floating museums. U.S.S. *Oriskany* (CV-34) was intentionally sunk off the coast of Florida as an artificial reef in 2006, and can be visited by experienced scuba divers.

During World War II, the U.S. Navy began construction of the subsequent *Midway*-class, of which the type ship U.S.S. *Midway* (CV-41) was commissioned on September 12, 1945, 10 days after the formal surrender of Japan. Her sister ships U.S.S. *Franklin D. Roosevelt* (CV-42) and U.S.S. *Coral Sea* (CV-43) followed shortly after. U.S.S. *Midway* participated in Operation *Desert Storm* in 1991, and is now a museum ship in San Diego, California. None of the numerous escort or light carriers of World War II have been preserved for prosperity.

The U.S.S. *Oriskany's* bow disappearing from the surface. The sinking took about 37 minutes. (U.S. Navy)

Since her sinking, U.S.S. *Oriskany* benefits marine life, sport fishing and recreational diving off the Florida coast. (David Benz)

Visiting one (or all) of the remaining *Essex*-class carriers (and the U.S.S. *Midway*) may give us an understanding of what it was like to live and fight aboard these mighty warships during World War II and beyond. Although we are now losing the generation that fought in that conflict, we sometimes have the opportunity to meet a veteran or his sons or daughters during reunions or special events. It should be an honor and privilege to listen to their wartime experience. When the day has come that the World War II generation has faded away, their memories will live on in books, films, interviews, personal memories and in the ships they have served on. Let us all help to preserve these historic vessels which make a tremendous contribution to educate future generations about the history of carrier warfare and its human dimension in World War II and beyond.

After her retirement, U.S.S. *Lexington* (CV-16) opened as a floating museum in Corpus Christi, Texas, in 1992. (Carol M. Highsmith, U.S. Library of Congress Collection)

U.S.S. *Intrepid* after her modernization with an angled flight deck in the 1970s. (U.S. Navy)

U.S.S. *Intrepid* as a museum ship in New York City harbor. She is now a popular destination for visitors from all over the world. (Alfred Hutter)

Nicely decorated, U.S.S. *Hornet* awaits her visitors for a special event. Actually, she should have been named *Kearsarge*, but when the first carrier *Hornet* (CV-8) sank in October 1942, the new ship under construction was renamed to continue the name *Hornet*. The original name *Kearsarge* is still engraved on the ship's keel plate. (U.S.S. *Hornet* Museum)

U.S.S. *Yorktown* (CV-10) at the Patriots Point Naval & Maritime Museum. In 1974, the Navy Department approved the donation to the Patriot's Point Development Authority, Charleston, South Carolina. The ship was formally dedicated as a memorial and museum on the 200th anniversary of the Navy, October 13, 1975. (Carol M. Highsmith, U.S. Library of Congress Collection)

Bibliography

Abe, Zenji, *The Emperor's Eagle* (Arizona Memorial Museum Association, Honolulu, Hawaii (United States), 2006)

Bauernfeind, Ingo, *Flugzeugträger - Flottenträger im Zweiten Weltkrieg* (Motorbuch-Verlag, Stuttgart (Germany), 2011)

Bauernfeind, Ingo, *Geleitflugzeugträger - USA, England, Japan 1939–1945* (Motorbuch-Verlag, Stuttgart (Germany), 2013)

Bauernfeind, Ingo, *Trägerflugzeuge des Zweiten Weltkriegs 1939–1945* (Motorbuch-Verlag, Stuttgart (Germany), 2014)

Bowers, Peter M., *United States Navy Aircraft since 1911* (Naval Institute Press, Annapolis, Maryland (United States), 1990)

Bishop, Chris, *Weapons of the Second World War* (Bechtermünz Verlag, Eltville am Rhein (Germany), 2000)

Delgado, James P., *Ghost Fleet - The Sunken Ships of Bikini Atoll* (University of Hawaii Press, Honolulu, Hawaii (United States), 1996)

Delgado, James P., Lenihan, Daniel J. (Principal Investigator), Murphy, Larry, *The Archeology of the Atomic Bomb* (U.S. National Park Service, Santa Fe, New Mexico (United States), 1991)

Judge, Sean M., *The Turn of the Tide in the Pacific War: Strategic Initiative, Intelligence, and Command, 1941–1943* (University Press of Kansas, Lawrence, Kansas (United States), 2018)

Parshall, Jonathan, *Tully, Anthony. Shattered Sword: The Untold Story of the Battle of Midway* (Potomac Books, Dulles, Virginia (United States), 2005)

Spick, Mike, *The Illustrated Directory of Fighters* (MBI Publishing Company, St. Paul, Minnesota (United States), 2002)

U.S.S. *Franklin* (CV-13) afire and listing after a Japanese air attack, off the coast of Japan, on March 19, 1945. Note fire hoses and crewmen on her forward flight deck, and water streaming from her hangar deck. (U.S. National Archives)

Index

U.S.S. *Hornet* at night, awaiting her next visitors in the morning. (Kevin Collins / U.S.S. *Hornet*)